PRAISE FOR ROBERT CALDERISI'S
THE TROUBLE WITH AFRICA
WHY FOREIGN AID ISN'T WORKING

"Robert Calderisi, a humanitarian who has had plenty of experience in Africa…and a few other authors are shaking up the aid establishment and making us all think about what works and what does not. That's painful, but also essential."—*New York Review of Books*

"His views may shock but they are well laid out… No one can deny his deep knowledge of Africa and honest desire to contribute to its development. His book is stuffed with anecdotes of African life which force us to put on our thinking caps again."—*Le Devoir*

"Those new to Africa will find this book a breathless tour across a continent four times the size of the United States. Calderisi's human touch draws the reader through…"—*Foreign Service Journal*

"A hopeful and important book. Calderisi's prose teems with admiration for the millions of resourceful Africans who scratch out a living despite the hurdles erected by their governments…"—*The Philadelphia Inquirer*

"Mr. Calderisi…clearly admires the drive and initiative of Africans freed of the disincentives he so well analyzes".—*The Wall Street Journal*

"This book should be in every academic library in this country – and every library in Africa."—*Library Journal*

"Calderisi is excellent company on the page. His life circumstances humanize him and help explain his emotional links with Africa. They also help relieve his grim account of the compounding man-made disasters afflicting the continent."—*Globe and Mail*

"A stimulating contrarian essay… An important addition to the conversation over Africa's future."—*Publishers Weekly*

"An unflinching personal essay by someone who has witnessed dictatorships in all their brutality."—*The Edmonton Journal*

"A refreshing, courageous and honest book. Most importantly, he avoids the mistake of many Westerners who fear sounding racist if they write plainly about Africa's failures."
—Andrew M. Mwenda, Political Editor, *The Monitor* (Kampala, Uganda)

"The author's love of the continent shines through every line, yet his bold suggestions will raise some eyebrows and provoke debate (as they should). The book ripples with good stories, mixes passion and reason, and is very often simply touching."
—Baroness [Lynda] Chalker, former UK Overseas Development Minister

"A hard-hitting, brutally honest personal essay about Africa. It is gripping, well-researched and fascinating. Corrupt and incompetent African government officials will fret over this but it is the bitter truth the African people would want told to the world."
—George B.N. Ayittey, Ph.D., Distinguished Economist at American University and President of The Free Africa Foundation, Washington, DC.

"A provocative and engaging look at problems of development in Africa. Everyone who cares about the continent will find ample room for thought…"
—Joseph O'Neill, Director of the White House Office of National AIDS Policy (2002-2005)

"This book is a 'must read' for anyone seriously interested in Africa. Well written, provocative and challenging, it deserves serious consideration by those seeking innovative solutions to Africa's problems. Some of its judgments are sharp, but so are its insights and recommendations."
—Julius E. Coles, President of Africare, a leading non-profit organization serving Africa

"The heartfelt cry of a lover of Africa…He was not born one, but he is nonetheless a great 'African.'"
—Martin Ziguélé, Prime Minister of the Central African Republic (2001-2003)

"This will become a landmark work for my generation – as important as De Tocqueville's *Democracy in America* for 19th century Europeans".
—Martial Ahipeaud, former President of the National Union of Students of the Ivory Coast

THE TROUBLE WITH AFRICA
Why Foreign Aid Isn't Working

ROBERT CALDERISI

Yale University Press
New Haven and London

For my parents
and
Jean Daniel

First published in paperback 2007

First published in the USA by Palgrave Macmillan

Copyright © Robert Calderisi, 2006.

For information about this and other Yale University Press publications, please contact:
    U.S. Office: sales.press@yale.edu   www.yalebooks.com
    Europe Office: sales@yaleup.co.uk   www.yalebooks.co.uk

Printed in Great Britain by MPG Books Ltd, Bodmin, Cornwall

Library of Congress Cataloging-in-Publication Data is available from the Library
of Congress

ISBN 0-300-12017-6

A catalogue record for this book is available from the British Library.

ISBN 978-0-300-12512-2 (pbk)

10 9 8 7 6

CONTENTS

ACKNOWLEDGMENTS

The opinions in this book are entirely my own. In writing it, however, I owe special thanks to Daouda Thiam, René and Alice Dégni-Ségui, Françoise Kadio-Morokro, Samene Djekouri, Martial Ahipeaud, Justine Agness Soumahoro, Albert Koua, Raphael Lakpé, Diegou Bailly, Honorat De Yedagne, Christophe Koffi, Franck Sidelin, Charles Mutashobya, Michael Holman, Jim Adams, André Bogui, Louise Gariepy, Jean-Paul Chausse, and Christian Fauliau. They were not directly involved in the writing but, without their comradeship and inspiration, I would now be resigned rather than impatient about Africa's future.

Early reviewers of the manuscript included Geoffrey Adams, Maria Calderisi, David Calderisi, Ronald Calderisi, Robert Charette, Paul Crawford, Pauline Fitzgerald, Neal Gripp, Keith Henderson, Anthony Ianicello, Peter Lee, Matthew McTighe, Brian Petty, Dennis Preston, and Jean Daniel Rossi. I hope I have done justice to their suggestions.

I am also indebted to Gabriella Pearce, whose advice, encouragement, and idealism enriched the book; to Rick Broadhead who embraced the project from the start; and to Marsha Abramson (who introduced me to Rick).

INTRODUCTION

There is nothing basically wrong with the Nigerian character. There is nothing wrong with the Nigerian land or climate or water or air or anything else. The Nigerian problem is the unwillingness or inability of its leaders to rise to the responsibility . . . of true leadership.

—Chinua Achebe, *The Trouble with Nigeria*, 1983.

Just after dark on August 1, 1999, two boys stole across the airport tarmac in Conakry, the capital of Guinea on the West African coast, and curled themselves up into the undercarriage of a Sabena Airbus bound for Brussels. They knew their chances of surviving were small. A young Senegalese had made a similar journey a year before—to Paris—and arrived stiff but alive, apparently protected by the heat of the nearby engines. But they were less fortunate. In the loneliness of the lower stratosphere, they were either frozen by the sub-zero temperatures or asphyxiated by the lack of oxygen. Their bodies were found lifeless after landing. The hand of one of the boys was still clutching a crumpled, handwritten message addressed to "Your Excellencies, the citizens and officials of Europe." It spoke of the "abuse of children's rights"—particularly in Africa's public schools. "It is only in the private schools that people can enjoy good teaching and learning, but it requires quite a lot of money and our parents cannot afford it because they are poor . . . .Therefore, we African children and youth are asking you to set up an efficient organization to help with the development of Africa . . . .If we are sacrificing ourselves and putting our lives in jeopardy it is because we . . . .need your help."[1]

The sequel was almost as sad as the incident itself. Guinea's ambassador to the European Union was shown on French television the next day sympathizing with the boys but trivializing their appeal to the world: "What they were saying was 'give us more aid', so we can prevent this from happening again." Two days later, the mayor of Conakry absolved his country's government of any responsibility in the matter. "This never would have happened if [the airline] Sabena and the airport authorities had been able to guarantee better security arrangements," he said.

The people of Guinea understood the message better. When the boys' bodies were returned home, a large crowd was at the airport to greet them, grieving and angry. One man moaned to French reporters, "These boys spoke for all of us." His disgust with his country's government was obvious.

The real tragedy was that this did not have to happen. In a sense, the mayor was right; but it was better schools, not better security, which could have prevented it.[2]

This incident was minor compared with the millions of Africans who die unnecessarily every year—just from AIDS and warfare. But to people still hoping for a glimpse of progress on the continent, the death of these two boys was like a dagger in the heart. It infuriated anyone who knew how much money and effort were already being spent to ensure some basic education for young Africans. And it forced close observers of Africa to ask themselves, once again, what was fundamentally wrong with the continent.

Since 1975, Africa has been receding to the margins of world affairs. That may be about to change. As international terrorists search for alternative safe havens, as new diseases like SARS and avian flu spread beyond their countries of origin, and as mass human migration begins to rival nuclear proliferation as the dominant challenge of the early twenty-first century, there will be rising interest in the West in containing the international ripple effects of failed states. Most of those states are in Africa.

Strategic considerations apart, Africa's immense human suffering continues to gnaw at the world's conscience. Yet the scale and origins of those horrors are barely known. Every twelve hours, the same number of people killed at the World Trade Center on September 11, 2001 (3,000) perish from AIDS on the continent. In a single year, 150,000 African mothers—half the number of people drowned or crushed in the 2004 Asian tsunami—die, just giving birth.

Some would argue that Africa's problems have been brewing for centuries. But, since 1975, they have grown more intense. Most Africans and sympathetic Westerners believe these problems are the legacy of history and foreign intrusions. Yet Africa has been making its own history since Independence and has been largely free of foreign domination since the end of the Cold War. Some blame globalization for making Africa poor. In fact, most countries on the continent have had only slight connections with the world economy, and these have grown even weaker. Instead of becoming entangled in the "treadmill" of international trade, Africa has fallen steadily behind, caught in a spiral of pride, anger, poverty, and self-pity.

Africa[*] has fascinated Westerners for a very long time. A seventeenth-century English writer exclaimed: "We carry within us the wonders we seek without us: There is all Africa and her prodigies in us."[3] More recently, Africa has depressed not only onlookers but Africans, too, many of whom have fled the continent to seek their fortunes or personal security in more rational environments. Yet Africa remains rich in talent, resources, and tradition. Much of its wisdom is oral, captured in aphorisms that speak volumes in a few words. A West African proverb warns that "One can only speak about the burden one is carrying." Another reminds us: "The stranger has big eyes, but he doesn't see."

Foreigners, including long-time lovers of Africa, need to be careful, even humble, when describing the diverse cultures and countries that make it up. Some would suggest that, except as a geographical term, "Africa" does not exist. In one writer's words: "The continent is too large to describe. It is a veritable ocean, a separate planet, a varied, immensely rich cosmos."[4] According to another observer: "You could drop the continental United States into Africa four times and the edges would scarcely touch. And of course it is infinitely more complex than the United States, less

---

[*] Throughout this book, "Africa" will mean the 48 countries in or below the Sahara desert. While the five North African states (Morocco, Algeria, Tunisia, Libya, and Egypt) are geographically and sometimes sentimentally linked with the rest of the continent, their histories and cultural traditions are profoundly different.

homogeneous, spectacularly more varied within itself, and more volatile."[5]

Unfortunately, Africa has exposed itself to generalization through its own spectacular failures. The very diversity of Africa makes the "African problem" more striking. It is the only region of the world where savage wars break out on a regular basis. It is the only continent that has grown steadily poorer over the last thirty years. And it is the only part of the globe where population growth has been out of control, making the general situation worse. It is no accident that two thirds of the world's AIDS cases are in Africa. African governments have largely ignored the problem. Even that great exception to African disorder, South Africa, has a president who insists he has never known anyone who died of the disease. Two other states that escaped economic and political catastrophe are considered by other African countries to be "un-African," rather than models to follow. Botswana, it is argued, is small and rich in minerals, while Mauritius has its Chinese and Indian minorities. So, taking Africans at their word, what does the rest of the continent have in common?

In most modern maps, Africa is at the very center of the world, with Western Europe bestriding it like a minor appendage or afterthought. A 1526 map of the world, prepared by the Florentine cartographer Giovanni Vespucci (nephew of Amerigo Vespucci), contains more detailed and accurate information about Africa than Latin America and Asia.[6] But in recent years, in a geo-political version of Continental Drift, Africa has fallen almost completely off the map.

With only ten percent of the world's population, one percent of international trade, barely enough diplomatic influence to match its small economic role, and modest military forces trained only on itself, Africa has become an oddity, a puzzle, and, of course, a thorn in the sides of Western immigration officials. Beyond church, aid, and tourism circles, the continent is mentioned only in connection with the international HIV/AIDS epidemic. Africa still attracts adventurers, anthropologists, zoologists, missionaries, idealists, and some romantics rather than the down-to-earth people who make the rest of the world run.

But few international newspapers still have correspondents in Africa. Except for South Africa, the continent is generally absent from economic and financial news and hardly appears even in brief digests of world events. If not for their colorful national dress at international conferences, Africans would scarcely be noticed on the world stage. Outside the oil and gas sector, most business people on the continent are monopolists, marathoners, or buccaneers. Serious investors have shunned the place for decades; stockbrokers do not think about Africa even in their sleep. In contrast, China attracts more private investment in a single year than Africa does in a decade.

Even more significantly, Africans themselves have been moving away in droves. At least 70,000 skilled graduates–the very people who could be leading an African Renaissance–abandon the continent every year. Until these gifted and enterprising people can be attracted to return, most of the world's peace-keeping efforts on the continent, and certainly most of its aid, will have little effect.

Why have I written this book? Several books have appeared on the subject of Africa recently and just as many on foreign aid. But this is probably the first book to tell the inside story of African development over the last thirty years through the eyes of a senior international official. Most aid professionals of my generation are still working as staff or consultants, and are not at liberty to express their views. I took early retirement from the World Bank to look after my aging parents, and even then I have had to wait two years to write about my experience under Bank rules that prevent former staff from publishing articles or books without its prior approval. As someone who has had a special—perhaps unique—vantage point on the subject, I feel obliged to share my experience, hoping it will serve the continent. I continue to care deeply about Africa and believe that it can reconnect with the rest of the human family with its head held high, if it shrugs off its illusions and gives full vent to its talent and resources.

My exposure to Africa has been varied. I first set foot on the continent in 1975 and have worked and traveled there extensively ever since. I lived in the two countries that sparked the greatest hope for Africa—Tanzania in the 1970s and the Ivory Coast in the 1990s. Most of my career was at the World Bank, the largest foreign aid agency on earth; I also worked for a national aid body (the Canadian International Development Agency) and an international institution in Paris (the Organization for

Economic Cooperation and Development), which coordinates the aid practices of wealthy countries. During three eventful years (1997–2000) as the World Bank's spokesperson for Africa, I contended daily with the anxieties, frustrations, and hopes of African business groups, journalists, students, women's organizations, human rights activists, and environmentalists, all eager to make a difference but wondering, as the new millennium dawned, why their tenth of humanity was being left behind. At the start of the new century, I was deeply involved in defending and supervising one of the most controversial aid projects in Africa: the Chad-Cameroon Oil Pipeline. And I am one of only a few international officials who regularly addressed large audiences in Africa and tried to answer their tough and often touching questions.

Another motive for writing this book is the renewed interest of the leading industrial countries in helping Africa. In July 2005, UK Prime Minister Tony Blair made Africa and global warming the overriding themes of the G–8 meeting in Gleneagles, Scotland. I hope this book can serve as a truly independent contribution to the debate provoked by those discussions.

This is a personal essay, drawing on contacts and conversations with literally thousands of Africans over the course of my career, ranging from small farmers to heads of state, with wide ideological and cultural differences. Some of the arguments in this book have been made by others,[7] but they will be supported by more recent evidence I have obtained as a senior aid official rather than as a journalist or scholar.

This book will also suggest some practical solutions. It is written with the love and loyalty that Africans expect of their brothers, but also impatience with the political correctness that has kept Africa in confusion and turmoil. While I have expressed my own views, much of what I have written will probably reflect the opinions of many others who have worked in Africa.

I believe it is now time to move beyond the hand-wringing and politeness that dominate most discussions of Africa, and to suggest concrete steps that Africans and the world can take to liberate talent and enterprise on the continent. This will involve sharing some unpleasant truths.

This book will be controversial in some circles. To begin with, it violates the cardinal rule among friends of the continent: "Thou shalt not say blunt things about Africa outside Africa." That this book is written by a non-African will also attract special attention. At best, I will be accused of being a "stranger with big eyes"; at worst, I will be charged with being part of that "neo-racist, anti-black intellectual current which is raging through the international media thanks to pretended specialists on Africa."[8]

Most people reading Western newspapers or watching TV will not be aware that Africa has steadily lost markets by its own mismanagement; that most countries—including supposedly "capitalist" ones like the Ivory Coast—have been anti-business; that African family loyalty and fatalism have been more destructive than tribalism; that African leaders and intellectuals play intentionally on Western guilt; that even Africa's "new" leaders are indifferent to public opinion and key issues like AIDS; and that, in recent decades, Africans have probably been more cruel to each other than anyone else has been. Nor is it generally known that, far from ignoring Africa, the world has made special efforts to help the continent, including writing off its debt continuously over thirty years.

Inevitably, in this book, there will be many references to the World Bank. Although I enjoyed working there immensely, it is not my purpose to praise or defend the institution. Nor do I wish to add to the criticism it continues to attract. But I do hope to shed fresh light on the controversies that surrounded the Bank's role in Africa in the 1980s and 1990s, as unfortunately that misunderstanding still affects current events.

This book will argue that Africa is now responsible for most of its own problems and that outsiders can help only if they are more direct and demanding in their relations with the continent. Forty years of foreign aid have established one unsurprising fact. Around the world, successful countries are those that have chosen the right policies for their own reasons and seen foreign aid as a complement to their own efforts rather than as a bribe for undertaking difficult reforms.

Most African politicians and intellectuals suggest that their problems have deep historical or foreign roots—in the slave trade, colonialism, the Cold War, high debt, and the behavior of international organizations. The first part of this book examines those factors skeptically and shows just how damaging home-grown dictatorships have been, drawing not on the nightmares of Liberia, Sierra Leone, Rwanda, and Somalia, but on less well-known countries.

The focus then shifts to African culture and values, and how these have been perverted to condone oppression on the continent. Part of that oppression—the so-called petty corruption that Africans face everyday—is so widespread that few people have the power or incentive to fight it. Western donors do not really fight it either, because they want to "sit at the table" with African governments and meet international aid targets, rather than asphyxiate political and administrative malpractice.

The second part of the book contains first-hand accounts of conditions in a series of countries. For a long time, two of them, Tanzania and the Ivory Coast, stood out from the general gloom. Five other countries that are relatively unknown in the English-speaking world (Chad, Cameroon, the Central African Republic, Gabon, and Equatorial Guinea) are members of a would-be economic "community" with very little in common. Their disputes illustrate just how little economics has mattered to most African politicians.

The book then examines some of the obstacles governments have placed in the way of individual initiative, as well as the West's difficulties in trying to help Africa. That section also offers some good news: that people-to-people aid and humanitarian assistance are much more effective in communicating values and shoring up African morale than official assistance. The story of the Chad-Cameroon Oil Pipeline points to a more intrusive way of investing in Africa's future, but is followed by examples of just how far apart the world and Africa's leaders are in assessing problems, let alone agreeing on the right solutions.

Is the outlook thus hopeless? I believe not. The final section of the book suggests ten ways of changing Africa and offers encouraging signs that Africans are beginning to take their future into their own hands.

Those who know Africa well may want to go directly to Chapter 12 before reading the rest of the book. There, I suggest that promoting more open political systems and a free press is more important than financial assistance. Few Africans share in the monetary manna they hear about on the radio, and many are discouraged from opposing bad governments when they see them propped up by generous Westerners.

With respect to aid, I propose an entirely new approach—focusing at first on just five countries (Uganda, Tanzania, Mozambique, Ghana, and Mali). These governments deserve much more than they are receiving at the moment, with fewer strings attached. I also propose that other African countries be helped only if they are kept under political and economic supervision.

Although I worked for more than twenty years at the World Bank, a bulwark of free trade and open markets, like most people there I do not believe in laissez-faire. Free markets will help Africa grow and a free press will help keep businesses and governments honest. But they will not put young girls in school, provide clean water, and fight HIV/AIDS ruthlessly. Good public policy is important for that. A conservative position would be to give up on foreign aid altogether and leave everything to private investment and the market. My suggestions are interventionist and radical, rather than slight extensions of experiments already underway.

I believe strongly in international efforts to promote freedom and spread wealth in the world. Like many economists, including Joseph Stiglitz in *Globalization and its Discontents* (2002),[9] I think that an open trade system is essential for reducing world poverty, provided that rich countries respect the same rules they urge on others. Like critics of globalization, such as Noam Chomsky in *Hegemony or Survival* (2003) and George Monbiot in *Age of Consent* (2003), I have confidence in the power of international public opinion to change the world for the better. But, in Africa, there is an important first step still to be taken.

Almost everyone in North America and Europe who shares my ideals believes that more aid, along with additional lecturing on governance, will help Africa. I want to puncture that illusion. Africans need breathing space much more than they need money. Not a Marshall Plan, but real backing for the few governments that are fighting poverty, plus political support for the millions of Africans who are resisting oppression and violence in the rest of the continent. Not just formal democracy, but "a society where people are free to lead their own lives without fear of either the government or what their neighbor will say."[10]

Some aid professionals will suggest that my assessment of forty years of international development efforts is simplistic and that my suggestions for change are unrealistic. I have certainly tried to simplify complicated subjects that are too important to leave behind a veil of jargon, and I have not run my recommendations through the sieve of political acceptability. I am merely offering practical solutions that in my view—after thirty years of working experience—stand better chances of success than ones that have been tried before. Unfortunately, in a climate of guarded discourse on sensitive subjects, it still takes nerve to write about such a broad subject in under three hundred pages. As the book is intended for the general reader rather than specialists, and to trigger a debate about new solutions rather than universal agreement, I have not tried to be subtle. But I hope most readers will find that I have treated the subject not just with deep conviction, but also with respect and occasionally a sense of humor.

Some of the judgments in this book may seem severe, but none of them exceeds the restlessness and disbelief that many Africans have expressed to me over the years. More than anyone, they know how much better they could be if they were not being hounded and blocked by their so-called leaders.

PART I

WHAT SETS AFRICA APART

CHAPTER 1

LOOKING FOR EXCUSES

More than half of Africa's people are under the age of eighteen. Yet, many of their elders, teachers, or governments are trying to persuade them that they are victims, rather than victors in a now-distant struggle for independence. Even Africans who were alive when that struggle was won are still wrestling with their demons.

In April 2005, a former culture minister of Mali—the Saharan country that boasts the legendary city of Timbuktu—wrote an "open letter" to French President Jacques Chirac. She said that Africa now wanted to stand on its own two feet. "The fight against poverty amounts to begging and submissiveness, leading to reforms that make us even poorer."[1] "The more the North 'cooperates' with the South, the worse off we become."[2] It is significant that she was writing to a foreign leader rather than an African one. Certainly, the pages of history can turn slowly at times, and French-speaking Africans have been especially reluctant to look homeward. Yet, many Africans, regardless of language or origin, ignore what is obvious around them and continue to see foreign governments or corporations as the major causes of their difficulties.

Some Africans acknowledge that their problems start at home and complain that the West has been too indulgent rather than too hard on their governments. The real-life hero of the Oscar-nominated film *Hotel Rwanda*, Paul Rusesabagina, has pointed out that in April 1994, the same month the Holocaust Museum was inaugurated in Washington, DC, 10,000 people a day were being massacred around him. Despite the phrase "Never Again" that rang throughout the speeches of dedication for the museum, the West did not intervene in Rwanda and is still "propping up African dictatorships."[3]

Even tangible expressions of Western generosity do not impress many Africans. The travel writer Paul Theroux met a political science teacher in the southern African country of Malawi who made no bones about his frustrations: "The tyrants love aid. Aid helps them stay in power and contributes to underdevelopment." "What if all the donors just went away?" Theroux asked him. "That might work," was the reply."[4]

Views vary widely in Africa, and increasingly new voices are being heard. But people of power or influence remain largely stuck in an outdated view of the world. Over a period of forty years, Africa has failed to develop. Even worse, its political and intellectual leaders still blame the continent's problems on factors as varied as an unjust international economic system, the slave trade, colonialism, the Cold War, crushing debt burdens, and even basic geography. On close examination, each of these explanations grows shaky and throws the spotlight back on Africa itself.

The most frequently cited "cause" of Africa's problems is that the world economy is biased against Africa. There is little doubt that small agricultural producers are at a disadvantage in international markets, and that measures that protect farmers in Western countries limit potential African exports or depress international prices (especially for cotton). But Africa has not been losing ground to competitors in rich countries; instead, it has surrendered markets to other tropical suppliers in Asia and Latin America. Most African countries have in fact let agriculture—their greatest wealth—decline steadily through over-taxation and other wrongheaded policies. African economies were certainly late-starters, but instead of pumping them up with steroids, governments have put shackles on their producers. In contrast, South Korea, a nation that was poorer than Ghana in

1960, caught up with the rest of the world, rather than complain about its handicaps.

Far from being biased against Africa, the international economy has engaged in affirmative action on its behalf. For decades, rich-country markets have been open to many African products, including some agricultural ones. Bananas are imported to Europe from former British and French colonies in Africa and the Caribbean, even though Central American fruit would be cheaper. The Germans, by far the largest consumers of bananas, are willing to pay the price. The US Africa Growth and Opportunity Act (1998) had a profound effect in some African countries by opening the US market to their textiles. This legislation faced domestic opposition, including objections from the inaptly named Senator Faircloth (Republican–North Carolina) who insisted that African countries first import cotton from the United States before sending it back as cloth. (Fortunately, his effort was defeated.) Half of the world's aid has been reserved for Africa. That money would have been better spent in India and China, which together have three times more people than Africa. It would also have reduced more poverty, because of better economic management and lower corruption.

There is now great pressure on rich countries to open their agricultural markets further. Tropical sugar cane would be cheaper for Europeans than locally grown sugar beets. Africa can also produce cereals and oilseeds. But, for the time being, the balance of interests is heavily against Africa. To protect its farmers, the European Union spends $350 billion* a year, an amount equal to Africa's entire annual income and fourteen times the aid the continent receives. Such subsidies not only help inefficient producers. In France, they also prevent rural depopulation, keep the countryside attractive, and protect the nation's most important industry, tourism. France has 70 million visitors a year—more than any other country on earth.

Africans jump the gun in complaining about European and US agricultural policies. International pressure will eventually create new opportunities for tropical farmers, but few African countries

---

* All currency references in the book are in US dollars.

will be able to take advantage of them. To make African production more efficient, significant reforms and investment will be needed first.

Unfortunately, "efficiency" has been a dirty word in much of Africa. It reminds people of the advice and arm-twisting they have received over 20 years from the World Bank and the International Monetary Fund. These institutions are the favorite targets of Africans. The Bank and the Fund are large, mysterious, and powerful, and so fond of technical jargon that their efforts to defend themselves often fall on rocky ground. All the same, they are an odd choice of villain.

To begin with, the World Bank is not a "bank" in the normal sense of the word but a financial cooperative owned by virtually all of the world's governments. It is a specialized agency of the United Nations and, with its staff of 10,000, the most important foreign aid body on earth. It has 1,400 people working on Africa—the largest single group of professionals anywhere promoting the continent's development. Many of them are African. In 1963, the popular writer James Morris described Bank staff as self-effacing do-gooders. "They may be excited by the unfolding of history all around them, but do not often let it show. They pride themselves upon their strictly businesslike approach to the needs of the poor nations, and would think it effete or namby-pamby to allow any breath of sentiment to creep between the ledger lines."[5]

The culture of the institution has changed since then. Crusty former colonial administrators have been replaced by smooth-talking economics Ph.D.s and business school graduates. But the Bank's self-image and sense of mission have barely faltered. Its purposes were obscured to the outside world by three colorless presidents between 1981 and 1995. In the decade after that, however, the hard-driving James Wolfensohn infused the institution with new energy and clarity.

Yet most critics of globalization, like Africans, still condemn the institution. Some do so in apocalyptic terms. In the words of one writer: "Zimbabwe's president, Robert Mugabe, is a brutal autocrat who has cheated his country of democracy, murdered political opponents and starved the people of regions controlled by the opposition. But the damage he has done to Africans is minor by comparison to that inflicted by the International Monetary Fund and World Bank."[6] Others have described the Bank as the "new maharajahs,"[7] "lords of poverty," and "masters of disaster."[8] The organization is even granted powers that it does not claim. One critic has suggested that the Bank's influence is more than economic; it has been "cultural, ideological and, in a not entirely metaphysical sense, religious."[9]

Like other large organizations, including genuinely religious ones, the World Bank has its faults. But it has also done some good. It may not be "democratic," but its member countries are deeply involved in setting the policies and approving the lending of the institution. Admittedly, most of the Bank's capital and voting rights are held by Western countries, but that is logical for an institution offering Western assistance and promoting an open society.

Its motives have also been disputed. The Bank feels that it is fighting world poverty; anti-globalization critics suggest it is serving Western interests. Both are right. The Bank and its sister institution, the International Monetary Fund (IMF), were founded in August 1944 at an international conference at Bretton Woods, New Hampshire, in the conviction of the Western powers that raising the living standards of the poorest countries would help everyone. The Bank's purpose was to promote the continued growth of world trade; the IMF's was to encourage the free flow of capital and orderly development of the world's currencies. Both sought to apply the lessons of the inter-war years during which a lack of international cooperation, including proliferating trade barriers and competitive devaluations, had hampered an improvement in the world's living standards. The Bank supported specific development projects like roads, power plants, and harbors (when private capital was not available for these), and later, a broad range of activities, including agriculture, schools, water supply, and family planning. The IMF acted as a global lifeguard, assessing the performance of individual economies (including the rich ones), offering advice on how to overcome occasional obstacles, and, in times of emergency, coming to the rescue by supporting a country's balance of payments. The United Kingdom received massive assistance from the Fund as recently as 1976.

In developing countries, the Bank and IMF worked closely together, for the obvious reason that development lending would not be very productive if it supported economies that were headed into trouble. There was creative tension behind the scenes and sometimes spectacular public differences, as in the case of Argentina in the late 1990s. Sometimes, the IMF's short-term objectives were at odds with the Bank's long-term view. By and large, however, their roles were complementary.

In Africa, the ongoing "crisis" of the 1980s and 1990s—a misnomer for what had become a permanent economic problem—confused the division of labor, as both institutions became involved in supporting government budgets. Their main instrument—and the principal target of African resentment—was the "structural adjustment" programs (or SAPs) introduced during the world recession of the early 1980s. Chapter 8 will discuss these programs in greater detail. Suffice it to say here that the new aid was given its strange name because it was intended to bring permanent benefits to Africa's economy rather than cover up temporary sores. Unfortunately, Africans confused the treatment with the disease, or regarded it as an operation performed with hatchets rather than scalpels.

The major adjustment of the period had nothing to do with the international institutions. Between 1970 and 1990, Africa lost half of its share of world markets to other developing countries, simply because those other nations were able to produce and deliver the same goods more cheaply. This represented a loss of income for Africa of about $70 billion per year. There was not enough money in the world—let alone in the World Bank—to fill this gap. It exceeded the amount of foreign aid being spent in all of Africa, Asia, and Latin America combined. In response, the Bank and other official donors shifted from supporting specific projects to providing immense sums to government budgets. These sums were linked to common-sense measures for stemming Africa's loss of markets.

African governments never explained to the public why they were negotiating with the international agencies—even though it was plain they had little choice. These governments—and sometimes the business establishment—did not believe in the reforms, agreed to them half-heartedly, or undermined them once aid officials looked the other way. As a result, the "crisis" appeared to be of somebody else's making, not their own.

The whole process went awry, in large part because of the way African governments kept their citizens in the dark. Few Africans knew that they were losing markets and that national budgets were barely large enough to pay for government salaries, let alone essential materials and supplies. All that Africans saw was the collapse of their infrastructure and public services. Already distrustful of their governments, Africans had even less confidence in distant institutions that talked about reducing poverty but seemed to make it worse at every turn. The real problems—Africa's high costs of production and distribution and poor investment climate—were obscured by the West's awkward efforts to help.

In a sense, the African public understood the situation perfectly. They were not seeing the effects of the reforms because those reforms were not being introduced, or they were being administered badly; in a small number of cases, the reforms were also misconceived. The World Bank was not being too "hard"; rather, the Bank was watering down agreements, or waiving conditions, in exchange for promises of government action at a later date. In Kenya, freeing up the national grain marketing system was an objective of the first structural adjustment loan (SAL); twelve years later, it had still not been done. There was no shortage of money for governments that were prepared to say the right words and sign the right documents. One generous country director at the Bank in the 1980s was nicknamed "Mr. Dial-a-SAL" for his willingness to support ailing government budgets. In just five years, he added $850 million in hard money to the Ivory Coast's debt burden. Yet, in a 1994 study of 26 African countries, the World Bank judged the performance of only one of them (Ghana) to be "adequate" by world standards.

Adjustment did not fail in Africa; it was never given a fighting chance. Africa was bleeding to death, but instead of worrying about the hemorrhaging, African leaders complained about the pain from the tourniquet. Naturally enough, economies took a very long time to recover and most African countries have still not returned to their income levels of the 1960s. The wounds of that period have never healed.

"Structural adjustment" was bad enough. But, for most Africans, it was just the latest in a series of indignities that the world had forced upon them, the most notorious of which was the slave trade.

Historians have argued for decades about the impact of slavery. Undoubtedly, it did psychological and economic damage to the generations immediately affected. But how great was it, and how relevant is it for later developments? The physical traces of this barbarism can still be seen on opposite coasts of the continent. In the west, they include the austere prison houses on Senegal's Gorée Island whence thousands of slaves were shipped to the Western Hemisphere. In the east, one can still see from the air the deep-green mango trees that the Arab slavers planted in Tanganyika along their route from the interior to the small port of Bagamoyo—which is Swahili for "the place where I lay down my heart."

The victims of the slaving raids, which affected large parts of the interior of the continent—not just areas close to the coasts—suffered grievously. Families were torn apart. Those who survived the journey were forced into hard labor in strange climates and lands. Many died on the way to the coast, in slave rebellions, or in stifling conditions on the high seas. It was a cynical, greedy, and brutal abuse of other human beings—abetted by powerful people in Africa. But the purpose of the slave trade was not to exterminate anyone. And it was not a crime of Europeans against Africans. "It was a crime of Europeans and Arabs *and* Africans and, in the truest sense, it was a crime of mankind."[10]

Those who suffered most were the people who were taken away. Most historians estimate that, between 1500 and 1800, 8–12 million people were carried off by the Atlantic slave trade.[11] If one includes the Arab slavers, who were active between the ninth and the twentieth centuries, the figure rises to 20 million people. Polemicists suggest that as many as 200 million Africans were affected, on the assumption that ten people died for every slave successfully transported overseas.[12] There is no way of documenting such numbers, even though the lower estimates are corroborated by shipping records. Hence, the impact on Africa's general population is also difficult to establish. But not everyone agrees that the damage was profound or permanent. In the words of one distinguished historian: "Africans *survived* the slave trade with their political independence and social institutions largely intact. Paradoxically, this shameful period also displayed human resilience at its most courageous."[13] What is even clearer is that, despite continued racism and poverty, most of the slaves' descendants in the Western Hemisphere lead better lives than their distant cousins on the other side of the Atlantic.

Even if this human trade left a lasting scar on the African mentality, why should it have impeded the continent's material progress? Slavery was abolished in the British empire in 1833 and in the French territories in 1858. More recently—just 60 years ago—six million Jews were systematically exterminated rather than just shipped to other countries. Yet it is not the common view that the Holocaust made the survivors less entrepreneurial and self-confident. Some would argue instead that this most recent chapter in an already dark history of persecution made the survivors even more intent on ensuring the security of the next generation.

Sensitive as the subject is, some Africans are willing to put slavery in its place. "Yes, there was the slave trade," says Jean-Paul Ngoupandé, a former prime minister of the Central African Republic and author of several enlightening books on contemporary Africa. "And many hide behind it to explain our difficulties, but I don't think it can explain, for example, the destruction of a country like the Ivory Coast, which had got off to a good start . . . It is the Africans of today who are responsible."[14]

The next "dark" chapter of African history came with the European settlers. One does not need to defend colonialism to recognize that some criticisms of it are grossly exaggerated. Other peoples, like the Indians and Pakistanis, have been less obsessed about their imperial heritage. It is also unlikely that the Africans would have acted very differently if roles had been reversed and they had had the technology, power, and opportunity to invade a relatively "empty" and defenseless Europe. Besides, to quote Mr. Ngoupandé again, "There is practically no country or civilization in the world which was not someone else's colony at some point in its history: France under the Romans for six centuries, Spain under the Arabs, etc."[15]

Like the slave trade, the impact of colonialism is also beginning to grow stale. The first African country to gain independence was Ghana in 1957. Most others were self-governing by
1965. Forty years later, it is hard to draw a clear link between
what the colonial powers did or did not do and what their
African successors most certainly did in their place. The smaller
colonizers did set a brutal example of government. During the
1905–07 Maji-Maji rebellion in Tanganyika, the Germans flayed
their opponents alive and hung them from trees. Belgium's King
Leopold II treated the Congo like his personal playground. The
Portuguese engaged in forced labor in Angola as late as the
1950s. But the major colonial powers, Great Britain and France,
were generally balanced in the treatment of the people they
ruled and, in various ways, respected their cultures and rights.
The British used "indirect rule" in Nigeria, relying on local
chieftains to ensure the smooth administration of the vast interior. In Tanganyika in the 1920s, a quasi-socialist British governor named Donald Cameron encouraged the Chagga people on
Mount Kilimanjaro to grow coffee–something the "natives"
across the border in Kenya were explicitly forbidden to do, under
pressure from the white planters. This led the Chagga to early
prosperity and a sense of enterprise and self-improvement that
has never been suppressed.[16]

In Kenya, Philip Mitchell, another colonial governor steeped
in the progressive ideas of the British Fabian Society and attentive
to the London Missionary Society as much as to the Colonial Office, forbade the sale of land and extension of credit to Africans.
Inspired by a history of rural exploitation in India, these regulations were intended to prevent Africans from becoming landless or
easy prey to unscrupulous moneylenders.[17] A Royal Commission
in the 1950s would criticize these rules as paternalistic and obstacles to the development of a free market. A laissez-faire approach,
they argued, might have led to greater consolidation of land, more
efficient agriculture, and even the prevention of the Mau-Mau uprising. Whatever the merits of the rules, they were a far cry from
the brutally self-interested management of tropical possessions
sometimes portrayed by critics of colonialism.

The British Empire was not monolithic. There was real tension between white settlers and colonial administrations, not just

between the colonizers and Africans. Commercial interests often outweighed enlightened reforms and missionary opinion. There was condescension, arrogance, and even racism. But there were also appeals to reason and higher ideals and occasional victories of benevolence over greed. One British administrator in 1930 argued that "native" interests should be paramount: "At the heart of western civilization lies the faith that human beings are ends in themselves. They have a value apart from any purpose which they may be used to serve. There is something in every man which is unique and incomparable, and which should command our reverence. Progress has consisted in the continuous widening of the field of opportunity for individuals to make the best of what is in them."[18] Few African leaders since then have been imbued with such sentiments.

The French administered their colonies almost in the same way they governed France, extending rights of political representation and citizenship to Africans. (This seemed illogical to the British, who never blurred the distinction between being British and being a British subject.) Two future African presidents (Léopold Senghor and Félix Houphouët-Boigny) sat in France's National Assembly. Houphouët was France's minister of health in five successive governments in the 1950s. He even boasted that he was the only minister to survive the reshufflings, passing "the key" to each new Cabinet. His death in December 1993 was an event in French–not just African–history. His funeral at Yamoussoukro, in the Ivory Coast, in February 1994 was attended by President Mitterrand and 11 of the 12 surviving French prime ministers. Senghor, after stepping down as president of Senegal in 1980, was elected to the French Academy as one of the 40 "immortals" entrusted with guiding the continued expression of French culture throughout the world.

It is true that some countries were left at Independence with few good schools and roads. Some started life as new nations too dependent on neighboring countries. In 1974, two-thirds of Mozambique's national income came from providing rail and port services to the racist regime in South Africa. Agriculture was unevenly developed, with more emphasis on export commodities than food crops. Boundaries were drawn in the wrong places, cutting whole peoples in half, like the Masai in the East (Kenya/Tanzania) and the

Akan in the West (Ghana/Ivory Coast). In some countries, like Rhodesia (later Zimbabwe), a white minority was left holding most of the land. But the record is better than many critics of colonialism would admit.

Europe certainly exploited Africa, in obvious and strange ways. In 1914, at the start of World War I, West African soldiers were pressed into service against German forces, with one French general blithely urging them to attack the enemy's positions early as they were not likely to survive the cold winter in any case.[19] But, for most countries, the colonial period was relatively brief—from the late nineteenth century to the mid-twentieth century. In fact, many later wondered whether the British and the French had left too early and should have assured a more orderly transition to self-government. The Portuguese just walked off. The colonels who overthrew Portugal's dictator in 1974 had no appetite for empire–leaving Angola, Mozambique, Cape Verde, and Guinea-Bissau to their own devices. France lingered longer than others–unofficially–and nurtured so close a relationship with some of its former territories that it was constantly being accused of neo-colonialism. Not everyone regretted this. By the early 1990s, West African parents—shocked by the steady decline of public services and order—were asking their middle-aged children: "C'est pour quand la fin de votre Indépendance?" ("How much longer is this Independence of yours going to last?") Among the only people feeling secure were the survivors of France's colonial wars in Algeria and Indochina who were receiving regular military pension checks from Paris.

The colonial experience also had positive effects that Africans are reluctant to acknowledge. Without the new technologies, habits, ideas, and education introduced by foreigners, the continent would have started even later on the path toward modernization. On the eve of Independence, a British writer noted: "Africans who imagine that all would have gone well for them without European intervention are probably in error, though excusably so; they underestimate their historical need for the revolutionary stimulus of other and more advanced cultures . . . The supplying of this revolutionary stimulus may be the only moral and material justification for colonial conquest: but it is a real one."[20]

Another benefit of imperialism is the former colonial powers' continued interest in Africa. Even countries without a colonial past—like Canada—have been drawn into supporting Africa's development through the Commonwealth of Nations, itself a major remnant of empire. As a result, people who have never set foot on the continent have a remarkable knowledge of its geography and challenges. (An elevator operator in Quebec City once asked a Nigerian friend of mine whether he was from Nigeria or Niger.) Germany, which lost all of its colonial possessions in 1918, still has a strong interest in Africa. So does Italy, even though its colonial history was very brief.

France has the strongest record of continued involvement in Africa. To be sure, some of its initiatives have been controversial. When Guinea refused to enter into a continued "cooperation" agreement with France on the eve of Independence, French officials stripped the country of everything it could, ripping even hospital equipment from its sockets, to punish this "ingratitude." Even after formal colonialism had ended, French forces overthrew governments and installed puppet regimes almost at will. French companies cornered the markets of the 13 countries that are "Africa" to the French—those that speak their language. Pharmaceutical companies bilked rich and poor alike by blocking the importation of generic drugs. And, as late as 2002, Air France was earning 60 percent of its overall profits from its African routes.

But France has also been the largest single source of foreign assistance to Africa. In the 1990s, its government was spending each year $400 per French household on its African programs, including paying the Ivory Coast's debt to the World Bank for 18 months. This was not publicly known in France, although few people would have objected, as a closeness to Africa is part of French identity. Some of that attachment is based on outdated images, more sentimental than probing, and is so far removed from today's realities that two French journalists have called it a love of "Africa without Africans."[21] Much French aid has been wasted on airports, hospitals, highways, and engineering schools that served only the elite and then deteriorated for want of proper maintenance. But as a result of France's continued interest in the continent, thousands of individuals have shared their knowledge and energy with Africans; to this day, they remain vital assets and allies.

Shortly after Independence, a European who knew the dark side of colonialism, tried to put the subject in perspective: "Africans would be far better off if they tried to learn as much from the colonial experience, instead of condemning it unilaterally. They might stop prolonging their errors and profit from their privileges."[22] A fellow author added: "Scores of stadiums, monuments, conference halls, luxury hotels, palaces, motorways are built, expensive jet aeroplanes purchased, steel mills planned, television services opened—while the peasant finds his ration of rice or maize becoming ever smaller. These circumstances are the products of policies controlled by men—African men—not by such abstractions as 'neo-colonialism'. And they can be changed by men."[23]

The Cold War is one cause of Africa's problems that stands up to analysis—within limits. The main charge is that the superpowers protected their shipping lanes and military bases, as well as their access to vital minerals and energy supplies in Africa, by shoring up dictatorships across the continent. But the number of countries directly affected by such tensions (Angola, Ethiopia, Mozambique, and Zaire) was rather small. The few military interventions that occurred were by proxy armies, with the South Africans fighting the Cubans in Angola in the 1980s and South Africans, again, supporting anti-government rebels in Mozambique. The Soviet Union intervened directly only once, bombarding the Eritrean port of Massawa from the sea during the Ethiopian civil war. The damage was terrible, but the initiative failed; Eritrea would eventually win its independence. Some foreign interventions were actually intended to dismember countries rather than keep dictators in power; France supported Katanga's unsuccessful secession from Zaire in 1960 and Biafra's attempted separation from Nigeria in 1967. African leaders, too, were just as interested as anyone else in keeping current regimes and borders intact. All but four African presidents supported Nigeria's war against Biafra and the Organization of African Unity elected Uganda's ruthless buffoon Idi Amin to the presidency of the Organization.

The Cold War also brought benefits. Decolonization was accelerated by US pressure on the former colonial powers, as well as by fear that the Soviet Union would exploit revolutionary elements in individual countries if independence was not granted. The Chinese, hoping to prove their moral superiority over the Americans and the Soviets, built a strategic railway linking Zambia with the Tanzanian coast. And there is little evidence that the superpowers did more damage than African states themselves. Libya meddled as much as the United States and the Soviet Union in other countries' affairs, and the superpowers' protective umbrella had its limits. By January 1968, there had been 64 military coups, attempted coups, and mutinies on the continent.[24] The worst proxy war—in Angola—went on well after the Cold War ended, thanks not to outside interference but to the thirst for power of a stubborn rebel leader, Jonas Savimbi. Nor did the end of the Cold War usher in a new political era; in fact, Africa overthrew very few of its dictators in the years that followed the fall of the Berlin Wall.

What about Africa's debt burden? Debt is a symptom rather than cause of Africa's slow development. It is not clear that Africa borrowed less wisely than other continents. Instead, it is the loss of $70 billion in annual export income that has made those debts unbearable. Furthermore, the world community has been forgiving Africa's debts for over a quarter of a century. There is nothing new about debt relief. What is new is the sheer scale of recent efforts. In 1998, Western countries agreed to write off $50 billion of debt—nearly as much as the World Bank had lent to Africa in the previous 50 years. In June 2005, rich countries agreed to cancel another $40 billion. Even earlier, individual countries had received spectacular support. In the mid-1990s, the World Bank refinanced $1.5 billion of previous borrowing by the Ivory Coast—a country of only 12 million people—with softer funds. These funds were drawn from the International Development Association (IDA) arm of the World Bank Group, which was intended to finance new projects in the poorest countries. Re-financing old debt was not an agreed purpose of IDA. But the action was consistent with the Bank's effort to deal seriously with African debt.

There are understandable differences between those who believe all debt should be "forgiven" and those who prefer to reduce it to a "manageable" level. The first point of view seems inspired by warm-hearted morality; the second, by dry economics. But there is also an ethical basis for questioning the merits of outright debt relief. Countries like Indonesia that have managed their debts carefully do not understand why African countries should be let off lightly. And Africans are not the only ones with a multiplicity of problems. Asians and Latin Americans, too, have faced profligate governments, unscrupulous lenders, unsuccessful projects, and gyrating international commodity prices. Like private firms in difficult circumstances, they have sought to restructure, reschedule, or in other ways lighten their debt loads. Few nations outside Africa have called for outright cancellation.

Nor will debt relief encourage a culture of credit on a continent where poor people—and poor women most of all—are the only ones who can be counted on to pay their debts. It is governments, not people, who benefit from global generosity. Debt cancellation is also expensive. Some international campaigners have suggested that debt relief is relatively painless and that Western governments never expected to collect past loans any more than African governments intended to repay them. They are wrong. Money devoted to reducing debt will not be available for starting new projects. With a higher rate of debt relief, African countries would certainly have fresh resources for a while by freeing up budgetary resources that would otherwise cover interest payments. But these would be absorbed quickly enough by routine government operations, by new debt that the same governments would take on, or by "leaks" of public money into private pockets. And Western efforts to channel debt relief to specific purposes have proved complicated. If there were democratic institutions in Africa, proper audit authorities, a free press, and better priorities in government, the benefits of releasing "old" money for new purposes might be worth the risk. But in current circumstances, debt relief adds acid, not oil, to rusty government machinery in some countries and reduces the scope for targeting outside assistance to purposes everyone would agree are noble.

In any event, since 1985, most new assistance for Africa has been in the form of grants or near-grants. All World Bank assistance has come from a special fund that allowed it to offer 40-year loans, without interest. The European Union, which controls the other large multinational fund for Africa, provides total grants rather than soft loans. Other countries would be pleased to have such help rather than lament the way the world is treating them.

Debt reduction will remain an important part of the world's response to Africa's problems, but it should not be taken for granted and it should not be offered lightly. Africa needs debt relief less than it needs to be relieved of some of its misconceptions.

Are there other reasons for Africa's failures? The continent certainly has a harsh environment. Despite being the cradle of humanity, its climate, diseases, soils, and insects stunted human progress from the very start. By some estimates, about 100,000 years ago as few as 50 people left Africa to settle elsewhere on the globe.[25]. By the beginning of the Christian era, that number had grown to 200 million. During the same period, Africa's population rose from about one million to only 20 million, half of them in North Africa. As one writer pointed out: "Both groups were descendants of the same evolutionary stock. Both groups inherited the talents and physiological attributes that evolution had bestowed during the preceding 4 million years in Africa. So why did the migrant population grow so much faster? Answer: because they moved out of Africa."[26] In a sense, Africa's departing professionals have been traveling a well-worn path in recent years; but it is not weather that has driven them away.

Africa has an unfortunate shape. It is the second largest continent after Asia (11.7 million square miles) and five times the size of Europe, but its coastline is barely a quarter as long. South of the Sahara there are few natural harbors and rivers navigable from the sea.[27] As a result, it has few well-protected, deep-water ports, which have been a key to economic development in other parts of the world.

There are too many countries in Africa—48 of them south of the Sahara, almost half of which (22) have fewer than ten million people. Markets are small, and weak transport links discourage internal trade. But Africans have been trading—or smuggling—goods across borders for decades and have been migrating to jobs wherever they can find them, at a pace that makes a mockery of official efforts at African unity.

Following the introduction of modern medicine in Africa, population growth has posed a new problem. But large populations in other continents have been a spur to innovation and investment, and Africans have never seen their large numbers as a reason for slow growth. Indeed, some African economists wish that their populations could be even denser.

◇ ◇ ◇

Africans' appeal to history to explain their difficulties has now developed a history of its own. In 1966, a European visitor bought some nuts in a Sierra Leone village store and encountered what has become a familiar complaint across the continent since then: "The village was surrounded by nut trees, but the only nuts sold were in tins imported from England. The storekeeper told me that this was because of 'imperialism'." Elsewhere, "Ministers and public servants are driving Mercedes and Cadillacs while the majority of the population are hungry; [large planes] are flying to the international airports, but village roads are impassable; air-conditioning is found in new palaces and offices, whilst mosquitoes return to the neglected slums."[28]

Slavery, colonialism, the Cold War, international institutions, high debt, geography, the large number of countries, and population pressures all have had an effect on Africa. But none of these can explain why the continent has been going backward for the last 30 years. African economies were expanding after Independence. They have been contracting until very recently and are growing again only very slowly.

 Ghana, Nigeria

◇ ◇ ◇

A possible antidote to all this finger-pointing is to look at a subject that has been a supposed priority of governments on the continent: African unity. It is also an area where foreigners have been largely inactive.

On the weekend of February 4–5, 1977, the East African country of Tanzania was preparing to celebrate an important national anniversary. With foreign leaders flying into Nairobi, the capital of the neighboring Kenya, for connecting flights to the Tanzanian capital Dar es Salaam, the Kenyans suddenly pulled the plug on the financially troubled East African Airways, grounding the few planes about to take off. The Tanzanians made hurried arrangements to transport their marooned guests by land. Then, in a fit of pique, the Tanzanian President Julius Nyerere closed the border with Kenya for several years. No other two nations on the continent had been so close. The East African Community (Kenya, Tanzania, and Uganda) was the most successful organization of its kind on the continent. Now, few African countries would be further apart, and Africa's most complete economic union came unstuck. Within a few years, once vibrant public corporations offering regional railway, port, postal, telecommunication, and banking services became historical curiosities. Since then, no other countries, with the possible exception of the West and Central African Franc Zone, have come close to regional unity in a true sense.

This failure of African countries to achieve greater unity is striking after 40 years of grand ideas, resolutions, organizations, and considerable money devoted to overcoming the continent's divisions. There are now 23 major regional organizations and innumerable smaller ones. The largest is the African Union (formerly the Organization for African Unity), headquartered in Addis Ababa, which has 53 members. Sub-regional bodies include the Economic Community of West African States (ECOWAS); the Common Market for Eastern and Southern Africa (COMESA); the Southern African Development Community (SADC); the Central African Economic and Monetary Community (CEMAC); and the Economic Community of the Great Lakes Countries (CEPGL). Some—like the Permanent Inter-State Committee for Drought Control in the Sahel (CILSS)—are focused on particular problems. Others, like the Senegal River Development Organization (OMVS), have only two or three members. But all are best known for pompous officials, padded budgets, stuffy reports, and incessant self-congratulation, rather than for any real progress in pooling national interests.

The Union of African Parliaments has been blunt about this. At its 21st annual meeting in August 1998, it complained about "redundant organizations," "overlapping functions," "unbalanced structures, non-competent appointments, non-payment of contributions and lack of resources," and asked member states to show greater political commitment to these bodies. It also suggested that African regional groupings should work more closely with each other.[29]

Even the World Federalist Movement—which is devoted to making national frontiers a thing of the past—has been sober about the chances for regional cooperation in Africa. An October 2001 background paper on the new African Union, the successor of the Organization of African Unity (OAU), complained that "the OAU has protected the interests of African heads of state without addressing the real problems. Because of the OAU's tradition of non-interference in the internal affairs of its member states, it has proved of limited use across a continent of constant conflict and widespread government corruption. [Nor has it done much] to address Africa's economies or to combat AIDS and other diseases plaguing the continent."[30] One bright spot was that the new African Union had pledged to abide by the African Charter on Human and Peoples' Rights and the Universal Declaration of Human Rights as well as the UN Charter. "However, there is no provision for the establishment of relevant institutions and only five states have ratified the protocol of the African Court on Human and Peoples' Rights."[31]

Is it realistic for Africans to aspire to some greater unity? Certainly. The large number and small average size of countries in Africa have stifled investment, trade, and growth and complicated social progress more generally. These disadvantages, and a flush of pride and solidarity at their sudden liberation from foreign masters, explain why a "Pan-African" movement was born at the very time most states were becoming independent. The wish for a broader "liberation" was very strong and reflected the powerful sense of kinship felt by all Africans. The founders of modern Africa knew it was a force that would not tread water.

Regrettably, they did not achieve very much. Ghana was the first African country to become independent in 1957. Its larger-than-life president, Kwame Nkrumah, set his sights immediately on leading the Pan-African movement. Unfortunately, he was also the first African leader to be overthrown by his army in 1966. Thereafter, the movement lost steam, although it remained a mantra for weary politicians wanting to lift the sights of their peoples beyond their immediate misery. Why the ideal has failed to make progress is closely connected with why Africa has failed more generally, especially economically.

Pettiness and egoism are part of the explanation. During 33 years in power, President Félix Houphouët-Boigny of the Ivory Coast never visited his next-door neighbor, Ghana. "They kept changing governments so often," he used to joke, "that I had to wait for the situation to settle down." But one Ghanaian leader was in office for 19 years. The real reason for Houphouët-Boigny's standoffishness was that he resented Kwame Nkrumah's arrogating the mantle of Pan-African leadership to himself. Different languages (French and English) and distinct colonial experiences also divided them, but these were less important than the discomfort of roosters crowing in the same small yard. The two countries are intimately related—the Akan people straddle both sides of the border—and they can accommodate each other, when necessary. In the late 1990s, a small kingdom in the eastern Ivory Coast (which, like other traditional structures, was granted limited local powers by the national government) elected a king from across the border in Ghana—a young military officer who knew barely a word of French. More importantly, the Ghanaian spoke Akan and his lineage was impeccable. Both countries would be better off if their two governments behaved as wisely as this little kingdom

Balanced economic unions are difficult to create. Countries with built-in advantages find it hard to share these with smaller or poorer neighbors, and it is far from obvious how public policy should affect the location of new industries or investments. But any attempts to tackle such technical difficulties would be a breath of fresh air, compared with the deep indifference of most African governments to the real interests of their peoples. Yet, to this day, the wrong reasons are being cited for the continent's decline. How can people face the future when they cannot even face the facts?

Some Africans *are* facing the facts—but they are in a remarkable minority. Jean-Paul Ngoupandé (whom I quoted earlier on slavery and colonialism) has stopped going to what he calls Africa's "Wailing Wall." He tells the story of being in San Francisco in 1965 and sending a money order and a suit to his father in his remote village in the Central African Republic. Ten days later, the package arrived, via the capital and a district town, with the last 15 miles covered by a postman on his bicycle. Forty years later, Central Africans living in France bring their letters to the Paris airport themselves and hand them to travelers flying home. Nowadays, Ngoupandé dares anyone "to send a money order through the capital to a village—even one close by."[32]

How could anyone have predicted in 1965 that most of Africa would be worse off at the beginning of the twenty first century than when it threw off the supposed shackles of European colonialism?

CHAPTER 2

AFRICA FROM DIFFERENT ANGLES

Africa has been in my blood since the age of fifteen. Like most young Canadians in the 1950s and 1960s, I had a vague awareness of the continent through geography, history lessons, and our British Commonwealth connections, which were relatively new and close at the time. I learned the names of countries and capitals that were to change very soon: Northern Rhodesia, Bechuanaland, Upper Volta, Dahomey, Ruanda-Urundi, Laurenco Marques, and Leopoldville.

But my real introduction to Africa was at Loyola College in Montreal in the mid-1960s, where Donald Savage, an inspiring man with a booming voice and hearty laugh, taught African history. In his spare time, he built up an East African Studies section in the college library and ran a summer orientation program for Canadian volunteers assigned to Kenya, Tanzania, and Uganda. I was fascinated by his intellectual and practical devotion to the continent, but not enough to take one of his courses on African history, a relatively new field at the time. Instead, I signed up for one of his more "respectable" offerings, British Victorian history. But I did not escape the continent that easily. One of my term papers was about Lord Lugard, a giant of British colonial administration and champion of "indirect rule" in Nigeria. In December 1967, I became the beneficiary of another colossus of British African rule—Cecil Rhodes—when I won a Rhodes Scholarship for the Province of Quebec. Professor Savage congratulated me from East Africa, where he was travelling on sabbatical, but also teased me for accepting the generosity of an "imperialist fink."

The next year, I was at Oxford with 67 other young men from the United States and the British Commonwealth, including India, Pakistan, South Africa and Rhodesia (then still named after our benefactor, but later to become Zimbabwe). The only black scholars came from Jamaica and the British Caribbean, as the Rhodes Trust had yet to recognize the newly independent countries of Africa as possible beneficiaries, and the two countries most closely linked with Cecil Rhodes, South Africa and Rhodesia, were still under minority white rule. A group of us asked to see the warden of Rhodes House, Bill Williams, about this; after all, it was 1968 and adding a few countries to the scholarship seemed a minor upheaval compared with those underway in the rest of the world. Williams, who had served as Field Marshal Montgomery's secretary during the 1940–43 North African campaigns, received us graciously but pointed out how hard it was to tamper with a final testament dating back to 1903. He hinted that it would be easier to add women than countries as beneficiaries, and even that would be difficult. (One of the quaint criteria for the Rhodes Scholarship was an interest in "manly outdoor sports.") Women were in fact admitted in 1977, and black Africans in 1986.

My next-door neighbor at Oxford was the British Caribbean Rhodes Scholar, Richard Jacobs. Later the ambassador to the USSR and Vietnam for the ill-starred radical government of Grenada of the early 1980s, he was black—and colorful, too. He joked that he was one of the few people to actually deserve the scholarship, as Rhodes's fortune had been made on the backs of black labor in the gold mines of South Africa. Together, on October 27, 1968, we attended the largest demonstration ever mounted in London against the Vietnam War. One hundred thousand people turned out. Richard took on other causes as well. With Bill Clinton (who was also a Rhodes Scholar that year) he marched into the main branch of Barclays Bank to protest against its involvement in the Cabora Bassa hydroelectric project near the Mozambique–South Africa border. It was non-violent protest at its best: they filled their arms with stacks of deposit slips and sent them fluttering into the air outside in the street.

By that time, I was firmly opposed to apartheid and already an admirer of Nelson Mandela, but I was not yet immersed in African causes. That changed over the next two years, as most of the close friends I made had African roots or came from developing countries. Jacobs and I would wander around Oxford with a Jamaican lawyer, a Sudanese forester and a dark-skinned Sri Lankan civil servant. At a time when immigration and race were already sensitive issues in British politics—the Conservative politician Enoch Powell had recently warned of "rivers of blood" if the country continued to let in Africans and Asians—our little group attracted attention. Once, a police car slowed down as it spotted us on a small street, and sped away only after I came into view.

After two years at Oxford, I began a Master's degree in African Studies at the University of Sussex on the south coast of England. My tutor was a slight man named Christopher Wrigley whose intellect and wit made up for his physical frailty. He had written a small history of Uganda, brimming with imaginative uses of colonial statistics and vivid anecdotes, one of which told of the prodigious interest of the Baganda people in Western education. A Scottish nobleman was fishing on the shores of Lake Victoria in 1898 and offered a nearby "native" some trinkets in exchange for bait. The man replied in perfect English that he would prefer a pen and paper instead.

In the summer of 1971, after I had completed a thesis on the history of the East African Union (Kenya, Tanzania, and Uganda), I considered a volunteer job, teaching schoolgirls African history at the 5,000 foot level of Mount Kilimanjaro. The school was part of a Catholic mission where, I was told, "you could have your teeth pulled and your sins forgiven in the same afternoon." Shortly after, I was also offered a job at the Department of Finance in Ottawa. I accepted this position, and resolved to go to Africa eventually as an economist.

My work at Finance was a powerful introduction to economic policy, political realities, and democracy. I saw how quickly the world was becoming "interdependent." (In the early 1970s, the word "globalization" was not yet widely used although people were already talking about the "global village.") And I was exposed to the challenges of economic development as a member of the Advisory Committee for Northern Development. The Arctic and

Africa had little in common, except for a sometimes harsh environment, but I learned some early lessons about how hard it is for governments to create jobs and how easy it is to create unintended dependencies among those they try to help.

In May 1975, I joined the Canadian International Development Agency, the government body responsible for managing Canada's foreign aid. In November of that year, I set foot in Africa for the first time at Wilson's Airfield in Nairobi, on my way to Johannesburg, South Africa.

It was an unusual trip for a Canadian. South Africa had been expelled from the British Commonwealth in 1961 for its racist policies and Canada had broken off all economic ties with it. The two countries still had diplomatic relations, but they were strained, as it was a Canadian Prime Minister (John Diefenbaker) who had led the charge to punish South Africa. The purpose of my journey was to visit three small countries that could only be reached by traveling through South Africa; in fact, two of them (Lesotho and Swaziland) were entirely surrounded by their large neighbor.

Our destinations were obscure. Botswana (once known as Bechuanaland) was mainly a cattle exporter but was soon to become a major producer of copper and diamonds. Lesotho (formerly Basutoland) was a rugged mountain kingdom, so poor that one of its few exports was human blood for South Africa's hospitals. It also exported mohair wool and–less willingly, through erosion–one percent of its topsoil every year, which traveled down into South Africa's already fertile Orange River Valley. Swaziland was also a mountain kingdom but, unlike Lesotho, was lush and relatively well-off, with sugar estates and forest plantations. The country's King Sobhuza II was the longest-reigning monarch in history. He had been on the throne since 1899 and was to stay there until 1982.

South Africa was on the verge of change, but few people recognized it at the time. Like any casual visitor, I was impressed by how prosperous, orderly, and apparently calm the country was, despite the forces I knew were just below the surface, threatening to tear the country apart. I saw no signs of black anger or resentment on the streets of Johannesburg and Pretoria.

Six weeks later, in January 1976, the largest black township, Soweto, exploded in revolt. No one could have known that this was the beginning of the end of white rule. The Soweto uprising dispelled the notion that the black population would be "patient" while the benefits of white-led progress trickled down to them. The disturbances went on for weeks, and by the end of the year 500 people had been killed. Afterward, political pressure for reform gathered pace. Unfortunately, many more people would be imprisoned, tortured, or killed in the struggle for freedom, but a sense was finally dawning that they were now on the winning side. In 1991, just 15 years later, one of Africa's great leaders, Nelson Mandela, was released from prison and began negotiating a new constitution for South Africa.

In December 1976, I was posted as First Secretary (Development) to the Canadian High Commission in Dar es Salaam, Canada's embassy in Tanzania. Now, five years after passing up the volunteer job on Mount Kilimanjaro, I had a ringside seat at the one of the great experiments in economic development. My two years there were rich in learning, but as a young diplomat I lived largely in a bubble, leaving the office at the end of the day to take my sailboat out into Msasani Bay or watch the sunset over a gin and tonic at the Yacht Club. I made only one close African friend, Charles Mutashobya, a young economist at the Ministry of Finance. (Two years later, he was shot dead on the campus of Georgia State University by an unidentified man sitting in a parked car.) The next time I lived in Africa, I promised myself, I would try to get off the beaten path.

In October 1978, I left Tanzania—and the Canadian government—to join the Organization for Economic Cooperation and Development (OECD) in Paris, which tried to coordinate the economic policies of the 24 richest countries on earth. My job was to suggest ways to simplify and harmonize the foreign aid procedures of the OECD countries and hence ease the administrative burden on developing countries. But it soon became plain that the largest donors—the United States, Japan, and Germany—were not interested in simpler procedures. They needed to demonstrate to their parliaments and publics that there were still "strings" on their generosity. They guarded their own forms and regulations jealously. Common donor standards and procedures, which would have reduced paperwork enormously in African and Asian capitals, were out of the question and remain an elusive objective to this day.

Cumbersome rules were also a good excuse for not increasing aid budgets.

I soon began to miss the concrete problems I had faced in the field, so within 12 months I joined the World Bank in Washington, DC, as loan officer for Tanzania. My work was fulfilling, but during the first four years, I missed the company of Africans. That problem was solved in October 1984, when I walked into St. Augustine's Roman Catholic parish, the "mother church" of African–American Catholics in the US capital. I ended up staying there for the next 18 years. I even joined the choir. At rehearsals each week, we would join hands and pray for those in need, down the street or across the world. Three centuries after their ancestors had been wrenched from their homes, these Africans showed the same profound sense of community, faith, and long-suffering that now keep a deeply troubled continent intact.

In August 1983, still based in Washington, I became one of the Bank's loan officers for Indonesia. On my long trips there, lasting five to six weeks, I did what I had not done in Tanzania: I took local buses into the countryside in my spare time to see how rural people lived. The sheer pace of Indonesia's progress was staggering, although it faced the same harsh tropical climate, soils, and diseases that many argued were the main brakes on Africa's development. Indonesia was not at the forefront of the East Asian "miracle." Like Africa, its institutions were relatively young, it depended on foreign technical assistance, and it lacked the infrastructure and efficiency of South Korea, Taiwan, and Hong Kong. But it was rapidly catching up. It had large oil and gas reserves and was one of the few countries in modern history to use them wisely. Between 1975 and 1995, Indonesia reduced the number of its poor from 60 percent to 20 percent of the population.

The blossoming of Indonesia is one of the least talked about successes in international development, partly because it was achieved by an authoritarian regime and partly because the financial crisis of 1997 revealed the corruption and cronyism that also underlay the Indonesian economy. Poverty increased slightly after the crisis, but the salutary effects of two decades of good economic management and public investment were still intact.

There was nothing accidental about Indonesia's success. Policy-makers had begun with "good housekeeping"—keeping indonesia

government deficits and inflation in check, borrowing wisely and paying on time, and acting pre-emptively to deal with new challenges. But the heart of their strategy was to invest a large part of their petroleum revenues in programs that would improve rural growth and incomes. These included strict family planning policies, rice "multiplication" programs (featuring high-yield varieties and improved agricultural services), rural irrigation, and adult literacy programs. As a result, the country—which had formerly been the largest rice importer on earth—became self-sufficient in less than a generation.

In May 1991, I was named chief of the World Bank's regional office in Western Africa, based in Abidjan, the capital of the Ivory Coast. As the country was one of the continent's few success stories, I was excited about my appointment. I had been absent from Africa for eight years, and was now eager to apply some of the experience I had gained in other environments. But, first, I had to overcome a personal hurdle.

I had been living with another man for over ten years. Until that time, the Bank had never posted a same-sex couple overseas. I had been testing the waters discreetly for a number of years to imagine the reaction, and the results were not encouraging. "Of course, you can accept a foreign assignment," a senior manager (who was also gay) assured me, "but Jean Daniel is going to have to live in a separate house." Other colleagues were more supportive. A former division chief of mine, a colorful Texan woman known for her brilliance and bluntness, told me that if she had a partner as presentable as mine, she would put him at the head of every diplomatic reception line in town.

I decided that, when the moment came, I would not make an issue of it. I saw no reason why my personal circumstances should get in the way of my professional life, and I certainly was not going to ask for permission to serve overseas simply because I was gay. My partner was more prudent. He wondered whether the institution would appreciate being taken by surprise; he also wanted to be more than a shadow lurking in the wings. "After all," Jean Daniel pointed out, "we're going to be living in a Bank-owned house." He wanted to feel free to walk through the front door.

So, when finally faced with the issue, I raised the matter with my boss, the Bank's vice president for Personnel and Administration, whom I was serving as senior adviser. "Well, you're certainly entitled to your privacy," he said, "but if I were the country director I would want to know about this in advance." With mild trepidation, I went to see my future supervisor, a former US Marine and reportedly a straight-laced Catholic. He could not have been more understanding. Remembering his early days in the military when he had been stationed at a US base in Germany without his wife—an experience he resented still—he told me to visit Abidjan, consult the Bank's current representative there, and see how my circumstances would sit with the government and local society. The reaction of the man I was to replace was also quite positive. Like the French themselves, French West Africans, were careful about protecting the private lives of public figures; they also had enough to hide on the sexual front not to want to ask pointed questions about others. Our current representative, a bubbly Latin American who had become quite popular locally, thought my nationality, personality, and experience would win people over immediately and disarm the sniggerers.

He was right. Within months of arriving, my personal circumstances were barely noticed. At the start, there were some awkward moments—for others, not for us. At our first diplomatic receptions, I would introduce Jean Daniel as my "friend." Ambassadors and their spouses would welcome him eagerly: "How long will you be staying?" "We'll be here at least three years," Jean Daniel replied. There were some awkward silences, throats were cleared, and then there were quick recoveries: "Oh, how nice." Within weeks, we were receiving joint or separate invitations to functions.

About the only way my personal circumstances affected my work was in my attention to HIV/AIDS. The disease had been identified just ten years before and was widely regarded in North America and Europe as a "homosexual" problem. In Africa, the virus was spreading like a brush fire among the general population. Like most gay men of my generation, I had already lived through the equivalent of a world war with close friends and friends of friends dying in large numbers without armor on a battlefield none of them had chosen. I also had first-hand experience of the disease as a night volunteer in Washington, DC, in 1986–89 at an AIDS hospice run by the sisters of Mother Teresa. I knew how devastating the disease would be in Africa. It was easy to project the numbers. But Africans were being complacent about it, and I wanted to shake them out of their disbelief.

My being gay also led to an interesting encounter. Barney Frank, the first openly gay member of Congress, who is regarded even by his enemies as one of the brightest people on Capitol Hill, visited West Africa in his capacity as Chairman of the House Sub-Committee on International Economic Affairs. He was not a friend of the World Bank. In the reception line at the US Ambassador's residence, he scowled at me and said: "This afternoon, the government has been grumbling about you people." "That's normal," I told him. "The World Bank isn't very popular with governments anywhere in Africa."

Later, I spotted him standing alone, nursing a drink, while guests circulated around him. I went up to him and said that, while I was not an American and had no reason to flatter him, I had been following his career with great interest for years. He looked at me a little doubtfully. "In fact," I went on, "I even quote you to foreigners who want to understand the United States." "What is it I said?" he quizzed me. "Well, in the 1982 mid-term elections at the height of the Reagan Revolution, when liberals were running for cover, you told voters in Massachusetts that Americans were conservative in general but quite liberal when they got down to the details." "I did say that, didn't I?" he remembered. "And I think it's still true."

The ice was broken. As we continued chatting, various members of the American community came up to us. Many asked how my summer holidays had been, and where Jean Daniel was. I told them that he was still in France and would be joining me soon. After I had been asked this several times, Barney turned toward me and said: "Well, I think it's time you met my partner," and he led me across the room to introduce me. Congressman Frank was on his first official trip with his other half, Herb Moses, and this had led to some amusing incidents. In Senegal, the government kept putting Herb in a car at the back of the motorcade and Barney had to go back, haul him out, and tell his hosts: "He's with me."

Both men were fascinated that the World Bank had stationed a same-sex couple overseas. (To this day, it is the only UN agency that extends domestic partner benefits to its employees.)

"Do you mind," Barney asked me, "if I comment on this favorably when I get back to Washington?" "Do you really have to?" I answered, squirming a little at having my private life made an issue—positively or negatively—in Congressional relations with the Bank. "I'd like to, if you let me," Barney answered. "I criticize people sharply when they do the wrong thing. By the same token, I think it's important to give positive reinforcement when people are on the right track." At the end of dinner, he asked me if I could show Herb and him some local sights the next morning, a Saturday. "I'm scheduled to visit the AIDS ward at the city hospital," he said, "and you know how little I need to learn about that subject."[1]

A couple of months later, I heard that the World Bank president had received a letter that he asked his staff to decipher. "It's the first time I've had a positive letter from the Congressman, and I don't know what he's talking about." In the letter, Congressman Frank expressed appreciation for the good support he had had from the World Bank's offices in Ghana, Senegal, and the Ivory Coast and wanted especially to commend the "progressive human resource policies" the institution was practicing in Abidjan.

Breaking new ground in this area proved to be an act of unintended audacity on my part. I knew that a successful assignment in Africa would lower some barriers and help overcome prejudices for other gay staff at the World Bank and elsewhere. But I was a reluctant pioneer. I raised the issue, not thinking it should be one, only because my partner Jean Daniel insisted on it. Little did I know that I would soon have to be audacious on a different front.

I had not done much public speaking in my career, but the country had just introduced a multiparty system. Now, a fledgling free press was trying to stretch its wings. Within days of arriving, I was being asked by reporters what I thought about the nation's future. I said that I would need at least six months to learn about the country before I gave any talks. However, I did agree to appear live on the television nightly news, and I surprised myself by how forthright I was that evening. The first question was, "What can the World Bank do for the Ivory Coast?" My answer: "You're asking the wrong question. You should be asking what you can do for yourselves, and how the rest of the world can play a small part to help." No one took offense, and I was invited back.

Conscious of the expatriate life I had led in Tanzania, I turned down an opportunity to buy a share of a beach cottage up the coast near Ghana. I did not want to spend every weekend sipping cocktails under the palm trees, and knew I would not meet many local people at the beach resorts. My instincts served me well. Within weeks, I was being invited to people's homes. Part of the reason was my status—people were interested in getting to know the World Bank representative—but part of it, too, was that I was available and curious. As will be plain from this book, the next three years were to be my richest experience of Africa.

Perhaps it was my knowledge of other poor countries, especially Indonesia, or a sense that African excuses were now wearing thin, but I was determined not to waste the opportunities I would be given to challenge government and even the general public. By June 1992, I was spending two-thirds of my time outside the office, visiting the countryside, composing talks, giving interviews, commenting on recent events, and manifestly not avoiding the press. This was not because of some daredevil taste for self-exposure but rather from a recognition that the greatest need at the time was for an open debate on national economic and social issues. People were being starved of basic information, and were confused about what was happening to them. There was an "economic crisis" but they knew little about it or what was in store for them. Facts and figures—and honest opinions—were so rare that people soaked them up like water on parched earth.

I made myself available, and people, in turn, opened themselves up to me. If I was out when journalists telephoned, I called back within a half hour of returning to the office. If they wanted an interview, I gave it the same day or, if I needed to prepare for it, the next day at the latest. I liked journalists, respected their profession, and understood the difficulties they faced, and it showed. In my first outing before 150 business people, I said that HIV/AIDS was one of the three most important issues the country was facing—and I still hadn't figured out what the other two were. I complimented the government's economic team, but also praised the "constructiveness" of the opposition. This must have seemed rather cheeky, as half the opposition's leadership was in jail for supposedly organizing a violent demonstration. But it was obvious that I believed what I was saying and that I was trying to stress the bright side of a difficult situation.

My first major speech, on the economic and social importance of fighting AIDS, was printed in the opposition daily. In it, I got right to the point. "I am not talking about the disease in the abstract. I have lost six close friends to AIDS." I explained that, at the hospice in Washington, I had accompanied fifty people on the road to death. "At first they were strangers, but very quickly afterward they became my brothers and sisters. I learned a great deal at their side about human suffering and courage. They also reinforced my natural inclination to be direct and even blunt about important questions in life, like AIDS itself."[2]

Other talks I gave were also printed in their entirety. These were on subjects that did not usually appear in the popular press—such as the importance of primary education, family planning, giving women access to credit, fighting corruption, and opening internal markets for farmers and workers, not just business. I never refused an interview, so my opinions appeared in some unlikely places, including papers to the far right and far left of the government. One day, the foreign minister, who had been reading the opposition paper, winced: "Boy, those are painful truths you're telling us this week." "Don't worry," I said with some relief. "Next Monday, you'll be able to read my economic predictions for 1994 in *Reveil-Hebdo* (a pro-government weekly)."

People at both ends of the political spectrum were impressed by the locations of some of the talks. These included movie theaters and open-air bars in large, poor neighborhoods far from the center of the capital, where diplomats and aid officials seldom ventured. I did not choose these places. That was done by the organizers, and I just went along.

For example, one day in central Abidjan, a young man came up to me, shook my hand, and said: "You're the World Bank representative, aren't you? I really enjoyed your speech at City Hall last month. Would you be willing to talk to a group of high school drop-outs?" I agreed immediately and suggested they come see me the following week to set a subject and date. They wanted me to talk about the financing of very small projects for the young. The topic was improbable, as a large international institution and $500 ventures were hardly an obvious combination. But so many young

Africans were curious about how to find their own way, sensing that connections in the right places were more important than talent in seeking employment, that I decided to give it a try.

At the appointed hour one Saturday morning, the same young man came round to the office to escort me to the hall where the talk was to be given. Immediately after getting into the car, he said that he had run into a problem. The local mayor wanted the event postponed, as he had hoped to attend and had prior engagements that day. "I told him that you were not a very complicated person, that you would not expect the mayor to be present, and that in any case this was *our* project, not the city's, and we wanted to proceed as planned." I broke out laughing at his initiative and independence.

I made the talk a young person's primer on development and the need for economic reform and competition. Africa, I pointed out, was not the only part of the world that needed to adjust to changes in the world economy. When I was a student in Montreal in 1965, only 5 percent of the national product of the United States—the largest and most diversified economy on earth—depended on international trade; now, two-thirds of all new US manufacturing jobs came from exports.

The audience was not merely happy with the talk; they were enraptured. The fact that I was willing, despite a supposedly "high" position and busy schedule, to rub shoulders with unemployed youth in a grimy hall far from the center of the city, to enlighten and encourage, was almost message enough. There were two hours of questions afterward, as well as some heart-rending statements by young people explaining their predicaments. One person liked my suggestion that, when it came to economic reform, we were all "in the same boat." He had been a student and rural social worker in the Ardeche region of France, and saw how hard it was for some French families to make ends meet. He no longer thought of a rich "North" and a poor "South," but of a world family struggling with similar problems of unemployment and uncertain markets.

During these discussions, it was plain how little the government was telling the public about national issues and how important outsiders were in promoting a more balanced public discourse. One day on national television, the Minister of Education accused the dean of the university law faculty and president of the national

Human Rights League of being a "troublemaker." This surprised me, as I knew the professor well and thought of him more as an Abraham Lincoln than a revolutionary. He had been urging me to give a talk on democracy, development, and human rights; so, a few months later, after the dust had settled, I did just that—with him in the chair beside me. Another way of promoting fair play was to ensure that the whole press, not just the state media, were present at public events involving the World Bank. When independent journalists were left off the invitation list by the government, no protest could have been more eloquent—or effective—than the last-minute call from my office to correct the "oversight."

I came to learn that the size of the immediate audience at these gatherings was immaterial. As one high school principal told me after a "disappointing" turnout of 60 students for one of my talks: "If we had known that you would be speaking in *French* to our English Club, there would have been hundreds of pupils here. In any case, you've probably talked to a million people indirectly today, as brothers will be telling cousins, and they, in turn, their cousins, that the World Bank representative is very positive about this country's future if we recognize our advantages and act on them."

Sometimes, my views produced wider ripples than I intended. In April 1993, I gave a talk to the National Chamber of Commerce and Industry on how to make the country's products more competitive. The speech was covered only lightly in the newspapers, but national radio and television, both of which interviewed me afterward, kept repeating my messages for three or four days. Ten days later in Washington, the World Bank president met with nine African finance ministers. The minister from Guinea waved a copy of the speech in front of him. "This was a tough talk," he said, "but I agree with every word of it. The World Bank needs to tell governments more of this kind of thing, if change is to happen in Africa and if we are to be able to explain it properly to our citizens."

At times, spreading a positive message meant taking some detours. Three days after the Chamber of Commerce speech, I gave a one-hour interview on national radio. I had been told that the questions would be one-third personal and two-thirds professional, but in the end, the proportions were reversed and some of the subjects were peculiar. "What do you think about death?" the interviewer asked. "What comes to mind when you think of your parents?" "What do your colleagues think of you?" "Have you ever fired anyone?" "Who are your favorite African musicians?" "What is your greatest weakness?" "Are you well-paid?" But I was still pleased to do the interview, as I had prepared some vivid examples of how the rural areas were suffering economically and what needed to be done about it.

At the end of the school year, a geography student came to see me to organize a talk. I asked him why he had chosen to invite me. "Because I heard you on the radio last month, and I told myself that if you could be so direct and frank over the air, I could certainly risk asking for an appointment." He continued: "What you do is a sacrifice, isn't it?" I didn't understand what he meant. "Well, it's obvious that no one *has* to answer the personal questions you were asked that night, and it seemed plain to me that you were doing it in order to move on to other subjects which you considered more important and that you believed in very deeply."

Often, I observed that there was a gap between what older and younger people were prepared to hear. My secretary, who was from Sierra Leone and by her own admission a member of the "old school" asked me why I was going to refer to corruption in a speech that evening. "Why not," I asked, "if it is an important obstacle to economic development?" "Because you're a diplomat," she answered, "and you should deal with these things deftly and indirectly." At about the same time, a young Ivorian friend asked me: "Why do you have to be so polite to the government? You're the only person I know who is prepared to say that the country is doing *something* right!" Between these two extremes, I found a lot of room to swim.

As a North American, I had a decisive advantage in a sometimes pompous and wooden environment. One local stricture was that no one could hold a public event without paying obeisance to the ruling party. The "sponsor" of one of my talks was the party's information chief. He arrived in a three-piece suit and tie, with a girth that would test a tailor's talents. The rest of us were in slacks and open-necked shirts. He thanked the group for inviting "such a humble person" (namely himself) to preside over the event. After the talk, he started the round of questions: "Mister Calderisi, we have listened to you almost religiously, but I think the World Bank has a communications problem. We know that things have to change, but why does the World Bank always insist on 'shock treatment' rather than gentle remedies?" Then, without waiting for an answer, he pleaded another engagement, excused himself, and left.

I had to answer hundreds of questions about controversial subjects, some of them quite hostile. But even the most stubborn questioners usually flashed a smile at the end if I tried to answer them honestly and carefully. Even when the pleasure was entirely mine, others were eager to show their appreciation. One evening, as I was fielding questions in a village by the light of a hurricane lamp, a young man slipped up behind me and unfurled on the table in front of me a four-page transcript from the national newspaper of a press conference I had given a year before. He had wrapped it carefully in plastic to protect it against the damp, and this seemed to be his way of saying that he was grateful I had come all this way to talk to them. I had been to nine villages that day and was getting tired. I didn't need that encouragement and couldn't acknowledge it except with a smile, as I was talking to someone in the audience. But I never forgot it, and it proved to me that even in remote corners of the continent there was an interest in knowing the facts and debating them openly.

Everywhere I went, I stuck to the same themes. For the Ivory Coast, I maintained, economic recovery would be smoother than for other countries. Economic reforms were necessary for *social* reasons, especially in the rural areas. An end to monopolies was in everyone's interest, even the monopolists. Economic growth would lead to development only with greater attention to population growth, basic health and education, and AIDS. And the government needed to build a consensus for change and introduce reforms fairly.

These messages transcended ideological and social boundaries. In a single week, I received positive comments about my talks from a human rights activist, a French pineapple grower, Italian missionaries, Ivorian entrepreneurs, the Papal Nuncio, a Canadian charity, and the Minister of Information. The only negative reactions were from French businessmen who felt I was being "harsh" about the lack of competition and efficiency in the country and too "favorable" to the informal sector. Amazingly, I was also told by a member of the ruling party's central committee that I was "too upbeat" about the country's future, undercutting his efforts to dramatize current difficulties.

Of course, it was hard to speak out without offending someone. And sometimes there was power in simply listening. I visited a poor neighborhood of Abidjan with a large group of journalists, whom the organizers had invited along. It was a squatter settlement. But I found the physical condition of the place less shocking than some of the stories I heard from my audience. They told of absentee landlords gouging their tenants for nonexistent services, policemen intimidating local activists, and mothers depositing dead babies in dumpsters (because they could not afford the "fees" for registering their deaths officially and burying them properly). I said very little, but the fact that I was hearing this, and appeared moved, became "news."

Unfortunately, some of the coverage was at the expense of the local authorities: "Why does the World Bank representative care enough to see poverty at first hand and the mayor doesn't even bother to join him for the visit?" I cringed at the holier-than-thou tone of the articles. Naturally, I expected to be reprimanded by the poor mayor; instead, the complaint came from a completely different quarter. At a bankers' reception a week later, the deputy head of the Central Bank, who knew me well enough to curse, blasted me: "What the *hell* were you doing in a neighborhood like that?!" I replied that, like other World Bank staff, I was simply doing my job. But it was plain that, to him, I had strayed well beyond the boundaries of prudence and good taste—and his notion of "development" work. The people I had visited in the poor neighborhood that morning were less surprised by my attention than the central banker had been. And, despite the misery around them, they had offered a humorous welcome. Crossing a two-plank "bridge" that floated precariously over marshy, sewage-filled ground, I was told that it would henceforth be named after me because I was the first "public figure" to have crossed it. Later, I was told that improvements were being made so that it could be worthy of its new title.

Throughout my tours of the country, I heard vivid stories that I simply repeated when I was back in the capital, using them to dramatize the unfairness of current economic and social policies.

Government officials, journalists, and other diplomats took notice. But amid all the mounting tension on the political front and continued wrong-headedness in the economic sphere, my greatest personal shock was at the lack of real interest in HIV/AIDS.

Some of the saddest cases I saw at Abidjan hospital were infected women in their 50s and 60s who had contracted the disease by simply sleeping with their husbands. Yet, many people still regarded AIDS as a "white man's disease." Cynics saw it as an "easy" answer to Africa's population problem—a solution that I compared to breaking up a traffic jam with a nuclear bomb. Still others felt, fatalistically, that this was another scourge that must be faced bravely, rather than fought off.

There were local heroes, of course, who tried to stem the tide. A young doctor at the AIDS ward set up a community organization to offer free tests and initial treatment to people, off the street. She called the clinic Espoir [Hope], and I helped publicize her efforts so that she could raise funds from outside agencies. But it was mainly foreign governments and private charities that were taking the issue seriously. Even the sisters of Mother Teresa were doing more than the national government to deal with the problem. With French aid, they constructed a large hospice in a poor neighborhood of the city and bristled with evangelical fervor in their efforts to inform and help.

At a garden party for the departing French Consul and his wife who had helped build the hospice, the Mother Superior came up to me, wagged a finger, and said: "Where have you been all this time? We haven't seen you at the hospice for at least nine months, and we *need* you. The other day, I asked the French Consul's wife to call you, because we had a young man who had just learned he was HIV-positive and he was taking the news very badly. We felt you could help him." "She did call me," I answered. "But I was in bed with the flu all day Saturday and Sunday." My partner Jean Daniel also made excuses for me. "You know, Sister, he has less time on his hands now. He is involved in *so many* things . . ." But she didn't look convinced, and I admired her tenacity. She made me feel guilty to have had the flu. She wouldn't have let it get the better of *her*.

In areas other than HIV/AIDS, especially the effects of national monopolies on the cost of living, I knew I was having an im-

pact when a reputable weekly newspaper published a three-part series on maritime services and shipping regulations. The first week,
the paper offered a balanced summary of the subject. The second
week, I was asked my views. Knowing the shippers would have
their say in the following issue, I pulled no punches: "Do you remember the nineteenth-century fable of the candle-makers who
persuaded the King to ban all windows so that people would be
forced to light candles during the day as well as at night? This is a
simple case of 'protection' for the few, at the expense of the many."[3]

The following week, the ship-owners said they were astonished
by the "ignorance and incoherence" of my arguments. "To justify
deregulation," they complained, "he suggests that current laws are
'old fashioned' because they date back 15 or 20 years. What does a
short period of time like that represent in the life of a nation?
Don't the laws of most Western countries date back more than a
century?"[4]

People stopped me in the street to apologize for the strong language the shippers had used. But I was delighted, not upset, that
there had been a detailed public debate about a central aspect of
economic policy, and that everyone's view had been heard.

A month before I left the country, in front of half the Cabinet,
the Minister of Transport said what he thought of me. "Mr.
Calderisi likes to be frank, so I want to be frank with him. He
spends too much time talking to private businessmen. The next
time he needs information about transport issues, he should approach government officials first." I didn't respond, as he was a
minister and I was just an international civil servant. Besides, the
reprimand was a backhanded compliment. All I could have said in
return was: "What's the use of economic reforms if only government officials understand them?"

The rebuke reminded me of how unfortunately dependent the
country had become on outside advice and money. It also suggested how narrow and difficult the "debate" remained on economic policy, despite the public fuss on shipping policy. Issues of
open government, a free press, and easy access to public information would be as important for the future of Africa as economic
management in the narrow sense. The right of international institutions to express themselves publicly on issues of national policy
was a fair subject for debate. But the public's right to comment

should have been obvious; here, and in other countries, it was being denied.

I had spent a great deal of time with journalists and knew how important a free press was for promoting understanding, fairness, and honesty in the economy, not just society. So, even then, I wished that aid programs could be switched off overnight if a single journalist was imprisoned purely for expressing his views. That did not seem practical at the time, but I have changed my mind since.

In July 1997, I became the World Bank's spokesperson for Africa, based in Washington. It was one of the many paradoxes of international aid that the institution most suspected, feared, and even reviled by many Africans was also considered the most informed and reliable on issues affecting the continent. The World Bank and IMF were seen as sometimes impersonal forces for change but also as one of the only counterweights to economic excess and one-party rule. This put the institutions on an unusual moral and political ground.

Criss-crossing Africa over the next three years, I heard familiar complaints about the dead weight of history and the role of the international institutions; but I also saw fresh signs that foreign aid was not helping many Africans. In Malawi, in April 1999, while I was visiting a road maintenance project, farmers left their fields and walked up to me to beg for money. That was the low point of my career. I knew the pride of rural people—and now I saw how desperate they were.

In July 2000, I was appointed Country Director for Cameroon, Central African Republic, Chad, Gabon, and Equatorial Guinea. In February 2001, I paid an official call on Cameroon's senior Catholic cleric, the Cardinal Christian Tumi, of Douala. He had been relentless in his criticism of the government's human rights record and the rigging of the last presidential elections, and was now considered a leading opposition figure—to the point of being refused a radio license for his diocese. Of course, the charges were ridiculous. As he explained, he was only speaking as a citizen: "I was *born* a Cameroonian, and *became* a Christian and priest. Why can't I have views about what is happening to my country?"

We spoke about AIDS. He thought the national infection rate (11 percent) was an underestimate, especially in the Northwest, where he was from. Only ten years before, there had been no cases. Now, there were at least five burials a week in his home village and most of those dying were under 50 years of age. The degree of hopelessness was extreme. One prostitute had told him recently: "I prefer to die of AIDS than hunger." As I left him, I hoped that his courage and down-to-earth views would make him Pope one day. Fortunately, Cameroon's president would have no say in the matter.

That night, I slept badly, hearing fireworks and sirens and people shouting in the street. I wondered whether these were demonstrations or the beginnings of a coup d'état; but I was too tired to drag myself to the window to see what was going on. The next morning, over breakfast, I was told that there had been a wedding at the hotel that night. A long and noisy one, I thought. At the office, I learned the truth. The central munitions dump of the capital had blown up at four A.M. and spewed smoke and flames for at least two hours. The area had been cordoned off for an investigation, but the official explanation was that women had been burning grass alongside the facility and sparks had leapt up onto the roof. No one believed the story—few people burnt grass in the middle of the night—but the incident was emblematic of the ignorance, uncertainty, dishonesty, and insecurity that rule African lives.

CHAPTER 3

THUGS IN POWER

The simplest way to explain Africa's problems is that it has never known good government. This was recognized over a century ago by the explorer Henry Stanley. In his memoirs of an expedition to rescue an embattled governor in the Sudan, *In Darkest Africa* (1891), Stanley used words that are dated but still accurate: "We may regret that [the Governor] did not possess that influence over his troops which would have compelled them to respect natives as fellow-subjects, to be guardians of peace and protectors of property . . ..The natives of Africa cannot be taught that there are blessings in civilization if they are permitted to be oppressed and to be treated as unworthy of the treatment of human beings, to be despoiled and enslaved at will by a licentious soldiery."[1]

No other continent has experienced such prolonged dictatorships. The record-holder is the president of Gabon, who has been in power since 1967. A close runner-up was Togo's dictator, in office for 37 years until he died in February 2005. Four other countries have had the same leaders for more than 20 years: Angola (1979); Equatorial Guinea (1979); Zimbabwe (1980); and Cameroon (1982). Like many of their contemporaries who were also in power a long time (Mobutu of Zaire, Houphouët-Boigny of the Ivory Coast, Sekou Toure of Guinea, Moi of Kenya), these men spent their entire careers enriching themselves, intimidating political opponents, avoiding all but the merest trappings of democracy, actively frustrating movements toward constitutional rule, and thumbing their noses–sometimes subtly, other times blatantly–at the international community. They ruled like kings and drew no distinction between their own property and that of the state. Some denied this. Mobutu, for one, insisted: "I cannot live outside the [government] budget. Where would the money come from?"[2] But Gabon's president was less coy, asking a French journalist in 2002: "Was the palace at Versailles built with money belonging to the French state or to Louis XIV?"[3] But let none of their citizens protest. Even now, in putative democracies in French-speaking Africa, it is a crime to "insult" the head of state. Imagine the dampening effect such laws have on political debate. Scores of journalists have spent time in prison or been murdered for exercising basic rights of dissent.

Modern African leaders are not the first to overstay their welcome. Paul Kruger, the first president of the Transvaal, which later became part of the Republic of South Africa, held office for 18 years. "Continued rule for half a generation must turn a man into an autocrat," thought Arthur Conan Doyle, the creator of Sherlock Holmes and author of *The Great Boer War* (1901). He reported that "The old President [Kruger] has said himself, in his homely but shrewd way, that when one gets a good ox to lead the team it is a pity to change him. If a good ox, however, is left to choose his own direction without guidance, he may draw his wagon into trouble."[4] One wishes that later African presidents could be described so indulgently.

In the early years of Independence, firm rule was tolerated and even encouraged by Africa's former colonizers, now its "partners" or patrons. They felt that Africans were not ready for elections and multi-party democracy. But the notion that Africans would have to wait for the political privileges of Westerners did not impress brilliant young leaders at the time. Unfortunately, many of them were cut down in their prime. One of the finest was Tom Mboya of Kenya, whose idealism, clarity, and promise died with his assassination in 1969. Others, like Thomas Sankara of Burkina Faso, were killed before they had a chance to test their ideals against hard realities. Despite their original intentions, these idealists might have instituted one-party states; but we will never know. The people who murdered them did so in their stead.

In the mid-1990s, a tide of political liberties finally seemed to rise across Africa; but hope quickly faded, even among sympathetic observers. The new leaders simply picked up where the old ones left off. In early 1998, when Bill Clinton made the first trip of a US president to Africa in 20 years, a fresh generation of politicians was being hailed as precursors of the "African Renaissance." They were Yoweri Museveni (Uganda), Paul Kagame (Rwanda), Meles Zenawi (Ethiopia), Issais Afewerki (Eritrea), and Thabo Mbeki (South Africa). They were an odd group. While modern in some respects, all but Mbeki had risen to power through the barrel of a gun. Within a year of Clinton's visit, Museveni and Kagame had invaded the eastern Congo, ostensibly to chase down former members of the extremist Hutu militia responsible for the 1994 genocide of 800,000 Rwandans, but also to plunder gold and other resources suddenly available for the taking. Within two years, Ethiopia and Eritrea were warring over a piece of barren land along their borders. Ten thousand young Ethiopians were sent to their deaths in a single battle, rushing the Eritrean front lines.

Thabo Mbeki was making headlines of a different kind. With 25 percent of his compatriots infected, he was questioning the origins of the HIV/AIDS epidemic, slowing research, and blocking access to potentially life-saving drugs. His hesitation and callousness probably hastened as many deaths as some of Africa's smaller wars. He was roundly criticized at home. Yet, as late as February 2004, the South African Minister of Health was recommending a diet of garlic, olive oil, and lemon juice to alleviate the effects of HIV infections. Even a monthly spoonful of olive oil, she insisted, would have significant effects on the immune system.[5]

Other "new" leaders have shown a streak of high-handedness. For example, in January 2002, President Obasanjo of Nigeria reportedly told the relatives of more than 600 people killed in an accidental explosion in Lagos to "shut up." Then, he added unnecessarily, "I don't need to be here."[6] Obasanjo's staff later explained that he was unaware the crowd was grieving—implying that he needed a special reason to be courteous to them.

African specialists, accustomed to measuring progress by the millimeter, will point out that in 1991 Benin was the first African country to replace one government with another by electoral means. The rarity of the event was stupefying enough. Elsewhere, military governments, dictatorships, and one-party systems still held sway. But even such advances were short-lived. At the next election, Benin's former dictator was back in power, perhaps somewhat wiser for his brief absence from the scene but certainly no promoter of fresh ideas and new blood. In Zambia, at about the same time, a relatively idealistic trade union leader, Frederick Chiluba, came to power by peaceful means. Within eight years, he was trying to amend the country's constitution to ensure himself a third term. It took great effort to block the amendment, but his opponents managed to do so eventually. Some were stubborn democrats; others, undoubtedly, were would-be autocrats themselves.

Any political progress in the last thirty years has been irrelevant to most Africans. Half of them live in just four countries: Nigeria (127 million), Ethiopia (64 million), the Democratic Republic of the Congo (51 million) and South Africa (43 million). The first three, with a combined population of almost a quarter of a billion people, have been in a political deep-freeze or outright civil turmoil for most of that time. Only two small countries, Botswana (2 million) and Mauritius (1 million), have enjoyed political freedom and economic progress from the start. South Africa, Botswana, and Mauritius have been the only African countries to appear continuously since 1980 in the World Economic Forum's International Competitiveness Tables—a guide to where hardheaded investors should put their money.

Most people on the continent are living in a penitentiary of sorts. Some guards are less severe than others. Some are open to calls for mercy and understanding. But, overall, life is made more fragile than it already is by the depredations and abuses of the powerful. Some of them cover their crimes with the semblance of democracy, while others behave like the African chiefs of old. In most of Africa, no one is safe, even from the supposed guardians of the peace. In some countries, people cross the street when they see a policeman or soldier coming their way—not from a sense of guilt but from a reasonable fear of being assaulted or robbed. In southern Chad, farmers grow their cassava far away from the road and do not fertilize their crops, worried that their plants will grow too high and be visible to military vehicles driving by. It would be difficult to find a closer link between human rights and economics.

NEOS

One does not need to be a technocrat to appreciate how frag-ile an economy is, and how destructive dictatorship can be. The poet William Wordsworth recognized this two centuries ago (1809): "The works of peace cannot flourish in a country gov-erned by an intoxicated Despot . . . ..Now commerce, manufac-tures, agriculture, and all the peaceful arts, are of the nature of virtues or intellectual powers; they cannot be given; they cannot be stuck in here and there; they must spring up; they must grow of themselves; they may be encouraged; they thrive better with en-couragement and delight in it; but . . . they are delicate, proud, and independent . . . ..A tyrant has no joy in anything which is en-dued with such excellence: he sickens at the sight of it; he turns away from it, as an insult to his own attributes."[7]

Early on, Africans perceived that their leaders were failing them. A prime example was Ghana's first president. In 1966, just nine years after the country's independence, Kwame Nkrumah was overthrown by his army. He had actually been in power since 1952, when he headed a government elected under the colonial administration. He was more a man of rhetoric and calculation than a man of principles, and power went to his head. As early as 1953, he told a visitor: "The ideological development here is not very high. There are but two or three of us who know what we are doing."[8] In 1958, he confided to someone else: "I don't want to make too much of myself, but in a way this nation is my cre-ation. If I should die there would be chaos."[9] That year, he intro-duced a Preventive Detention Act that allowed him to lock up his opponents for up to five years without trial. He had predicted such a measure in his autobiography: "Even a system based on so-cial justice and a democratic constitution may need backing up, during the period following independence, by emergency meas-ures of a totalitarian kind. Without discipline, true freedom can-not survive."[10]

In Nigeria, the same year, troops killed the prime minister and governors of three important states in the dead of night. At first, no one knew what was happening; but when news of a military takeover spread, there was rejoicing in the streets. Nigeria was only five years old, but the public was already fed up. One political party issued a communiqué which mixed exasperation with cele-bration: "The mad rush of our politicians toward self-enrichment disgraced Nigeria's name abroad . . ..A ruling caste had arisen in our country, which based its power on the sowing of hatred, on pitting brother against brother, on liquidating everyone who held a view different from theirs . . ..We salute the new regime as if it had been sent down by God to liberate the nation from black imperialism."[11] Yet, nearly 30 years later, a sense of resignation and déjà vu had set in across Africa. There were eight more changes of government in Nigeria before a president was properly elected at the end of the twentieth century.

In late October 1993, a coup d'état in Burundi—insignificant to the rest of the world—depressed political reformers in Africa to the core. Violence was nothing new to the small ex-Belgian colony, where two rival tribes had been massacring each other for as long as anyone could remember. But elections the year before had been among the few clean and undisputed votes in the history of the continent, returning a president from the majority tribe for the first time since Independence. People took notice right across the continent. When the army, dominated by the minority tribe, overthrew and killed the president, it said it was prepared to organize new elections, presumably on condition the country elected someone the army liked. At the other end of the continent, the editor of the main opposition paper in the Ivory Coast and a man of deep conscience, culture and conviction, wrote: "This continent is really cursed. We may even have to accept that Africans are a bad copy of the human race. We always make ourselves look ridiculous in the eyes of others . . ..What have we done, for our Creator to pour such uncompleted beings into these green spaces? We can only wait for evolution to change us. Until then, all we can do is cry . . ."[12]

This cri de coeur was not self-hatred so much as the echo of a persistent struggle catching its breath. The author of the article, Raphael Lakpé, would later be imprisoned for six months for being disrespectful to his country's president. Over a beer, the day after his release, he was philosophical about his plight although he was finally inclined to throw in the towel after a long career as a journalist and find some other way to provide for his children's education.

The same week, the Ivory Coast's students union called a two-day strike to protest the killing of a high-school student by police. He had been demonstrating against a $2 fee imposed on parents by the school principal and was helping a girl who had stumbled while fleeing the police. He was shot twice on the spot. No one could understand why armed police had been sent to control unarmed children.

That was October 1993. Any month in Africa since then has been as replete with tyranny and injustice. For example, in May 2004, Sudan's government signed a peace with rebels which it had been fighting for decades, but pursued a separate conflict in the western region; Namibia's president told a rally that some white people were "snakes" who wanted to re-colonize the country; in Malawi, a 70-year old economist and protégé of the former head of state was sworn in as president after an election that most observers judged unfair; and Robert Mugabe, Zimbabwe's president, called Nobel peace prize winner Desmond Tutu an "evil and embittered little bishop," after Tutu criticized him.[13]

Fortunately, at the local level, Africans have been able to resist some of the tyranny around them, often without violence and sometimes even with a sense of humor. A few years ago, African women journalists meeting in Senegal told two remarkable stories of such resistance.[14]

In 1996, a group of women in the Northern Province of South Africa, one of the poorest regions of the country, banded together to establish a vegetable garden for extra income. Concerned about the women's growing independence, their husbands convinced the local magistrate to cut off their water supply, using an obscure bylaw. The women built a casket, carried it to the magistrate's office and, wailing furiously, dug a grave on the grounds outside to bury him symbolically as he looked on. The man fled screaming from the building to the safety of his house, but did not reconnect the water. A few days later, the women acted again. They marched back to the magistrate's office, and as he watched agape from his window, they took off their clothes. Three hundred naked women were too much for him, and he promptly restored their water supply. In turn, they promised never to undress again.

A Chadian journalist at the same conference had prepared a television documentary on female genital mutilation (sometimes described politely as "female circumcision"). Her express purpose was to shock young girls into resisting the procedure. The film included graphic scenes of girls having their clitorises cut with a razor blade in a courtyard, with female relatives chanting dutifully around them. When the film was aired, religious leaders claimed that showing women's private parts was contrary to Islam, and implied strongly that the journalist should be killed as a service to God. Fortunately, she was out of the country and, when she returned, no one from her family was at the airport to greet her. She called her producer, who sent a car. At home, she found her parents and cousins terrorized about leaving the house. The television station appealed to the president to have the imams lift their fatwa, but there was an election campaign underway and he was unwilling to confront them. Two months later, he persuaded them to lift the order, not because it was wrong, but because it would tarnish the country's reputation abroad.

Other opponents of tyranny have been stubborn government officials across the continent, who have tried to do their duty despite daunting conditions—including low or late pay. I once visited a rural development project with a group of young civil servants, who sought villagers' views of the project with conspicuous respect. The schedule they kept was extraordinary. One day, we missed lunch, had a token dinner, and compared notes until 11:30 P.M. The next morning, we were off again at 6:30 to visit some more remote villages and were in meetings until 8 o'clock that night. Just before calling it a day, the young team leader asked the local project coordinator why he had been 45 minutes late that morning. Apparently, the man had run out of gasoline and service stations didn't open very early. That excuse didn't satisfy his supervisor: "You're supposed to be a *planner* and planners think ahead. Why didn't you check your gas tank before the stations closed yesterday?" To me, this seemed a little harsh after what had still been a long day on the road. But those were his standards, and apparently he lived up to them himself. Certainly, no one else was surprised by his reaction. A few months later, this dedicated official was demoted because he refused to cave in to a new Minister's demand that project contracts be given to her friends.

Not all African leaders have lacked vision and integrity. Three of the greatest–Nelson Mandela of South Africa, Leopold Senghor of Senegal, and Julius Nyerere of Tanzania–were world statesmen. Unfortunately, few African politicians have followed their example. Mandela's story is well-known. While much of Africa was struggling to keep its head above water, Mandela was spending 27 years in South African prisons. He did not molder away into despair and apathy. Instead of resenting his imprisonment, he learned his jailers' language, Afrikaans. His patience and stature were such that, in the end, it was his country's white minority government that had to accept the terms of his release, rather than the other way around. In his five years (1994–1999) as president of the "new" South Africa, he displayed all the gifts, instincts, and values that his countrymen had expected. He retained his sense of proportion. And he kept his humility.

By early 1998, Mandela's government was building 500 houses a day and had provided clean water to nearly 5 million people. But this was not enough. At a conference in Johannesburg in March of that year, he recounted a visit to his home village and his shock at the conditions in which people there lived. "I saw some women taking water in containers from a large stagnant puddle. I asked them if they hadn't noticed the algae on the surface and the tadpoles swimming underneath, or the women washing themselves up the hill with water which then ran off into the street. 'Yes', they said, 'but we don't have a choice.' 'What are you going to do with this water?' 'Cook with it and drink it,' they answered. 'I hope you're going to boil it,' I protested 'Boil it?' they said. 'With what? Look around you. Do you think we have electricity? And look towards the horizon. Can you see any trees? We use dried cow dung for fuel, and we have little enough of that. It produces more smoke than heat.'" Mandela continued: "I wanted to fall on my knees and beg their forgiveness for my ignorant questions."[15]

Nelson Mandela also took daring risks for peace. In 1995, South Africa's rugby team won the World Cup. After the game, Mandela strode out onto the field and donned the national team's sweater—once a symbol of white domination. There was still only one black player in the Springbok line-up. No other politician in the country could have pulled off this gesture. It stunned and touched the nation. I asked a former South African police officer whom I met on a plane once whether he, too, had been moved by this gesture. "Let's just say that Mandela was well-advised." I insisted on hearing his personal reaction. "Well," this former defender of white rule admitted, "it began to lighten my cynicism about the change of government."

Léopold Senghor was above all a poet and a man of ideas—
some of which seemed contradictory even to his admirers. He was
a champion of "Negritude" but also a deep lover of everything
French and founder of the French equivalent of the British Commonwealth, *La Francophonie*. When he was elected a member of
the French Academy, he felt obliged to defend the honor. It would
have been "discourteous" to refuse, he said. Senghor was brought
up to believe in self-control, good manners and patience—the last
of which, "more than one thinks, is a particularly African
virtue."[16] At Catholic seminary, he pressed for better living conditions for the students and was turned down for the priesthood for
not showing a "spirit of obedience." "I accepted this, of course," he
wrote, "but I poured out every tear I had in my body."[17] He went
on to study French literature in Paris, write a thesis on the poet
Charles Baudelaire, and teach classics in Paris and Tours.

Throughout his life, he tried to demonstrate—sometimes in
the face of shaky evidence—that Africa was the source of all world
culture, including writing and art. He confirmed the existence of
African poetry in a German prisoner-of-war camp during World
War II. One of his guards was an Austrian philologist, interested in
African languages. "One day, he played a tape for me on which, he
said, he had recorded some stories. Once I had heard it, I jumped
for joy, hugged him and shouted 'Eureka!' . . . What he had played
was not a story but a poem containing regular meters sustained in
the background by beats on a drum."[18] Another of his foibles was
to comment, as only a Francophone could, on the imperfections of
the English tongue. "While softened and enriched by Latin,
Greek, and French borrowings, its pronunciation has kept the
roughness of German and its literature the disorder of the Teu-
tonic mind."[19]

His politics were a mild version of African socialism. During
his two decades (1960–80) as president of Senegal, he gave the
state a leading role in economic development but avoided the totalitarian excesses of other French West African countries like
Guinea and Benin. He introduced a one-party state but later, in
1976, allowed the formation of opposition parties and left office of
his own volition in 1980. Thereafter, he could be seen at the airport lining up for a flight like everyone else; he had led a life of
comfort but did not seek any permanent privileges. His legacy was

stability and some political and economic inertia, but that was more than most African leaders would leave behind.

Senghor was so revered by French-speaking Africans that one young journalist wrote effusively about him even after being refused a formal interview. "What can one say to a man who has said almost everything? He has told us that our future will be a common one or we will have no future at all. That we are brothers on this planet and should manage our resources collectively . . ..Will this man be heard? Or will he be ignored like other prophets in their own time?"[20]

Julius Nyerere of Tanzania was more controversial–at least outside Africa. He studied in Scotland and translated Shakespeare's *Julius Caesar* into Swahili, but he was less of an intellectual than Senghor. Instead, he was a formidable idealist. His experiment with "African socialism" in Tanzania inspired an entire generation of Africans and liberal Westerners, and gave eager aid officials around the world something to pin their hopes upon. Robert McNamara, the apparently hardboiled former US Defense Secretary, famous for his "body counts" during the Vietnam War and president of the World Bank for 13 years (1968–81), became one of Nyerere's greatest devotees. He lost patience with the man eventually, appalled by the state of the roads he saw in northern Tanzania during a final visit and by other aspects of an economy that remained anemic despite the vast sums of aid the country was receiving.

Like other African leaders, Nyerere had trouble giving up power. President from 1961 to 1984, he left office peacefully–a rare event in Africa even then. He still dominated the ruling party and country from behind the scenes thereafter. Yet, he earned the lasting affection of his people. As a former schoolteacher, he found his presidential salary of $5,000 quite adequate. He was stubborn about his egalitarian political ideals. He went to early Mass almost every morning. There was never a whiff of scandal surrounding him and his relatives. And he promoted standards of personal behavior that were well beyond the capacity of most human beings. He could irritate his compatriots while also inspiring them. He was like St. Francis of Assisi who, when he found some of his friars building a house for themselves, jumped up on the roof, began tearing off the tiles, and screamed, "This is not why I created our order." Many of Nyerere's compatriots, while wanting to believe, had doubts about the socialist model. Many government officials could not live up to their president's high standards, and corruption began to spread. But Tanzanians never lost their loyalty to the "Father of the Nation."

One of the reasons for that loyalty was the clarity of his values and his willingness to say things which other African leaders would not. In 1978, on the 17th anniversary of Tanzania's independence, Nyerere denounced the Organization of African Unity's pandering to Uganda's dictator, Idi Amin. "Blackness has become a certificate to kill with impunity," he said. Referring to the tens of thousands of Ugandans the dictator had killed, Nyerere pointed out that Amin had slaughtered more people than the white-minority governments of southern Africa in their protracted wars against black nationalist guerrillas.[21]

Late in life, Nyerere was asked if it was true that the Masai people still voted for him at each presidential election, although his name was no longer on the ballot. "Yes," he chuckled, "because for them a leader is chosen for life. They see no reason why modern elections should get in the way of that. Like the gazelle and the wildebeest, they also have trouble respecting national boundaries."[22]

His reputation also knew no boundaries. When he died in October 1999, another World Bank President (James Wolfensohn) eulogized him fervently: "While world economists were debating the importance of capital output ratios, President Nyerere was saying that nothing was more important for people than being able to read and write and have access to clean water . . ..His political ideals, his deep religious convictions, his equally deep religious tolerance, and his belief that people of all ethnic and regional origins should have equal access to knowledge and material opportunities have marked his country—and Africa—forever."[23] Wolfensohn's words struck such a chord with Tanzanians that their current president repeated them in his own funeral speech for Nyerere at the National Stadium.

Such leadership has been as rare as water in a desert and, for most Africans, the wait for intelligent government continues. Even a change of generations or players does not always bring relief—if only because old habits, expectations, and role models die hard. In September 1982, at the World Bank's annual meetings in

Toronto, I attended discussions with 22 African delegations. When the Zairean delegation walked in, I wanted to hide under the table. They looked as if they had jumped off the screen of a B-rated mobster movie and had not had a good night's sleep in years. Two decades later, a *Financial Times* article described the country's new rulers as "a rogues' gallery of gangsters and opportunists"[24]

Transfers of power have seldom been easy in Africa; many have been savage, others comical. For example, during the first half of 2002, Madagascar had two presidents, because the defeated one refused to resign—having been in office almost continuously for 20 years. Even apparently radical and peaceful change can prove disappointing. In December 2002, Kenya breathed a sigh of relief when the 24 year rule of Daniel Arap Moi ended peacefully. The new president was Mwai Kibaki, a minister of finance and vice president under the old regime who allegedly had changed his stripes. Unfortunately, just 13 months later, in January 2004, the Kenya Union of Journalists and Foreign Correspondents Association of East Africa denounced a government crackdown on small "illegal" newspapers that were critical of senior figures.[25] In April 2004, draft revisions to the constitution intended to curb the power of the presidency and the plundering of public assets were blocked by a faction close to the new president.[26] In July 2004, the British envoy to Kenya told businessmen that the new government had signed corrupt deals worth almost $200 million. "They may expect we shall not see or will forgive them a bit of gluttony. But they can hardly expect us not to care when their gluttony causes them to vomit all over our shoes."[27]

On the other side of the continent, another passing of the torch was so bizarre that even most novelists would not have dared to invent it. Togo is a narrow West African country of only two million people, tucked between Ghana and Benin. In the early 1990s, despite dictatorship and a high exchange rate, the economy bustled along, driven by the sheer intelligence and get-up-and-go of its business and professional class. By the end of the decade, many of them had indeed got up and gone—some of them to drive taxis in Paris.

In February 2005, the country's ruler, General Eyadéma—in power since 1967—died on his way to Europe for medical treatment. True to form, the army installed the general's 39-year-old son as the new head of state. But they had forgotten something. The country's constitution stipulated that the speaker of the National Assembly should become president, pending the holding of national elections within 60 days. When the international community reminded them of this, the army fired the speaker and replaced him with their favorite. The National Assembly was also persuaded to change the constitution and do away with the requirement to call elections. The African Union, European Union, France and the United States dug in their heels and—for a while—appeared to get their way. The new president agreed to hold elections, which he rigged and won in April 2005. The opposition protested and violent demonstrations erupted in the capital, ending 800 lives, and the runner-up also declared himself president. The country soon returned to the deceptive calm that reigns throughout much of Africa. There was little more the international community could do.

Another exasperating transfer of power took place in Malawi in 2004, when the outgoing president failed to have the constitution amended so he could run for a third term. Instead, he designated his own successor in the next elections. In May 2005, the outgoing president fell out with him and apologized publicly for "imposing him on the country."[28]

Only two countries in black Africa have been liberal democracies from the start: Botswana and Mauritius. I first visited Botswana in November 1975. Already, it stood out as a glittering exception in Africa. Still run largely by British technical experts who negotiated hard and set high standards of personal behavior, the country was on the verge of a major transformation from a cattle to a diamond economy. But it was not losing its head in the process. The government insisted that the foreign experts train their successors as part of their job. Soon, the director of Economic Planning was replaced by his "counterpart," who later became the country's president. No other country in Africa has had the same success in managing technical assistance, although dizzying variations of it have been tried across the continent.

I observed little hierarchy or pretension in Botswana. The country was small and the elite never strayed very far from their origins on the farm. On my first visit, I was invited for a barbecue on a Saturday evening at the Minister of Finance's modest home.

He was in the back garden in a sport shirt turning the meat over on the coals himself. It was a local specialty, pony testicles, and I asked for mine to be well done. Like the finance minister, the country's president, Seretse Khama, was modest and admired. In a region where race was a lightning rod of tension and oppression, he had married a British woman and quietly promoted tolerance of diversity and free expression.

Botswana may have been blessed. As one writer put it, "During the two decades after the war, the 'winds of change' brought independence to most of Africa. It blew harshly in some countries, for example the Congo and Algeria, where it caused waves of devastation. Over Bechuanaland, the wind was mild and the British Government withdrew in 1966 in a climate of good will."[29] These foundations proved lasting. Since 1970, no other developing economy on earth—including the East Asian "tigers," Korea, Hong Kong, Taiwan, and Thailand—has grown as fast. Unfortunately, the country's blessings have been followed by a curse. Thirty-seven percent of Botswana's adult population now carry the HIV virus—the second highest infection rate in the world. Life expectancy has plummeted to 34 years.

Mauritius—an island off the southeast coast of Africa—is much smaller than Botswana but has done even better economically. Botswana is about the size of Texas; Mauritius is 11 times the size of the District of Columbia. Yet, without oil or diamonds or other natural resource windfalls, Mauritius has the highest income per person in all of Africa. An open political system, stable government, and good economic policies, including the encouragement of private investment, have made the difference. So has imported labor and entrepreneurial talent; more than 70 percent of Mauritians are of Indian or Chinese descent. Other Africans point this out, almost as a way of writing off the country's progress. But the rest of Africa should also be encouraging the inflow of skills and capital from other continents, rather than chasing their own people away.

The only other country on the continent that combined political and economic openness and attracted steady private investment, Tunisia, is now going backward. A country that introduced equal rights for women as early as the 1950s and where, even now, more than half of university students are women, regularly restricts access to the Internet, ostensibly to prevent Islamist agitation. Yet, with a straight face in November 2003, the Tunisian president made the head of the World Internet Organization a Grand Officer of the National Order of Merit. The sycophantic official newspaper beamed: "It is hardly an accident that Tunisia has been chosen to host the second phase of the World Summit on Information Technology in 2005. It is a consecration of the good choices our industrious country has made under an enlightened leadership."[30] In private, Tunisians complain bitterly about political surveillance and repression, claiming with ironic exaggeration that half of the country's ten million people are police officers.

Still, economically, Tunisia remains an inspiration to countries south of the Sahara. The staff of the African Development Bank, which was forced to move its headquarters to Tunis after the outbreak of civil war in the Ivory Coast, were simply astonished when they arrived. "This is not Africa," some of them said, staring at the skyscrapers, broad streets, and lack of peeling paint. Tunisia is also looked up to by struggling professionals south of the Sahara. Early in the new century, a Cameroonian architect wrote to a building magazine as follows: "Of the 198 architects in my country, only four are keeping their heads above water, and you can imagine how. Two are leaders of the Order of Architects and are on all the big projects. I am doing odd jobs which have nothing to do with architecture. But I have great hope that your magazine can one day change mentalities so that we can become like Tunisia."[31]

Other countries have started on the right track, only to be thwarted afterward. Both Uganda and Ghana had highly developed administrative and professional classes at the beginning of Independence, owing in large measure to the early educational efforts of Christian missionaries. Makerere College in Uganda was one of the finest institutions of learning on the continent. Ethiopia had a strong civil service tradition that survived even the bloody regime of Mengistu Haile Mariam (1977–91). In the 1980s, Ethiopia's publicly owned companies were actually serving the public and making money. Ethiopian Airlines was one of the few companies with trans-continental flights that business travelers and officials could rely on. But, then, Idi Amin destroyed the Ugandan administration in 1971–79. Military governments did similar damage in Ghana. And, in Ethiopia, civil war and economic hardships wore down the administrative culture. By the late 1990s, few civil servants in western and central Africa were receiving their salaries, let alone proper training, equipment, and encouragement. By then, the African exodus was reaching a fever pitch and African talent bled away. Sometimes, that talent was drawn to unlikely places. In the South Pacific in 1989, I came across a group of 30 Ghanaians offering technical assistance to the government of the Solomon Islands.

Other countries came through a firestorm with their national spirit intact and a determination to transform themselves. Mozambique, for example, fought hard for its independence and in the process also freed Portugal from dictatorship. In 1974, young Portuguese officers, disgusted with the deaths of so many comrades in a senseless colonial war, overthrew their own government in Lisbon. Mozambique started life with a lopsided economy and a very small administrative class. Soon after Independence, it faced another prolonged war against domestic rebels supported by South Africa. The civil war maimed and killed thousands, and littered the countryside with landmines that continued to kill people long after the peace was signed. These hardships would have drained the resolve and resources of most nations. Instead, Mozambique came together again and the elected government has tried to use its resources responsibly. Pragmatism has replaced hard ideology. A surreal sense of history remains—most streets in the capital are named after revolutionary heroes like Mao Tse Tung and Ho Chi Minh—but canniness has trumped nostalgia. In 2003, for example, the government invited white farmers expelled from their lands in Zimbabwe to bring their experience and enterprise to Mozambique. The only limitation was that their new farms should not adjoin each other and become the nucleus of a white community.

Tanzania, too, has moved from being a one-party state to one where diverse political views are expressed without intimidation. It is one of the few countries in Africa that has never had a coup d'état. Tribal rivalries have been kept in check and there is a sense of continuity and pride in national institutions. Unfortunately, such inspiring examples are rare, and it is truly remarkable that democrats and human rights advocates are still active across the continent. Most of them are weary or in danger, and need the world's help.

With international pressure and the right leadership, political breakthroughs are possible on the continent—as South Africa has shown. There, the foundations were already in place. The rest of Africa has seen the dark side but ignored the positive aspects of that country's history. True, South Africa has always been in a category of its own. As early as the late nineteenth century, its economy was already larger than that of the rest of Africa combined. As recently as 2000, African statistics carried the qualification: "excluding" or "including" South Africa. Despite decades of international sanctions, its economic success, modern infrastructure, and highly developed institutions have always made it look un-African. Remarkably, too, its press and judiciary remained generally free even in the darkest days of apartheid.

In fact, the society of South Africa is one of the most complex on earth, more comparable to India than to other countries in Africa. It is highly charged, bristling with talent, ambition, tension, and historical grudges. But the political transition that occurred there in 1991–1994 remains one of the wonders of the modern world. The scale of South Africa's achievement was summarized by Allister Sparks, former international editor for the Johannesburg *Rand Daily Mail*: "An equivalent settlement in the Middle East would see Israel, the West Bank and the Gaza Strip consolidated into a single secular state which, before long, would be ruled over by a Palestinian majority government and in which Jews could live in peace and security as a minority group."[32]

It would be naïve to view the country too rosily. Immense political pressures are building up behind the scenes. After Brazil, South Africa has the worst income distribution in the world. Pressure on large white farmers to give up some of their land to blacks could prove as explosive as in Zimbabwe. The ruling party is a magnet for the corrupt, not just the talented. And government agencies are beginning to adopt the Orwellian tone of other African countries. In May 2002, the Minister of Safety and Security stopped publishing crime statistics because they were too embarrassing; his official reason was that he did not want to "demoralize" the public.[33]

Yet, South Africa, Botswana, and Mauritius should be constant reminders that the rest of Africa is capable of much better, that checks and balances like a free press and a strong legislature are curbs to natural African—and human—excesses, and that despair can be turned into hope.

Unfortunately, the canvas of African politics remains dark, and well-publicized efforts to brighten the outlook have themselves receded into the general shadows. In late 2001, the presidents of Nigeria, Senegal, and South Africa persuaded their fellow heads of state to endorse a New Partnership for Africa's Development (NEPAD) under which they would police each other's progress toward greater integrity, democracy, and respect for human rights. The Partnership was endorsed with fanfare at the G–7 Meeting of the leading industrial nations in Canada in June 2002. But, despite glaring opportunities to deliver on this refreshing promise, Africa's leaders utterly failed the test. In particular, they refused to rein in the Zimbabwean president, Robert Mugabe, who had given a whole new meaning to the term political brutality. And, as late as 2005, the three leading NEPAD countries had failed to ratify the African Union's own Anti-Corruption Convention.[34]

Africa's excesses–and excuses–are bad enough. But Africa's friends have sometimes made matters worse by trying to explain away such behavior. Europeans have likened state formation in Africa to their own drawn-out processes of national integration, comparing warfare and tough rule in Africa to the fifteenth-century War of the Roses in England and the sixteenth-century Catholic–Protestant struggles in France. While this comparison seems credible, there is also something contradictory about it. People have claimed that Africa can leapfrog into economic progress by bypassing certain stages of technological development. So, why should the continent learn from other countries' economic advances but not their political mistakes?

An appropriate rejoinder to historical relativists is Winston Churchill's verdict on the seventeenth-century English dictator Oliver Cromwell: "Not even the hard pleas of necessity or the safety of the State can be invoked. Cromwell . . . debased the standards of human conduct and sensibly darkened the journey of mankind. Cromwell's Irish massacres find numberless compeers in the history of all countries during and since the Stone Age. It is therefore only necessary to strip men capable of such deeds of all title to honor."[35]

Of course, there is no close parallel between the brutality of African leaders and the ruthlessness of twentieth-century dictators like Stalin or Hitler. Certainly, no government in Africa has tried to run a totalitarian state, with the possible exceptions of South Africa and Tanzania–and they were not able to pull it off. But the international community resisted the Great Dictators and has since tried to raise standards of respect for human rights around the world. Economic sanctions and the plain flexing of political muscle have led to some bright spots on the world scene–such as the independence of East Timor in 2002 after nearly 30 years of illegal occupation by the Indonesians. But millions of Africans have died cruelly and unnecessarily, many of them very recently. And even the most hardboiled strategist can hardly argue that Africa's states and economies have been strengthened as a result.

CHAPTER 4

CULTURE, CORRUPTION,
AND CORRECTNESS

Many Africans have denounced their governments—sometimes from exile abroad. The Nigerian, Wole Soyinka, who won the Nobel Prize for Literature in 1986, has been one of them: "African dreams of peace and prosperity have been shattered by the greedy, corrupt and unscrupulous rule of African strongmen . . ..One would be content with just a modest cleaning up of the environment, development of opportunities, health services, education, eradication of poverty. But unfortunately even these modest goals are thwarted by a power crazed and rapacious leadership who can only obtain their egotistical goals by oppressing the rest of us."[1]

That much is understood. What is less clear is why so many good people accept bad government. I believe the answer has three parts: culture, corruption, and political correctness.

Culture is a delicate ground to cross in Africa. Most Africans are loath to admit that character has anything to do with their arrested political and economic development. It is just as difficult to generalize about Africans as it is about North Americans (Canadians, Americans, Mexicans) or Europeans (English, French, Germans).

As one writer suggested in 1962: "Variety in Africa is largely man-made. On a landscape that is vast, monotonous and vaguely repellent, the most striking features are the works and ways of men."[2] In my own experience, Ghanaians can be irreverent and even jolly, Malawians austere, Ivorians formal, South Africans intense and complex, Senegalese talkative to a fault, Malians tight-lipped, Chadians sober and proud. Kenyans are open-hearted, while their neighbors, the Tanzanians, are more reserved. Yet some African traits are common enough to escape controversy. Although language, history, and geography separate them dramatically, Nigerians appear to feel a greater kinship with Mozambicans than Chileans do with Brazilians at opposite ends of their own continent.

Of course, the African character has adapted to a new environment. Already in 1972, a British observer warned: "African life is rapidly changing. The rising generations are adopting alien ways with alacrity and rapidly losing their own."[3] Population increases, economic hardship, globalization, and HIV/AIDS have put new pressures on traditional values. Some have proved unbudgeable; others have waned; still others have re-emerged, as new generations discover the wisdom of inherited practices, in much the same way that second- and third-generation immigrants in North America have reclaimed their Italian, Greek, and Irish heritages.

If contemporary Africans are uncomfortable with the subject of the African personality, an earlier generation was quite loquacious about it. One of them was Léopold Senghor, the first president of Senegal, who coined the word "negritude." His concept seems simplistic today and triggered objections even in the 1960s. The Nigerian writer Wole Soyinka poked fun at the concept: "A tiger doesn't have to proclaim its tigritude."

Senghor thought the European and African worldviews were fundamentally different. The European "distinguishes the object from himself. He keeps it at a distance. He freezes it out of time and, in a way, out of space. He makes a means of it. He destroys it by devouring it. "White men are cannibals,' an old sage in my own country told me. 'It is this process of devouring which [whites] call humanizing nature or more exactly domesticating nature . . ..They don't take into account that life cannot be domesticated."

In contrast, according to Senghor, the African is "shut up in his black skin. He lives in primordial night. He does not begin by distinguishing himself from the object, the tree or the stone, the man or animal or social event. He does not keep it at a distance. He does not analyze it. He turns it over and over in his supple hands, he fingers it, he feels it. The African is a pure sensory field. Subjectively, at the end of his antennae, like an insect, he discovers the Other."[4]

Few modern-day Africans would recognize themselves in this description. Senghor's language was thick with the French philosophy of the time, especially existentialism. And he raised eyebrows on all sides. Nadine Gordimer, a white South African and another Nobel Laureate for Literature (1991), was appalled by Senghor's views as they contradicted her efforts to promote greater understanding among Africa's different races. "The apprehension attributed to the whites," she complained, "is racist and derogatory, and that attributed to the blacks is obeisance to a romantic primitivism that so easily can be used by whites to 'prove' that blacks are childish and backward. Of course, Senghor's thesis is that . . . the human must not lose his/her invaluable sensuous connections with all creation . . ..The existential state he claims for [Africans] is strikingly similar to the concept of living in tune with universal energy extolled in a great philosophy-cum-way-of-life, at the other side of the world, the [Indian] Vedanta."[5]

Senghor's view implies that Africans were so much at one with the world around them that they were unable to see that they could improve their lives. If this is true, development planners were knocking at the wrong door during the first four decades of African independence.

A British psychiatrist active in Kenya during the 1950s and 1960s used less poetic language than Senghor but started from the same premise. The African, he found, was integrated completely into the world around him. "Within his society he is seldom at a loss and is courageous, loyal, stoical, socially self-confident and eloquent, courteous, and very sensitive to the feelings of others. All this is clearly admirable, but it is achieved at the expense of integration at the personal intellectual level. A man is not expected to think for himself except in regard to the practical details of living and lacks principles of general application on which such integration could occur. He thus becomes intellectually conventional and does not see himself as a self-reliant unit with sustained responsibility for all his deeds, past, present and future, but rather as a puppet pulled by interpersonal strings . . ..Whether or not intellectual curiosity, independence of thought, initiative, and personal responsibility for one's acts are to be regarded as virtues, they are certainly required for successful living in the Western way."[6]

The Nigerian novelist Chinua Achebe suggests that the Western ethic is captured in Descartes' phrase: "I think, therefore I am." According to him, the African approach to life is to be found in the Bantu saying: "Humans are humans because of other humans."[7]

These distinctions may seem dated and debatable now, but Africans certainly claim values that set them apart from other peoples. One of them is generosity and hospitality, best seen at the village level. Rural habits of sharing still inspire urban Africans who are old enough to remember life before 30 years of economic hardship frayed the social safety net of their childhoods.

More than in Senghor's portrayal, Africans would recognize their parents and grandparents in the following account of Huron and Iroquois practices in seventeenth-century North America: "All were prompt to aid each other in distress . . ..When a young woman was permanently married, the other women of the village supplied her with firewood for the year, each contributing an armful. When one or more families were without shelter, the men of the village joined in building them a house. In return, the recipients of the favor gave a feast if they could; if not, their thanks were sufficient. Among the Iroquois and Hurons—and doubtless among the kindred tribes–there were marked distinctions of noble and base, prosperous and poor; yet while there was food in the village, the meanest and the poorest need not suffer want. He had but to enter the nearest house, and seat himself by the fire, when without a word on either side, food was placed before him by the women."[8]

This urge to share can be heart-warming—and extreme. A Polish visitor to East Africa witnessed an extraordinary example of this in the 1960s:

> Individualism is highly prized in Europe, and perhaps nowhere more so than in America; in Africa, it is synonymous with unhappiness, with being accursed. African tradition is collectivist, for only

in a harmonious group could one face the obstacles thrown up by nature. And one of the conditions of collective survival is the sharing of the smallest thing. One day a group of children surrounded me. I had a single piece of candy, which I placed in my open palm. The children stood motionless, staring. Finally, the oldest girl took the candy, bit it into pieces, and equitably distributed the bits.[9]

Africans can be generous on a global scale, too. In 1998, a village in Mali raised funds for a small town in rural Quebec that had suffered damaging storms that year. And in late 2003, Mozambique's Red Cross raised $600 to help the victims of forest fires in Portugal. Judging by the sizes of the contributions, most of the donations came from poor people. Mozambique's 30,000-strong Portuguese community hardly responded at all.[10]

One does not need to believe in the myth of the noble savage to accept that pre-modern cultures had remarkable values, some of which are disappearing. And some of those values, such as generosity, always had their limits. Idleness was not encouraged. Loafers were expelled rather than sustained at the village's expense. And sharing did not extend far beyond one's own clan. Although linguistically related, the Iroquois were sworn enemies of the Hurons and exterminated them in just a hundred years. But the sense of community among Africans has been remarkably strong.

Other African values are also self-evident. Few cultures place such a high importance on family. The individual is incomplete without reference to his parents or to her brothers and sisters. No blood relationship is too faint to be respected. The "extended" family moves beyond one's own siblings to larger groups like the village and ethnic group. When a stranger is introduced as someone's "brother," he will be asked: "Same father, same mother?" This is not a reference to widespread sexual shenanigans. Instead, it covers the very real possibility that the person is only a cousin or friend or half-brother through family misfortune (the death of a first wife or a first husband's disappearance). Divorce is very rare in Africa, as few wish to abandon their family responsibilities publicly. But families are rearranged continuously, and grandmothers and mothers-in-law are often the only ones who keep them intact.

By and large, Africans are preoccupied with the here and now. From the very start, Ministries of Planning were a pious hope in the African environment and have always run into problems. Despite promising beginnings and sometimes strong ministers, planning agencies have usually been eclipsed by the greater budgets and patronage of more powerful government bodies. In rural areas, farmers plan for tomorrow by protecting their grain from the elements or rats in wicker containers that they stand on stones or hang from the trees. But, in almost every other respect, Africans enjoy life as it is, rather than fret about the future. This pleasure takes many forms and acts as a mysterious buffer against the misery that otherwise would swamp whole families, villages, and provinces.

African joie de vivre has always impressed visitors. As one tourist noted in the 1930s, this lightheartedness serves many purposes: "Africans dance. They dance for joy, and they dance for grief; they dance for love and they dance for hate; they dance to bring prosperity and they dance to avert calamity; they dance for religion and they dance to pass the time. They dance with a verve, a precision, an ingenuity which no other race can show."[11]

Seventy years later, one would think that this conviviality might have faded. In fact, cheerfulness can survive in unlikely places. Nigeria is one of the most disorganized, violent, and corruption-plagued countries on earth. Yet, in September 2003, an international survey found that it had the highest percentage of happy people in the world, followed by Mexico, Venezuela, El Salvador, and Puerto Rico. The United States ranked 16th and Great Britain 24th.[12] Africa's spirit is reflected in its music. In the words of a seasoned observer of another large and troubled country: "If Congo has failed in most sectors, music must qualify as its one, most glorious exception . . ..The mystery is how conditions so depressing can give birth to tunes so infectiously light-hearted, so innocent in tone."[13]

Family and fun are certainly important, but so is respect for one's elders; in fact, many Africans venerate age—and authority in general—to an extreme degree. Wisdom and experience are certainly appreciated, but they are not prerequisites for influence; instead, ignorance, dishonesty, and stubbornness are common features of leadership. Some of this patience with flawed superiors is breaking down under the pressures of urbanization and poverty, but young people rarely speak out in a large group. They wait for older and more established figures in the community to express themselves first, or they resort to three-cornered conversations, using a go-between to make themselves understood. In traditional settings, old people are looked after devotedly by their families, reminding everyone of the need to care for each other but also of the importance of sheer seniority. In addition to respecting earthly authority; Africans are deeply religious. While other cultures honor God, read scriptures, and pray at least once a week, most Africans–not just Muslims–practice their faith every day. They are also superstitious.

So far, one might say, there is little to distinguish Africans from the Italians or Spaniards of the 1950s and 1960s, whose own family ties, love of life, and respect for age and authority did not prove insuperable obstacles to strong economic growth.

But there is a darker side to the African character that Latin peoples have not experienced to the same extent. Family loyalty can be tyrannous in Africa. If it is not spontaneous, concern for family may be brutally imposed. If someone succeeds, however modestly, relatives will often insist on sharing in the fruits of that accomplishment. This was already a social convention in the 1960s, when one observer noted: "Whoever breaks this rule condemns himself to ostracism, to expulsion from the clan, to the horrifying status of outcast."[14] There has been little change since then and, for similar reasons, Africans are not savers. Those who accumulate capital can be considered traitors to their family rather than investors in its future well-being. Small enterprises across Africa have failed time and again because one of the partners absconded with capital to meet immediate personal needs.

Even respect for one's elders has contributed to the downfall of the continent. Africans accept dictatorship and high-handed elected officials as their lot. In the words of a leading Nigerian businessman, who has fought hard against political and corporate corruption, "The leader is usually looked upon as one who should wield power and authority to personal advantage. Politicians compete for public office not so much to serve all the people as to win positions of power and privilege."[15] Some of this deference has an ancient lineage, as many national leaders are only a generation or two removed from traditions of village leadership: "The roles of chief and high priest tended to be combined, and in many tribes this led to the glorification of the chief as a living god who embodied the whole vital force of the tribe."[16]

Loyalty operates in both directions and, to this day, exacts a high price. Subordinates overlook the willfulness and pettiness of their superiors, in exchange for having their own limitations condoned by their bosses. Even modern African managers can put on airs, expect loyalty without earning it, and give poor performers third and fourth chances to redeem themselves.

Africans can be discreet—and prudish. At least in public, people do not discuss sexual matters. This is one reason AIDS has spread so uncontrollably. As late as 1999, the former first lady of Mozambique (and Nelson Mandela's second wife), Graça Machel, scandalized her relatives by referring publicly to the fact that her brother had died of AIDS. They felt she should have consulted them before doing so.

Another virtue which is double-edged is the African love of language. Turns of phrase that seem dated and formal in Europe add a near-literary flourish to African newspaper articles. Even illiterate people in French-speaking West Africa pay scribes in the marketplace to write letters of love or supplication, worthy of Cyrano de Bergerac. A taste for hyperbole can be entertaining but unfortunately also divisive. Politicians and church leaders rain fire and brimstone on those who disagree with them. In August 2003, when a diocese in New Hampshire elected an openly gay bishop, some Anglicans around the world applauded the decision, while others disagreed with it. But the Archbishop of Nigeria condemned the event as "a Satanic attack on God's church".[17] It is difficult to back down from such extreme positions.

Africans' religious convictions can also work against them. Dark forces, not just benign ones, look over their shoulders. Most uneducated Africans are fatalistic. In their world view, there is little they can do to control events. They accept and submit. When children die, many parents do not even wonder why. Instead, they console themselves and others with the phrase: "God giveth, and God taketh away." This acceptance of a supernatural order makes Africans less likely to challenge harsh realities in the present life. In effect, their faith prevents them from burning with social justice.

This acquiescence can shock visitors from abroad, including those with African roots. Like French Canadians visiting France for the first time, African Americans find something missing in their motherland. What they cannot find is their own sense of impatience, ambition, and sheer human pluck after centuries of being oppressed. Not willing to accept their lot, they have ardently tried to change it. African Americans will quote Scripture against injustice in *this* world rather than feel they must suffer it willingly and wait for the next life.

This acceptance of hardship is a central feature of the African personality and eclipses some traditional explanations of Africa's slow development. For example, are Africans intellectually different? The French writer André Gide was concise enough on this point: "The less intelligent a White man is, the stupider Black men seem to him."[18] The accomplishments of Africans in free societies around the world are proof of their talent. Doctors, lawyers, scientists, engineers, and managers who emigrated have more than held their own in highly competitive environments; some have become pace-setters in their fields. Many professionals have stayed and excelled at home, but they have attracted jealousy or have become frustrated at the lack of moral and material support from their employers.

Are Africans lethargic? Not the women who walk many miles a day carrying wood or water on their backs, or the children trudging similar distances to school. Is tribalism the stumbling block to progress? Ethnic ties in Africa are a magnified expression of family loyalty that become a fault line at times of economic distress. Like religion in other lands, tribal attachments can indeed be a convenient lever for a divide-and-rule ploy by cynical leaders. But, like nationalism, such solidarity is not necessarily a destructive force. The core of Africa's cultural problem lies elsewhere.

Africans are patient and long-suffering to an extent probably unparalleled on earth, except in Buddhist countries. Indeed, anyone who knows the daily lives of most Africans must marvel that only 20 percent of the continent's people are still in civil turmoil. And those wars are largely the result of small groups vying for control of a nation's resources rather than mass movements of protest against unjust governments. Many Africans have sacrificed their lives to win freedom for others, but most are passive and unwilling to interfere with what they see as the natural wheels of life. In this respect, they are like the rest of us. Few people in free countries write letters to the editor or campaign actively to change laws. But the extent and duration of dictatorship in Africa are such that military force is not enough to explain it. The ability of Africans to put up with difficulty and mistreatment is reflected in the historically low incidence of depression and suicide on the continent.[19]

Africans can be brutal to each other, especially in groups. But, individually, they do not tend to be terrorists or ideologues. No social cause is great enough to interfere with the enjoyment of what they have and the acceptance of what they lack. As one exasperated Congolese priest put it in the late 1990s: "People cling to life and are not yet at the stage where they will fight for the quality of that life. They feel as long as they are surviving, that is enough."[20] This equanimity is attractive on the surface but ends up being a curse in disguise. If their basic needs were met, there would be no cause for concern. But Africa has suffered grievously over the last 30 years. It has more than doubled its population and lost half its income. Disease is spreading. School attendance is dropping. Vaccination programs are sporadic. Food security is uneven. And Africa is the only region of the world that has grown steadily poorer since 1970. Stoicism may be a virtue, but it is literally killing Africa's sons and daughters.

If African culture keeps people firmly under control, corruption has woven a web that binds their ramshackle states together. In his essay, *The Trouble with Nigeria*, Chinua Achebe bemoaned the extent to which dishonesty was considered the prerogative of the high and mighty. "For, by the same token, discipline will be seen as a penalty which the rank and file must pay for their powerlessness."[21]

Ironically, a root of corruption is Africa's strong family ties. Family pressures are so pervasive that Africans joke about them—or run away from them if they can. At the top of the pyramid of patronage are ministers and senior government officials who face queues of cousins, acquaintances, and constituents outside their door, even on the weekend, to air their complaints or seek material support. But one does not need to be rich to attract attention.

In Abidjan, my day-guard once planned a trip to Burkina Faso (his home country to the north) to visit his mother and son for the first time in ten years. It was delightful to see how much he was looking forward to the trip. But he feared some unlucky event would prevent it, and he was right to be nervous. A cousin working as a night guard for a local firm fell asleep, and bandits struck while he dozed. The owner suspected his employee was an accomplice, arranged for the man to be arrested, and offered to lift the charges once the firm was reimbursed for its losses (about $200). This was almost exactly the amount my own guard had saved for his trip. There was no question of not rescuing his relative; the family code was that sacred. And, to his family, my employee's monthly salary of $160 made him a wealthy man. I lent him the money, but with his family ties and luck, it remained uncertain until the very last minute that he would ever make his trip.

Our guard was not corrupt, but he might have become so, given the opportunity. He certainly knew that better-off people cheated when they could. I have done so myself. In 1978, at the end of my diplomatic posting in Tanzania, I sold my car through the State Motor Corporation. Like its counterparts in the Communist countries of Eastern Europe, the Corporation had exclusive rights to dispose of imported automobiles. Prices were fixed, but enterprising buyers could fiddle with the system, and many did. An Asian businessman offered me a $2,000 "bonus" for my car, and I accepted it. I did not keep the money. Instead, I settled a long-standing debt for my mother at a department store in Montreal. I had no remorse for what I had done. The extra money was probably still less than I could have received in a free market for vehicles. I was benefiting only from the absurdity of state intervention in the sale of cars. And it was not obvious that anyone had been hurt by my behavior.

It is with such apparent innocence that much corruption has developed in Africa. This is not to excuse or condone it. On the contrary, corruption is so endemic on the continent that, in my view, the rest of the world must now radically change the way it tries to help Africans. For years, Africans have called for a "Marshall Plan"–a huge aid program that will finally set them on the road to palpable economic development. In the meantime, massive resources have been seeping away or just carted off by grotesque figures like Zaire's President Mobutu and Nigeria's General Abacha. This loss has been so commonplace that in 2000 the newly elected government of Nigeria was prepared to let Abacha's children keep $100 million as part of a settlement to recover the $2–3 billion that their father had amassed abroad. Many Nigerians were appalled by this munificence and, fortunately, the settlement later broke down. Very little of this money has returned to where it belongs.

Up to a point, in other countries, corruption has been tolerated as a "cost of doing business." In Africa, it has had no positive features at all. Near the end of his life, even the stern schoolmaster, Julius Nyerere of Tanzania, was fond of telling the well-worn tale of the difference between Asian and African corruption: The story began with an African minister who visited a colleague in Asia and was impressed by the man's lavish home. "How did you afford all this on a minister's salary?" he asked. Pointing through his living-room window, his host said: "Do you see that large bridge in the distance?" "Yes," replied the African. "Well, part of its budget came my way," the Asian explained. The next year, reciprocating the visit, the Asian minister asked the same question. "Do you see that road down in the valley?" asked the African. "No," he replied. "I see nothing." "Exactly," explained the African. "I financed this house instead."

Even more harmful than cheating on major contracts has been the so-called petty day-to-day corruption that Africans experience everywhere. They may have to hand over two weeks' wages to obtain a death certificate for burying a relative, a month's farming income to have a child admitted to school, more "tips" to the schoolteacher to have their son or daughter seated in the first few rows (important in classes of 150 or 200), and the like. These practices have been much more than a nuisance. For decades, they have sapped the energy, dulled the enterprise, and darkened the entire outlook of many Africans.

Corruption hurts the poor most. One day, my day guard in Abidjan—the same one who had to rescue his cousin from jail—was attacked on his way to work. Thieves took his watch and broke his arm, but did not get away with any of his money. In the next few days, he was less lucky with the police and doctor. The police wanted to be "rewarded" for filing a report. The doctor charged $12 for X-rays and a cast, but $80—half a month's salary—for a medical document certifying to the guard's employer that he could not work, and another $80 six weeks later, to confirm that he was better.

To make matters worse, culprits are seldom punished. At about the same time as my guard's misfortune, Italian Catholic nuns at a regional hospital outside the city were asked to advance money to feed the patients for three months. The government budget was $3,200, but the sisters did everything for $1,300. When the public money arrived, the hospital accountant disappeared with it, leaving both the state and the sisters in the lurch. Later, the thief was offered a similar job somewhere else.

A corrupt judicial system is another millstone around Africa's neck. In fact, dishonest judges are as bad as the dictators. Efforts to clean up the judicial system—training judges, computerizing records, strengthening the role of clerks—have borne little fruit because the politicians have found it more convenient to have a crooked and malleable judiciary than an independent one. As a result, although numerous judges have gone to France, Canada, and the United States for professional courses, many have returned to their sordid practices once they were back on the bench. In this, as in other respects, South Africa has been the sterling exception.

Lawyer groups across the continent have fought hard to counter this rot, but their pleas have gone largely unheard. Some activists have been jailed for contempt of court (a strange inversion of responsibilities!) and many lawyers have had to tone down their protests to earn a living.

At a business club meeting in Abidjan in the mid-1990s, entrepreneurs complained directly to their guest of honor, the Minister of Justice: "If you take away a sense of confidence in the law— which is one of the pillars of society—you create a parallel system of justice instead. In industrialized countries, it is true, there are examples of corruption and miscarriages of justice which make the headlines. But these are rare and the judicial system restores public trust fairly quickly afterwards. But in a young country, the consequences are amplified and lead to frustration and fear in business circles. We used to complain that justice was 'arbitrary' and unpredictable. Now, it is thoroughly predictable: all decisions go against business . . ."[22] Instead of getting to the bottom of the problem, the minister summoned the club president to her office—three times—to have him apologize for raising the issue in public.

Like well-to-do Africans, some Westerners have tried to put corruption into context. Reacting to news that Ghana's Kwame Nkrumah had siphoned off $6 million for his own purposes (admittedly a modest sum by later standards), an eminent British historian referred to eighteenth century European politicians who were also corrupt but served their country well and were "cheap at the price": "No matter how gross or self-indulgent Nkrumah's methods may have been, his intentions and his successes cannot be regarded as negligible. I suspect that he will prove to have been well worth his graft, if not his tyranny."[23] Those Africans who pay the price of corruption are unlikely to share that judgment.

All the same, it is pointless to rue the past. Practical judgments are now more important than moral ones. Very few Westerners would behave differently from Africans in the same circumstances. Imagine being a minister of finance, trying to raise a family of five or six on a salary of $500 a month, while being exposed to Western standards of living through television or international travel, and surrounded by less competent colleagues who have already sent their children to American or French universities and have handsome apartments in London or Nice. Only the rarest of human beings could resist such temptations very long. Remarkably, many still do. One way of honoring that resistance is to close the yawning gaps in government rules–foreign and domestic–that allow officials to rob public money with impunity.

Corruption is endemic in Africa for the same reasons as elsewhere. But it hurts the continent more than other regions, is more brazen, and is accepted more readily. As much of the elite is involved, and the poor are powerless, there is little pressure for change. Even when people at the top become too greedy and cut off opportunities for others, those below them have little interest in shaking the ladder they are standing on. People in power or professional positions are more likely to lose than gain from political upheaval. Even opposition groups do not want to change the system very much, as they await their turn to exploit it themselves. It is hardly surprising that anti-corruption campaigns rarely bite. Their purpose is public relations and the intended audience is largely foreign.

If character keeps Africans fatalistic and corruption binds their elites together, political correctness in the West adds a final touch to Africa's misery. This correctness takes several forms. The first and most harmless is a general sympathy for a continent that has grown steadily poorer over the last 30 years. Those who sense that their own well-being is connected with that of others, are reluctant to criticize Africa—any more than they would berate the unemployed for being out of work. They accept that reducing poverty will take time. In the meantime, they contribute massively to private charities that deal with the problem at the grass roots level.

A second aspect of Western feelings toward Africa is the historical or racial guilt of the former colonial countries like France, Germany, and the United Kingdom. Many of their citizens accept without much argument that the colonial period destroyed some "golden age" in Africa and, by creating artificial borders, doomed independent governments to lasting problems. They feel obliged to compensate the continent for the damage Western interests have done. Many Americans also feel some responsibility as distant beneficiaries of the slave trade.

A third strand of political correctness is the suggestion that Africa is actually better-off than it seems and is dealing admirably with its many problems. Some believe that Africa has much to teach the West, and that it is Europe and North America that are in trouble. Africans are viewed as having a sense of proportion, community, and resilience. In the words of one European, "Africa can teach us solidarity. Our modern democracy is not very human. Trade unions are breaking up, churches are emptying, associations are falling apart. The only healthy 'communities' are private companies . . ..Africa may not have real political parties, but it is bristling with other forms of cooperation: families, ethnic groups, savings associations, churches, sects, Masonic lodges . . ."[24] Some foreign visitors try to be reassuring: "Consider the Zambezi River, and the Tonga people who dwell along its shores. Daily, they must struggle with hardships that most [Westerners] can barely imagine, but they do not seem to be immobilized by pain or grief. Instead, their lives seem ordered, calm, imbued with purpose. They seem to be at peace with themselves, their communities, their world. They seem to be getting along just fine. And maybe, in a way, they are."[25] Others are more balanced in their assessments of African conditions: "There is a deceiving sense of timelessness to the stillness of rural life."[26]

A fourth variety of political correctness is expressed by those who question globalization. Many wonder how international trade can help poor, defenseless countries; they doubt the claim of economic theorists that a "rising tide will lift all boats." They see little evidence that prosperity is spreading in the world and are more concerned by the still-wide income differences between countries. Their concerns are deep and widely shared, even among economists. Others go further and portray the global economy as a moral battleground, where corporate profits are "blood money," the World Trade Organization is a "war machine," and rich countries are waging a "world war against the poor."[27]

Whether expressed in mundane or extreme forms, Western sensitivities have allowed African intellectuals to shift responsibility for their problems to others. Some of Africa's guilt-mongering comes from eminent sources. The great Nigerian novelist Chinua Achebe bears a strange grudge against the Polish–English writer Joseph Conrad, who described African culture in his famous novel *The Heart of Darkness* as the "incarnation of suppressed rage." Achebe also resents the French missionary Albert Schweitzer's reference to Africans as "my brothers, but my *junior* brothers."[28] According to Achebe, the Western belief that Africans are fundamentally different affects the way foreigners deal with Africa and how Africans try to help themselves. "I am not a whiner," he has said. "In fact, I hate whiners, and I know Africa's faults. But who created Mobutu and kept him in power apart from the CIA and who is paying the price now?"[29] Achebe forgets that he has been among those who argue that Africans *are* very different. Conrad and Schweitzer probably reflected their times more than they influenced them. They may have been condescending but it is in no way clear that they were racist. Nonetheless, great men like Achebe, who have shown their own humanity and disappointment with African governments, are entitled to criticize the West. Unfortunately, the charge of "racism" also comes from less exalted lips—like those of Robert Mugabe, the president of Zimbabwe.

In 2002, Zimbabwe was suspended from the 54-member Commonwealth of Nations following the manipulation of election results, the harassment, imprisonment and assassination of opposition politicians, the closure and burning of the offices of independent newspapers, and the murder of white farmers resisting the takeover of their land. In December 2003, Zimbabwe withdrew from the Commonwealth altogether, to avoid being evicted by what President Mugabe and his sympathizers described as "white racists"—the UK, Canada, Australia, and New Zealand. Arguing for "constructive engagement," President Mbeki of South Africa sought Zimbabwe's immediate re-admission to the Commonwealth. President Obasanjo of Nigeria sent emissaries to Zimbabwe's capital to try to persuade Mugabe to rejoin the club. Ironically, Mbeki and Obasanjo were the architects of the New Partnership for Africa's Development, which had promised that African presidents would apply peer justice to the continent's political problems.

In Mugabe's eyes, Western countries were "racist" because they were concerned about the 60 white farmers who had lost their lives in the government's campaign to seize agricultural land. Zimbabwean zealots—not seeing their own racism—found it obnoxious that the lives of a "handful" of stubborn people weighed so heavily in international opinion. Reality was lost in a fog of recrimination and rationalization. Millions had been killed by dictators, civil war, disease, and famine since Africa gained its independence. Some minorities, like Uganda's Asians, had been expelled out of economic jealousy. But there were few parallels for the brutal elimination of a small group of people whose contribution was vital to the health of an entire economy, and who had been promised the protection of the law following the introduction of majority rule. As it happened, thanks to the ruthlessness of this desperate government, none of the small farmers who took over the stolen lands would be better off for very long. In fact, in late 2004, newly installed black farmers outside the capital got a taste of their own medicine, when they were forcibly evicted by ruling party stalwarts eyeing the land for themselves.

In trying to be generous, Africa's friends perpetuate confusion about the roots of the continent's problems and the limits to which outsiders can help. Like African governments, they end up mincing their words and dodging the facts. But the facts are now too obvious to ignore.

For one thing, racism is alive and well *within* Africa. In the mid-1980s, the largely Arab and Berber government of Mauritania expelled thousands of dark-skinned Senegalese workers and traders, sending them back to their own country. Fifteen years later, the same government refused to accept a resident representative from the World Bank because he was black. The Bank's vice president for Africa, himself a black African, had to swallow his disgust and comply. Elsewhere on the continent, in Sudan and other countries, slavery and forced labor survive to this day.

Since the slave trade, no people—white, yellow, or brown—have been as vile toward Africans as Africans themselves. The Hutu slaughter of 800,000 Tutsis in 100 days in 1994 was not the fault of the international community—even though latter-day critics suggest that UN or US intervention could have stemmed the killing. Instead, it was the product of decades of imagined and real slights. Western influence, including a century of missionary activity, was powerless in the face of ethnic hatred. About 85 percent of the Rwandan population were Roman Catholics; even priests urged their congregations to join in the bloodbath, or did so themselves. The forces at work were larger than Christianity and—with apologies to Achebe–reminiscent of Conrad's "suppressed rage."

In recent years, a number of observers have tried to burst the bubble of polite commentary on Africa. African Americans have been among the first iconoclasts. The comedian Whoopi Goldberg put it simply enough: "I've been to Africa, and let me tell you, I'm an American." The *Washington Post* correspondent in Nairobi in the early 1990s, Keith Richburg, was deeply scarred by events he covered in Somalia, Ethiopia, Liberia, and Rwanda. His memoir, *Out of America*, ripples with anger: "Excuse me if I sound cynical, jaded. I'm beaten down, and I'll admit it. And it is Africa that has made me this way. I feel for her suffering, I empathize with her pain, and now, from afar, I still recoil in horror whenever I see yet another television picture of another tribal slaughter, another refugee crisis. But most of all I think: Thank God my ancestor got out, because, now, I am not one of them."[30]

In 2003, the French journalist Stephen Smith capped 20 years of African reporting with a book entitled *Négrologie* (a play on the French word *nécrologie*, meaning obituary). His judgments make mine seem tender by comparison. As he puts it bluntly: "One cannot embroider or exaggerate what is happening in Africa: the only unity there is one of pain and suffering."[31] "Since Independence, Africans [however unconsciously] have been steadily building the case for re-colonization. If that was the goal, they could not have done better. Yet, even in this, the continent is failing. No one is interested anymore."[32]

Certainly, Western indifference is growing. Shortly after the Rwandan genocide, I asked a French friend, who is a priest, why NATO had intervened to stop "ethnic cleansing" in the Balkans but not lifted a finger to stem a larger genocide in the Great Lakes Region of Africa. "Because Bosnia and Kosovo are in Europe," he said, matter-of-factly. Europe certainly has problems closer to home. But part of the West's detachment derives from a sense of helplessness at the scale of the continent's problems and how little Africa's own governments are doing about them.

Africans criticize Western double standards, but African hypocrisy is just as deep. Peacekeeping forces might have saved some lives in Rwanda, but they would not have altered the basic equation. This is not mere opinion; it is borne out by subsequent events. French forces intervened briefly in 1995 to stabilize the Rwanda–Zaire border, where the massing of refugees and some rumbling volcanoes were creating a literally explosive situation. But a new war soon emerged in Central Africa, provoked in part by the overflow of ethnic hostilities in Rwanda. Almost four million people have since died from fighting or famine in that struggle.

In the late 1970s and early 1980s, two of South Africa's neighbors, Zambia and Zimbabwe, complained that Western countries were ignoring international sanctions against the white regime. Those denunciations already seemed hollow at that time, as these so-called front-line states were secretly importing canned goods and other essentials from South Africa. They regarded this cheating as pragmatic. Meanwhile, more distant countries like Tanzania were proud to demonstrate their solidarity and incurred real sacrifices by refusing to trade with South Africa, the largest economy on the continent. Given such hypocrisy, are Africans really in a position to teach morality to anyone?

At about the same time, another example of African double standards could be found in the northeastern corner of the continent, known as the Horn of Africa. At midnight in November 1977, I met the Somali dictator Mohamed Siad Barre at his barracks in Mogadishu. He railed against his neighbor Ethiopia, which he regarded as the last colonial master, for having attended the Berlin Conference that carved up Africa in 1884–85. It was odd that he should complain about his neighbor's imperialism. He was supporting ethnic Somali rebels in Ethiopia's Ogaden province who were fighting the central government, and Somali maps showed the province already incorporated into a Greater Somalia. It was not the only annexation in Barre's sights. The star on the Somali flag had five points: two were for the former British and Italian Somalilands that were fused together at Independence in 1960, and the other three represented the Ogaden, Northern Kenya, and the small neighboring state of Djibouti, all of which had Somali populations. In 1990, Barre slipped out of the country to escape being overthrown. After that, instead of "rescuing" Somalis in neighboring states, he had to watch his own country implode under the bloody rule of warlords. For the next 15 years, it was the only country on earth without a government of any kind. Not only were Somalis living overseas now stateless; their very country was, as well.

Some would argue that the events of the 1970s and 1980s are now distant; but Africans are still making their own kind of history. In the late nineteenth century, when the British explorer Henry Stanley saw a Pygmy man and his wife in the Ituri forest of Central Africa, he was able to put aside the prejudices of his age and regard them as his ancestors. "In him was a mimicked dignity, as of Adam; in her the womanliness of a miniature Eve."[33] In 1961, an enthralled Scottish anthropologist named Colin Turnbull wrote a best-selling book about the Ituri called *The Forest People*. Africans showed them some respect, too. "The Pygmies have long been called *premiers citoyens* (first citizens) in the Democratic Republic of the Congo, a title that not only assumes their primordial existence in the forest but also accords them the privilege of not paying taxes."[34] In late 2002, a UN inquiry found that rebels belonging to the Congo Liberation Movement had killed, raped, and robbed civilians, sprayed live-stock with automatic fire, raided fresh graves to look for treasure, and eaten human flesh. Their principal victims were the Ituri Pygmies, who were suspected of acting as forest scouts for rival factions. "For a long time," an aid worker told the French news-paper Le Monde, "the Pygmies have been looked down upon by other ethnic groups, even though they are the 'first citizens' of the country. The fact that they are now being eaten has con-vinced them that they are not regarded as human."[35] Some wit-nesses later retracted their stories, claiming they were pressured by government agents into discrediting the rebels.[36] The fact these witnesses were believed at all is a sign of the real horrors Central Africa has been suffering. Along with human beings, truth is another victim of the lying and intimidation at the heart of the political struggle in the region.

The Congo has been a trouble spot for as long as anyone can remember. But, in early 2004, a place unknown even to most Africans suddenly became a household word in the West. At Dar-fur, in western Sudan, Arab militiamen on camels and horses killed an estimated 50,000 people, most of them black, in the space of a few months. Almost 1.5 million people were displaced and nearly 200,000 refugees fled across the border into Chad. The militias were avenging rebel activities the year before, and were being armed and encouraged by the government. By late 2004, an international outcry led to a United Nations Security Council res-olution threatening sanctions against Sudan's oil exports if the government did not take steps to end the violence. Weeks went by as diplomats discussed whether the killings were "genocide" or not, so as to justify stiffer penalties. As the debate proceeded, more people died.

Smaller horrors continue elsewhere—even in countries sup-posedly at peace. In the first six months of 2004, opposition to polio vaccination by religious and political leaders in northern Nigeria caused the disease to spread to ten other countries, some of which had wiped it out previously. Extremists claimed the vac-cine made girls infertile and that Western countries were trying to reduce the Muslim population. The World Health Organization was forced to test the product in two other countries, South Africa and India, before a program to vaccinate millions of Nigerians below the age of 5 could continue.[37] "It's a totally unnecessary public health tragedy," a senior UNICEF official told reporters. Another UN official lamented: "We could see thousands paralyzed at a time when the disease should be eradicated."[38] Nigerians eventually agreed to use a vaccine imported from another Muslim country, Indonesia.[39]

In Zimbabwe, the same year, the government prevented the United Nations World Food Program from delivering relief supplies. As one observer said: "Last year, about half the country's 12 million people were getting such assistance. No longer. [President] Mugabe says the country is having a bumper harvest and relief is no longer needed, but it is hard to determine whether this is true. Mugabe has shut down the country's main independent newspaper, *The Daily News*. The World Food Program has been denied permission to assess crops. Other sources of independent information have also been muzzled."[40] At the same time, church leaders were reporting that, all around them, large numbers were dying of hunger and disease. The year before, Mugabe had refused US assistance on the grounds that American corn was genetically modified. He had also steered United Nations food aid to his supporters. Consequently, other Zimbabweans faced starvation whether the country accepted international assistance or not.

Such behavior is still condoned in Africa because many people do not know the facts or refuse to accept their significance. Perhaps most alarming is that many people believe that their leaders are entitled to their faults as long as the continent continues to be subjected to Western "oppression." Even in the country that has been the great exception to Africa's rules, South Africa, self-pity and nationalism can outweigh sympathy for the victims of real oppression. In April 2004, at the start of President Mbeki's second term, Mugabe was the only foreign dignitary to receive a standing ovation from the crowd attending Mbeki's inauguration. Meanwhile, back home, Mugabe's new minister of finance was being charged with corruption.[41] In October 2005, Mugabe was applauded again—this time in Rome at the 60th anniversary of the United Nations Food and Agriculture Organization—when he compared US President George W. Bush and UK Prime Minister Tony Blair to Hilter and Mussolini.

The political correctness of South Africans is just as damaging to other Africans as Western "compassion." Nelson Mandela has criticized Mugabe, but his example has failed to spread. Africans continue to accept bad governments for three reasons. Their culture induces them to respect their elders and accept their fate. Patronage and corruption have a complex stranglehold on national life. And Westerners prefer to speak politely about Africa's problems, not wanting to alienate decision-makers. Or, when their words are severe, their actions do not measure up. Africans are the ones who suffer the consequences.

PART II

STORIES FROM
THE FRONT LINE

CHAPTER 5

TANZANIA

African Socialism

Even politically correct Westerners have sometimes grated on African nerves by emphasizing the continent's difficulties rather than its accomplishments, or appealing to Africa's shame rather than its pride. Like most young nations, in the 1960s, Africa nurtured great dreams, the greatest of which was African unity. Almost as important was the possibility of achieving self-reliance after decades of interference from others.

Early in the life of modern Africa, one country, established in 1964 as a fusion of the British protectorate of Tanganyika and the Muslim island state of Zanzibar, made self-reliance its overriding goal. That experiment, and the remarkable man who led it, are an important part of the African story. They may seem distant to younger readers, but they left an indelible imprint on two generations of Africans and aid planners alike. They also shone a bright light, and later a shadow, on the world's efforts to help the continent.

Tanzania is the land of Mount Kilimanjaro, the tallest mountain in Africa (19,340 feet). As you approach it across the Masai plain, it rises slowly from the horizon until it almost floats above the ground, a symbol of strength and tranquility. Tanzania is also known for the Ngorongoro Crater, beautiful in itself but famous for its wildlife. Further to the west is Olduvai Gorge, where Louis and Mary Leakey labored on a barren sun-blasted hillside for 28 successive summers to find traces of the earliest ancestor of man. A simple plaque on the site—nothing more—marks one of the greatest acts of scientific perseverance in human history. Foreign eccentrics also passed this way. At Moshi cemetery, near Kilimanjaro, the geologist who gave his name to the southern summit of the mountain ("Gillman's Point") is buried with the following epitaph: "To the memory of Clement Gillman, 26th November 1882–5th October 1946, who led a commonsense and therefore happy life because he stubbornly refused to be bamboozled by his female relations, by his scientific friends and by the rulers spiritual and secular of the society into which without his consent he was born."

However, most of all, in the 1970s the world was watching Tanzania as a laboratory of African socialism. Other countries like Guinea and Benin in West Africa had slavishly imitated the Soviet Union, believing in heavy-handed police states and a "dictatorship of the proletariat," where presidents did the dictating. Tanzania was different. Like most African countries, it was a one-party state but, at least at the start, the ruling elite was disciplined and serious. It relied on an elaborate network of "cells," one for every ten households in the country, to stay in touch with local opinion. (Later, the cell leaders would be accused of spying on and suppressing inconvenient points of view.) Tanzania boasted other advantages. There was common sense and even self-criticism at many levels of government. There were certainly political excesses at the regional and local level, but also checks and balances built into the system. And, at the very top, there was a strong sense of direction from a president everyone could be proud of.

Julius Nyerere had high ideals, a strong sense of public service, a gift for expressing himself, and a stubbornness about reaching his goals. Like many Africans, he loved language, but he was neither pompous nor overbearing. His speeches and writings were as clear as water, and they stuck to the principles he had enunciated early in his career. Their most famous expression was the Arusha Declaration of 1967, named for a town nestled in the shadow of the Mount Kilimanjaro. In this document, Nyerere set ambitious goals for his country. It started with a simple declaration of human rights and socialist principles, then burst with ideas, many of which still make sense for all of Africa.

Foreign aid, the document said, was not the answer to Tanzania's problems. "There are many needy countries in the world. And even if all the prosperous nations were willing to help the needy countries, the assistance would still not suffice."[1] Nor would borrowing help. In Nyerere's view, "Whether it is used to build schools, hospitals, houses or factories, etc., it still has to be repaid. Where, then, shall we get it from? We shall get it from the villages and from agriculture. . . . If we are not careful we might get to the position where the real exploitation in Tanzania is that of the town dwellers exploiting the peasants."[2]

Agriculture, not industry, Nyerere insisted, must be the basis of development. Personal effort was also important. "People, through their own hard work and with a little help and leadership, have finished many development projects in the villages . . . Had they waited for money, they would not have the use of such things."[3] This did not mean that people should be left to themselves. Good policies and leadership were also essential. "Leaders must set a good example to the rest of the people in their lives and in all their activities."[4]

No other politician in Africa had laid down the challenge so firmly and unpretentiously. Unfortunately, there was also some condescension in the Arusha Declaration: "The energies . . . . wasted in gossip, dancing and drinking, are a great treasure which could contribute more towards the development of our country than anything we could get from rich nations."[5] The document also expressed a suspicion of private investment and enterprise, in line with emerging official thinking across Africa. But the merits of the Arusha Declaration far outweighed its faults, and gave aid donors the confidence that at least one country was charting its own path and tailoring its expectations to international realities.

Nyerere's socialism (called "Ujamaa," or "familyhood") was inspired by traditions of African solidarity and Christianity rather than Marxism. He was not doctrinaire. When collective production failed in a number of model Ujamaa villages, he told the ruling party to abandon the idea. But his followers sometimes used rough methods to promote his ideals. After the government tried unsuccessfully to coax the rural population into larger villages so as to improve their access to public services, the ruling party turned up the heat—literally. According to a sympathetic Westerner: "As soon as a house was burnt in the first village, the news spread over a radius of sixty miles, and finally the local population relocated—not willingly, but without physical violence, except on rare occasions."[6]

To be fair, Nyerere was also tough on his colleagues. A rigorous "leadership code" prevented senior officials from earning income on the side. Nyerere's own wife had to give up a prosperous poultry business. Some officials left the party to go into business full time; others stayed, but resented the rules. As one observer put it: "I think there is a real asceticism in the President and such a deep conviction that people have confidence in him. Everyone knows that he doesn't profit from politics. He is disinterested."[7]

Paradoxically, because of its insistence on becoming self-reliant, Tanzania received very high levels of aid. Enrollments in primary schools surged and adult literacy programs sprouted up across the country. The government promoted rural projects rather than "prestige" investments to such an extent that the capital, Dar es Salaam, deteriorated into one large slum. But, as Nyerere predicted, there was never enough money. In 1977, despite record-high prices for coffee (one of the country's principal exports) and Tanzania's first balance of payments surplus ever, people in the capital had trouble finding meat, a cholera epidemic spread quickly throughout the country, and industries were short of spare parts. Eager aid donors also made questionable decisions.

From December 1976 to October 1978, I saw the unfortunate consequences of generous aid as First Secretary (Development) at the Canadian High Commission (Embassy). One day, I read a World Bank proposal for a shoe factory in the middle of the country which was to export its products to Italy. Although deeply sympathetic to the government and its goals, I was dumbfounded. The document praised Tanzania's social policies but tiptoed around emerging economic problems. These included low prices for farmers, inefficient processing factories, and the "villagization" program that had relocated 70 percent of the rural population in just three years—all of which had led to sharp falls in production of the principal export crops (cashews, cotton, sisal, coffee, and tea). I doubted that Tanzania was ready to enter the international market in light manufactures, let alone undersell Italian shoemakers in their home market. But, like many onlookers at the time, I assumed the World Bank had better access to information than we did. Alas, within a year of opening, the factory was operating at only 4 percent of capacity and exporting nothing; it was even having trouble delivering the few shoes it made within Tanzania. Years later, the Bank recognized that it had used "heroic" assumptions. As Nyerere had predicted, the country's farmers–whose income was dropping–would eventually pay back that loan.

The World Bank was not the only agency getting itself into trouble. I planned a $60 million program to supply Tanzania's aging railway system with new rail, locomotives, and wagons at a time when Canadian manufacturers were facing a slump. What better marriage of interests could there be, we thought, than saving jobs in Canada while improving a major transport corridor in eastern Africa? To ensure that we were not just taking commercial advantage of the situation, appropriate engineering and economic studies were done; but Canada almost certainly provided more equipment than was needed. There were no spectacular consequences. The aid was more dispersed and hence less visible than the shoe factory at Morogoro and a massive pulp and paper plant that the World Bank was also planning. But, the railway had trouble assembling trains in crowded marshalling yards, and management improvements lagged well behind the replacement of equipment.

In 1977, ten years after the Arusha Declaration, Nyerere published a candid assessment of progress. As usual, he used terms that could be understood by schoolchildren, not just specialists. Significantly, he mentioned industry, not agriculture, first. In 1967, hardly any of the country's cotton was made into cloth; by 1975, Tanzania had eight textile mills. Primary school enrollments had nearly doubled. Over five million people—about a third of the population—were taking adult literacy courses. The number of rural health centers had more than tripled. Three million rural people had access to clean water. Differences in personal income had been narrowed. The villagization program was almost complete.

But agriculture—the heart of the Arusha Declaration—came almost last in the accounting. In Nyerere's words, "The majority of our traditional crops are still being grown by the same methods as our forefathers used."[8] Food production was not keeping pace with population and government-set farm prices were too low. As Nyerere put it, "We have continued to shout at the peasants, and exhort them to produce more, without doing much to help them or to work with them in a relationship of mutual respect."[9]

Without knowing it, he put his finger on what was becoming a general African problem: "Over the last ten years we have done quite well in spreading basic social services to more and more people in rural areas. More remains to be done; but we shall only be able to do it if we produce more wealth. And we have not been doing very well on that front." World conditions had not been helpful; import prices were high and export prices too low. "But," Nyerere insisted, "we must not use that—or the drought years—as an excuse for our own failures."[10] The country was not being efficient. State companies were absorbing wealth, not creating it. Productivity was falling. In the Tanzanian president's words, "We employ some 'Sales Managers' who sit in their offices and wait for customers to search them out . . ."[11] Nyerere recognized that workers, too, had developed bad habits: "We have virtually eliminated the discipline of fear; it is quite hard for a manager or employer to dismiss a worker, or even suspend or fine him for dereliction of duty. But in Tanzania it is not unusual for a manager to be locked out by the workers!"[12]

Nyerere saw that the government was growing faster than the rest of the economy, leading to the budget problems that were to plague Tanzania—and the entire continent—during the 1980s and 1990s. Foreign aid was funding 60 percent of the development budget. For Nyerere, this was far too high: "It can be justified as an emergency operation . . . to increase production, not to supplement our living standards. The intelligent farmer does not eat his seed-corn, and especially not borrowed seed! . . . [Our] friends are willing to help us only because they respect our determination to help ourselves, and to try to build a society based on human equality and dignity."[13]

Like most of the world, I was mesmerized by Nyerere's ideals and clear-headedness. My letters home brimmed with a sense of moral adventure. But they also betrayed some misgivings. In May 1977, I reported that coffee farmers on Kilimanjaro were *proud* to be capitalists and were chafing at the checks on their enterprise. I recognized that "some of the most important developments here are invisible to outsiders, especially those who feel they can throw money or machinery or expertise at a problem." Such doubts did not prevent me from being glib. In June 1977, a colleague at the US embassy questioned the wisdom of putting Canadian money into emergency grain storage rather than rice production in the southern highlands. I asked if he was aware that Tanzania could expect another bad harvest in a year and a half if the normal four-year cycle prevailed. "Yes," he said. Did he really expect the country to grow sufficient amounts of experimental rice to head off a famine? "No," he acknowledged. I persisted: "Well then, do you think that the threat of starvation should be kept alive just to encourage maximum production in the meantime?" Undeterred, the American answered: "I wouldn't put it quite that way, but essentially—yes." At the time, I thought him heartless; now I see his point.

Not everyone was cheering the government on. Maoist-leaning Canadian volunteers told me that the authorities were "oppressing the peasants, reinforcing neo-colonial dependence on world commodity markets, and having far too much to do with the World Bank." Marxist political scientists were saying that Tanzania had not done enough to "capture" the peasantry for the modern economy. "It is fashionable," wrote one, "to criticize African governments for being too coercive and authoritarian, leaving little or no room for civil liberties . . . . If governments were to depend on participatory and grass-roots approaches alone, there would be no modernization, no development."[14] At the other end of the political spectrum, the *Wall Street Journal*'s view was that the emperor had no clothes. The world should see through "all the hot air and poppycock that has been penned by or about Mr. Nyerere. . . . [Tanzania] is a shabby place that has betrayed the hopes of its people and now lies hooked on foreign aid. . . . [It was] helped along this path by a bunch of starry-eyed do-gooders without much appreciation for how the world works."[15]

Corruption was also taking off, even though at first Tanzania seemed to have kept the disease in check. "Corruption is no doubt spreading," a Catholic missionary reported in 1981. "But it's called by its name and has to hide. It cannot become a system of government, as it has in neighboring countries."[16] Yet, the same observer recognized that "family solidarity" was already ruining the economy: "A teacher will not hesitate to leave his class to buy some vegetable oil for his family. A company director will bloat his payroll to hire relatives, neighbors, friends . . . If a civil servant's father falls ill in a remote village, the son will hire a taxi to take him to the city. This will cost thousands of shillings, many times his monthly salary. Either he can borrow it, which merely puts off the problem, or he can acquire it by illegal means."[17] A Swedish political scientist described this as "the economy of affection."[18]

Nonetheless, Tanzania continued to receive so much aid that soon it was having trouble repaying its debts—even those on very favorable terms. As a result, some donors already felt obliged to write off some debts. In April 1978, Canada announced the cancellation of $80 million of obligations. This caused barely a ripple in the Tanzanian press. A few months later, after I mentioned the debt relief to a young reporter, the news was splashed on the front page of the Swahili-language paper Uhuru [Independence]. I learned about it over breakfast, when my cook thanked me for "my" generosity—and then asked for a raise. The news also went out on the international wires, leading to prickly letters from home. One man from Vancouver attached clippings about the debt relief and new credits for Zaire, Upper Volta, and Gabon. Then, he let me have it: "Within a few weeks, Canadians playing Santa Claus have given away over $250 million for aid. You nincompoops can't spend it fast enough. . . . As a taxpayer, I am getting sick and tired of how you big shots squander our money." I flinched, but his punch hit home.

Debt relief from individual countries was not enough to help Tanzania. By 1981, high oil prices, low export earnings, poor weather, and mounting debt service were strangling the country. (Tanzania had also invaded Uganda and overthrown Idi Amin—a victory which was a gift to the world, but cost a whole year's exports.) Each week, the government was literally having to choose between paying the World Bank or buying another shipload of emergency grain. Quite naturally, the government chose wheat over debt and the Bank was forced to suspend most of its projects. Six months later, the country was on the verge of a formal default that would have been the first in the history of the international institution. As the World Bank's loan officer for Tanzania, I urged the head of the finance ministry not to make this new kind of history. "Why don't you pick on Argentina and Brazil?" he told me. "Because they've reneged on the private banks but are still meeting their official obligations," I replied. He was astonished. Shortly after, the Bank's vice president for eastern Africa visited Nyerere with a letter from the Bank's president appealing to his sense of international solidarity. Nyerere was deeply insulted. "How can you doubt our intentions?" he asked. "If we had the money, we would certainly pay you."

The logjam broke, Tanzania paid its arrears, and the privilege of being the World Bank's first defaulter went to someone else (Nicaragua, in the following year). But Nyerere's heart was broken. From leading the battle for a new international economic order and fighting cynicism with simple ideals, he had been forced into the grubby position of facing the debt collectors. Within three years, he would leave office saddened and frustrated.

He had reason to be exasperated. Tanzania's friends had given him conflicting advice. First, they praised him for emphasizing primary education, then complained about the neglect of higher education. In the mid-1970s, following a disastrous drought, the government was encouraged to increase food prices and achieved self-sufficiency in maize (corn) within three years; later, it was scolded for biasing farmers against export crops like coffee and tea. In 1977, outsiders urged the country to relax its import controls to allow industry to buy badly needed raw materials and spare parts; shortly after, donors said that the government had acted too late, just as the international coffee boom was ending. All this advice sprang from the best of analysis and intentions, but priorities and perceptions had changed sharply. And the country was still far from its objective of self-reliance.

The World Bank, which had lionized Nyerere and bankrolled large parts of the country's development plans, now began to distance itself from well-intentioned but heavy-handed government intervention. The winds of Reaganism and Thatcherism were sweeping through the corridors of aid agencies around the world. Little had changed in Tanzania. It remained a very poor country with few options for development. Too many expectations had been placed on a single country. It was unfair to punish Tanzania for a change of mentalities or ideology in Western capitals. But the clock had run out on noble experiments. A worldwide recession and low international commodity prices were cramping Africa's options even further. It was important to get back to brass tacks: offering farmers a fair return for their efforts, promoting private investment, and doing everything possible to use public money more efficiently. Nyerere himself understood the problem but seemed to think that appeals to national pride rather than real economic incentives would make the difference to farmers. Other African governments, however, could not even see the problem. Countries could not feed themselves on social services, or pay for them indefinitely, while Africa's economy was rotting away.

In 1997, 30 years after the Arusha Declaration, and 20 years after Nyerere's assessment of results, the World Bank organized its annual aid meeting in Dar es Salaam (which usually took place in Paris). The government was calling for more aid in general, a larger donor share of individual project costs (already running at 80–95 percent), and more debt relief, including contributions to a special fund to help pay off obligations to the World Bank and other official lenders. Some countries attending the meeting were already contributors to the World Bank; so they were being asked to pay twice for the same original purpose. In an unintended understatement, Tanzania's president, Benjamin Mkapa, told the gathering that "disengagement from donor dependency will not be accomplished in the twinkle of an eye." He cited a survey of 50 villages showing that only one in five households felt they were better off as a result of economic changes; almost 40 percent thought they were worse off.

Yet some things were changing. South Africans had taken over the brewery and cigarette company, Indians had bought the Chinese bicycle plant, and Tanzania's population had nearly doubled (from 17 million to 33 million) in 22 years. Local humor remained strong. Near the pier on the sea front, where small jetfoils now whisked visitors to islands off the coast, a makeshift wooden bench under a shade tree bore the sign "VIP/Non-Residents Lounge." Some businesses had prospered. I visited a handicrafts cooperative founded in the early 1970s that was now ten times its original size. As I paid for a basket at the front of the store, the manager came up to me with a big smile on her face. "Karibu [Welcome], Robert!" she said. We hadn't seen each other in 14 years.

In May 1998, Julius Nyerere visited the World Bank. I met his car at the front door and gave him the ancient Swahili greeting: "Shikamuu" ["I kiss your feet"]. "Marahaba" ["I am graced"], he replied with a gentle smile. Over lunch, the Bank's vice president said that he had become interested in Africa and development because of Nyerere. "Ah," the visitor replied with a laugh, putting his arm around the man's shoulders, "I misled a lot of young people in my time!" Turning serious, an African staff member said: "I have been re-reading your speeches from the 1960s and they still ring true. Obviously, there was nothing wrong in your vision. Where did we go astray?" Nyerere leaned his head gently into his left hand, refusing to be glib: "I don't have a full answer to that question. Some things certainly went right—we knitted a nation together, gave it pride, and educated a large number of our children and adults. But some ideas needed to await their proper time. People weren't ready. But you [the younger Africans] now have a chance to give those ideas new life."

He suggested that Africa and the international institutions should work differently together. "We've had our faults, but you [the World Bank and the IMF] have been running Africa for the last 10–15 years—not literally, but essentially, as national budgets have shrunk, African debt has grown, and political options have narrowed. Whatever mistakes we made, we made together. Now, we must find the humility to correct them hand-in-hand."

Later, he addressed about 200 Bank staff, whose affection for this father of modern Africa was palpable. He was still clear, modest, and idealistic. Asked about the sale of publicly owned companies to private investors, he answered: "I understand the rationale for privatization now, but part of it still strikes me as simple thievery." Two-thirds of the audience, mostly Africans, jumped to their feet in applause. It was plain to most people there that Nyerere still spoke for the entire continent.

He had made mistakes—many of which he admitted—but some of his shortcomings were noble compared with the achievements of other leaders. And the lessons Tanzania had learned by aiming high were still proving valuable to the rest of Africa and the world.

CHAPTER 6

IVORY COAST

The End of a Miracle

Except for the equator they are close to, Tanzania and the Ivory Coast have almost nothing in common. They are 3,000 miles apart, one on the east African coast, the other on the west. Culturally, linguistically, and ideologically, the distance between them is even greater. Despite its poverty, Tanzania was seen by international observers as the model of African socialism. Because of its economic success, the Ivory Coast was considered the showcase of capitalism. Where Nyerere was unpretentious, modest, and idealistic, the Ivory Coast's first president, Félix Houphouët-Boigny, was formal, rich, and practical. Yet, like the tortoise and the hare, Tanzania made slow and steady progress while the Ivory Coast got off to a strong start, then floundered.

The contrast is even more striking as the Ivory Coast, like South Africa, had been a rare exception on the continent. Prosperous and stable, and a magnet for private investors, from 1960 to 1990, it had been a haven for job-seekers from nearby countries. A 1991 survey at the main hospital in the capital found people of 24 nationalities receiving care. For most of the nation's life, enlightened immigration policies and a relatively open economy kept living conditions ahead of increases in population. Low prices for cocoa, the country's major export, and an overvalued currency caused difficulties in the early 1990s. The country may not have been the "miracle" people spoke of, since human effort, good soils, and a convenient location had certainly helped. But, overall, the Ivory Coast had managed itself admirably by African standards.

The miracle ended on December 24, 1999, when the army overthrew the government. Although a common event elsewhere in Africa, this was high drama for the country—its first coup d'état since Independence in 1960. In fact, when the BBC reported a "coup," I thought they were mistaken. I knew the country well, as I had headed the World Bank's office for Western Africa in the capital, Abidjan, between November 1991 and December 1994. Yet, when the news was confirmed, I felt relief rather than dismay.

Since I had lived there, relations between different communities in the country, and between nationals and foreigners, had turned poisonous. The former shelter for immigrants had become obsessed with something called "Ivoirité"—a concept of nationalism that implied that anyone born outside the country's borders (as defined in 1960) was suspect. In a country once proud of its religious tolerance, this new doctrine also suggested that Muslims, the largest single group in the country, were inferior to Christians and should have fewer civil rights.

Just how tense the situation had become was brought home to me in April 2000 in the VIP Lounge at Abidjan's airport. I usually preferred to go through the main terminal rather than enjoy the courtesies—and delays—of the diplomatic route. But my local hosts had organized the visit. Shortly after I sat down, an official from the Ministry of Foreign Affairs entered the lounge with the Chinese ambassador. Recognizing me, the official rushed over and welcomed me effusively. Then, pointing to a former Minister of Culture and his wife who were sitting nearby, he asked if I had talked to them yet. When I said no, he dragged me over and pressed me into small talk with the one-time politician and poet.

"What do you think of recent events?" he asked. I pussyfooted around the subject, saying that I hoped the general who had taken power would not develop a strong taste for high office and would allow new elections relatively quickly. The former minister smiled faintly. When he left, I told the Foreign Affairs official how impressed I was to see the portrait of Houphouët-Boigny still in place. (The picture of his deposed successor had been removed.)

"It was easy for him to like immigrants," the diplomat snorted. "He needed them to work on his coffee and cocoa estates. The rest of us have no use for them!" I was chagrined. If a government official was denouncing the country's George Washington in the VIP Lounge, what must people be saying in the streets? Later in the week, I was aghast to find that even good friends in the human rights community had the word "Ivoirité" on their lips.

In this highly charged environment, the new president, General Robert Gueï, made all the right moves. In his first broadcast to the nation, he apologized for disrupting Christmas and a Muslim feast as well. He expressed regret to two neighboring countries, Mali and Burkina Faso, for the forced repatriation of hundreds of their nationals a few months before. He promised to be a unifier. And he quoted some of Houphouët-Boigny's favorite aphorisms about brotherhood and understanding. Made banal through constant repetition years before, these appeals to common sense and civility now seemed almost magical.

His speech was also a reminder that the cast of political characters changes slowly in Africa—and then usually through coups, or assassination, rather than the ballot box. Less than three years later, this man would be lying in the street outside his home with 19 bullet holes in his body. Ten years before, he had been at the heart of a different controversy.

In January 1992, just after I started living in Abidjan, the country won Africa's soccer championship for the first time. The national team's performance was lackluster—scoring only once in four games and winning through shots on goal in overtime. But the victory was so heartening that the country went berserk. The president declared a two-day national holiday and gave every member of the team a villa and $20,000. Then, after the holiday, he announced that he would not punish the army officers whom a National Commission of Enquiry had found guilty of beating and raping students at the university—arguing that no one had died and that other African countries had seen worse examples of violence. The man judged ultimately responsible for the criminal acts was the Army chief of staff, General Robert Gueï.

By mid-February 1992, the country's joy had turned to anger. Student strikes paralyzed the university, as well as colleges and high schools across the country. The government responded by arresting student leaders. In the middle of this uproar, the president went to Paris to attend an award ceremony at the headquarters of the United Nations Educational, Scientific and Cultural Organization (UNESCO). The Houphouët-Boigny Peace Prize—which he had personally funded—was being given to South Africa's outgoing president Frederick de Klerk and his designated successor Nelson Mandela. To celebrate, the government announced a National Week of Peace.

In the middle of that week, on February 18, a demonstration led by the main opposition party went awry when a small group broke away from the crowd and burnt vehicles and smashed windows in central Abidjan. The government arrested over 300 people and charged them with willful damage of public property. The contrast between pardoning soldiers for rape and coming down hard on demonstrators was too bitter to be lost on even the most casual observer. All of this was indeed milder than events in other African countries: the same week, 17 people were shot dead by police in Zaire during a peace march led by Catholic priests. But in the Ivory Coast, a country that had always prided itself on being "different" and orderly, a sense of shock and anxiety set in.

Those imprisoned included the opposition leader, a mild socialist by the name of Laurent Gbagbo, and the president of the Ivorian Human Rights League, René Dégni-Ségui (who was soon to become a close friend). Kept behind bars for six months, they refused to apologize for the damage done, arguing that it was the work of troublemakers in the pay of the ruling party. The government certainly never apologized to them.

Although it had introduced multiparty elections in 1990, the Ivory Coast was still largely a one-party state and there were limited opportunities for public debate. There was an irreverent opposition press, but radio and television were reserved for the ruling party, and political demonstrations were forbidden after February 1992. Human rights activists were often intercepted at the airport on their way to conferences overseas, and sent home. In May 1993, the government cancelled a "Rule of Law" conference organized by the Center of Legal Studies as being "too dangerous." These curbs on political expression, and the opposition's efforts to win points for "good behavior," blocked understanding of public opinion and forced passions and frustrations into other channels.

On November 1, 1993 (All Saints' Day), the city of Abidjan exploded in an orgy of soccer violence. Disappointed at losing a key match in neighboring Ghana, and hearing rumors that Ivorians were being attacked on the other side of the border, mobs prowled the city in search of Ghanaians, about 200,000 of whom lived in the country. The Ghanaian receptionist at our office called for help from a police station in his neighborhood, where he had taken refuge with 20 members of his family. A crowd was trying to break into the station, and there was nothing we could do, except call the chief of police to ask for reinforcements. Our security guard saw a woman set on fire and another group of men attacking a woman and her two children with broken bottles mounted on sticks. In another part of the city, a friend saw thugs dragging people off buses and stopping cars, looking for more Ghanaians. Altogether, about 500 people perished in the massacre.

Ivorians were victimized, too. A young friend called me the next day to say that he had been awake until 1:00 A.M. His apartment had been stripped of everything, because he had sheltered 13 Ghanaians there. All he had left was the clothes on his back. His pregnant wife had been sent off to relatives elsewhere in the city just in time.

For decades, Ivorians had relished their relatively peaceful history. Now, there was mounting discontent not just with immigrant workers but also with an elite trying to protect their standard of living while asking others to make "sacrifices." At about this time, the editor of the only respected newspaper in the capital described the country as "a powder keg sitting on a time bomb." The government accused him of being alarmist. In a sense, both were right. The editor had underestimated the patience of his countrymen— but, six years later, his prophecy was to come true.

A major reason for the unraveling of the national fabric was the failing health and weakening political grip of the country's founding father. Like Marshal Tito of Yugoslavia, Houphouët-Boigny had kept his country's centrifugal forces under control for more than 30 years. He had used force to repress secessionist movements—sending the army to massacre 6,000 people in several villages in the western region in 1970—and applied his considerable charm and wealth to cajole opponents into submission.

By the end of his life, his early ruthlessness was largely forgotten and expunged from the official histories. He was widely seen as an avuncular figure with a Midas touch in politics, not just business. With his immense personal fortune—at least $2 billion—he had purchased a sumptuous mansion in Paris and had personally funded a $400 million air-conditioned replica of St. Peter's Basilica in Rome in his home village of Yamoussoukro. His palace resembled Versailles, complete with gilded panels and Louis XVI furniture. He would frequently charter a Concorde to ferry him and his retinue to France, where he stayed for six months at a time. Although he owned vast cocoa and coffee estates, few people really believed he had earned his fortune honestly. Yet few held this against him, and like the political murders earlier in the country's history, the origins of his wealth had faded into the mists of time.

He was proud of his place in history. In 1992, he told me of a conversation he had had with British Prime Minister Margaret Thatcher in 1983. After dinner at 10 Downing Street, Mrs. Thatcher asked him condescendingly: "Why aren't English-speaking African heads of state mature and far-sighted like you?" "Madame," he replied, "it is because of your mistakes in running the colonies. The French let us sit in their National Assembly and (in my case) serve in five successive Cabinets in the 1950s. My Anglophone brothers never had a chance to learn the trade before Independence." Staring at the Iron Lady's sparkling jewelry, he added: "So, when the necklace started to choke them, they tore it off."[1]

At home, Houphouët was a towering figure. In neighboring countries, he was regarded as an important ally and, like European monarchs of the past, regularly married off members of his large family to regional power figures. In France, he had close relations with the political establishment and was a major contributor to France's main political parties. Elsewhere, Houphouët's reputation was less solid and he was regarded as being on the wrong side of history. For example, his insistence on maintaining contacts with racist South Africa was resented by other Africans. His closeness to the former colonial power and his predilection for placing many French nationals in positions of influence in the Ivory Coast also made him suspect. But, as one of modern Africa's founding fathers, he was held in high regard by his fellow leaders. In 1975, when it became known that Fidel Castro intended to denounce him as an "imperialist stooge" at a meeting of heads of state in Algiers, the host president, Houari Boumedienne, went to great lengths to protect Houphouët-Boigny. Castro was to speak on the fourth day of the conference. Already, on the first and second days, the organizers began cutting the electricity briefly at selected moments. Speakers grew accustomed to the interruptions and waited patiently for the microphone to come back on. When Castro mounted the podium, he did the same, but the power was never restored and he had to cancel his speech altogether. It was an amusing but heartfelt tribute to an African elder at the expense of a Latin American upstart.[2]

In December 1993, it was Houphouët's personal entourage who switched off the lights—this time on his life. The president had been ailing for two years, and was brought back from a Geneva hospital on a stretcher. Few people outside his immediate family had seen him, and it was widely assumed that he was being kept alive artificially. In a wink to history, those close to him pulled the plug on his life support on the 33rd anniversary of Independence, while letting the country think that his death was natural.

In the weeks leading up to Houphouët's demise, the country's famous stability seemed to be fraying at the edges. The international community grew nervous. The UN system updated its emergency communications system, assigning Zodiac walkie-talkie codes to each agency head to allow them to talk to each other secretly, if necessary: Cancer for the World Health Organization, Pisces (Fish) for the Food and Agriculture Organization, Gemini (Twins) for the population group, Libra (Balance) for the World Bank, and so on. (The IMF, which was absent from the code-setting meeting, was christened Scorpio.) In late November 1993, the president of the African Development Bank asked whether his 1,200 staff and their families could also be placed under the UN's security umbrella. Until then, like the rest of Abidjan's international community, the Bank had been so confident of the country's rock-solid political situation, that they had never drafted an emergency plan.

The tension kept rising. Everyone knew the president was dying, but people could only speculate about how close the end was. The main opposition paper announced the president's death one day, retracted its story, and then began burying him ahead of time. "Houphouët is not coming back. We have a country to build, and we can't spend time scanning the sky and cocking our ear for the sound of the Concorde bringing our President home. There is a limit to everything. A country which depends on a single individual does not inspire confidence. Just ask investors."

The succession had been planned meticulously for years; in fact, the country's constitution had been amended several times to spell out what would happen. The designated heir to the "throne" was Henri Konan-Bédié, the speaker of the National Assembly, who was rumored to be Houphouët's illegitimate son. Instead of applying the Constitution, the main opposition party was calling for a government of national unity. The prime minister himself seemed attracted to the idea. His relations with Bédié were sour and he was obviously reluctant to give up power. During the last week of November, the country's fate seemed to be hanging by a thread. Bédié was in Yamoussoukro waiting for nature to make him president. People close to the prime minister hoped that a Council of State would be set up under him, to prepare constitutional changes and new elections in about a year's time. Tension vied with humor. Bédié's aides asked the head of the national television service to stand by for a special broadcast, once their man assumed the presidency. The TV manager replied that, as far as he knew, the constitutional arrangements for succession did not assign a role to state television. A surprise was in store for him.

Some observers were certain that calmer spirits would prevail. One reason for their confidence was that the prime minister and acting president, Alassane Ouattara, prided himself on being a technocrat rather than traditional politician. He was also the standard-bearer for a younger generation disgusted with the political practices of the past.

Still, in a country run like a village, there was astonishment at the absence of official information. There had been no government statement on the president's condition for ten days. A brief TV bulletin reminiscent of Maoist China announced that a small group of ruling party "elders" had met to discuss "the current situation." People held their breath, while events that normally would have worried them—such as strikes by hospital, university, electricity, gas, and water staff—barely attracted their attention.

So there was little surprise at midday on December 7, when the prime minister interrupted the 1:00 television news to announce that Mr. Houphouët-Boigny had died at 6:30 that morning. He declared an official mourning period of two months, invited the Supreme Court to meet and declare the presidency vacant, and asked ministers to continue exercising their functions. There was no reference to Mr. Konan-Bédié. Instead of applying his usual pragmatism to maintain stability, Prime Minister Ouattara began playing with fire.

That evening, for the 8:00 television news, the usual anchorman was replaced unexpectedly. Sitting next to his replacement was the constitutional successor to Houphouët-Boigny, Konan-Bédié, who had forced himself into the studio with a handful of soldiers to announce that he was assuming office immediately. Appearing solemn and even angry, Bédié asked the nation to put itself at his "disposal."

Then, as the anchorman began the next item—a government communiqué on that day's Cabinet meeting—there was a disturbance in the studio, and the item was dropped. Sweating and obviously embarrassed, the announcer explained that the rest of the broadcast would consist of a filmed tribute to the dead president. At about that time, the French ambassador (who had been in Abidjan for 16 years and was nicknamed "the Viceroy") roused the Vatican envoy, who was the dean of the diplomatic community, from an early sleep and dragged him and five other ambassadors to Bédié's home to pay their respects to the "new president." A film clip of the visit was shown on the late evening news.

The next day, the morning papers were slow to arrive, suggesting more confusion (especially at the government-controlled *Fraternité-Matin*). The BBC French-language radio service at 6:00 A.M. referred to a "struggle for power" between Ouattara and Bédié, but Radio France Internationale at 7:00 A.M. carried only Bédié's statement announcing his assumption of power.

For the next 24 hours, there were no more public announcements, but Radio France Internationale finally acknowledged a "fight" for the succession. The BBC reported that Ouattara had met with senior military staff, all of whom pledged loyalty to the "government." But the Cabinet was beginning to disintegrate. The Foreign Minister told a reporter that the government was finished and Bédié was the rightful successor to the president. Meanwhile, the main opposition paper kept thumbing its nose at the "self-proclaimed" president, and even within the ruling party there was consternation at the indecorous turn of events. One young official remarked to the state newspaper how unfortunate it was that Bédié had assumed his responsibilities on television. "He should have waited for the Supreme Court to act. It was a question of a few hours or a few days at most."

The city was eerily quiet. I called the Minister of Finance to express my condolences on the death of the president, but my secretary was told calmly that the minister was attending the "usual" Thursday morning cabinet meeting. Behind the scenes, the prime minister, a Northern Muslim, was trying to divide the army along religious and regional lines, hoping to keep his hold on power. He was certainly not putting himself at the "disposal" of his arch-rival.

He was fighting a losing struggle. The Army chief of staff, Robert Gueï—the same man who had escaped punishment for violence at the university two years before and was to lead the first coup d'état in the country's history six years later—urged his troops to stay in their barracks and avoid a bloodbath. On December 9, the acting President Alassane Ouattara stepped down, his reputation a little tarnished—except within the Muslim community.

For the next few weeks, foreboding was replaced with a sense of relief. The opposition parties, although shut out of the new government, kept their peace, promising to "bury the dead respectfully." Oddly enough, it was the ruling party's newspapers that quarreled. The pro-Ouattara paper questioned the choice of some new ministers, calling it "a return to the old cronyism," while the main Party paper asked the pro-Ouattara camp to learn some courtesy from the "real" opposition papers.

The daily tributes to the former president in the state media were so insistent that their inspirational purpose wore off quickly. On a tour of western villages later that month, I did not hear a word of grief—except about the economic situation. Even an official briefing at the Ministry of Foreign Affairs about the funeral arrangements seemed oddly casual. A senior official asked the assembled ambassadors for a gift of 200 cars and 50 motorcycles ("from Japan and Germany, if possible") to escort visiting delegations. "Our resources are not what they used to be," he explained.

The irony of asking for help to bury a gentleman worth at least $2 billion did not seem to dawn on him. Or, perhaps, it was another sign of the charmed life the country had led until then.

The funeral mass on February 7, 1994 was a physical test, as well as an emotional one. Scheduled to last three hours, it dragged on for seven, largely because the French president Francois Mitterrand insisted on being the last person to enter the famous basilica. Accordingly, his plane circled in the air above the airport while other heads of state slowly made their way to the pews. There were 7,000 people inside the air-conditioned church and 11,000 outside in the sun. Whether caused by sun stroke or genuine affection, there were soon reports of apparitions of the dead president in surrounding villages. Through it all, the state media continued their barrage of homage, some of which was preposterous and even pagan. One paper said: "We have lost more than a great chief; we have lost a god." Another intoned: "There have been three great prophets since the beginning of time: Moses, Mohammed and Houphouët!"

Some Ivorians may have been deluded about the greatness of the former president. Many more were gracious and prepared to give the new man a chance. Yet Bédié lost no time in turning a still pond into a maelstrom.

Comparisons of the two presidents proved hazardous. Within two weeks of the funeral, one opposition paper asked: "If Ivorians were unafraid of demonstrating before the giant Felix Houphouët-Boigny, why will they worry about doing so in front of a dwarf?" The editor was promptly thrown into prison for a year, and his paper was shut down for three months, for "insulting" the president. The message was clear. Not only was the new man as vain as his predecessor; he was not about to tolerate rabble-rousers. Two months later, after the main opposition paper called for a general strike to make the country "ungovernable," the government jailed two more journalists, including the deputy leader of the opposition party. Defending these strong-arm tactics, the president's prime minister said rather airily: "Well, you know, he's not out to win a Nobel Peace Prize."

The next few months set the tone for the following five years. Some actions, like the imprisoning of journalists and students, were deliberate and meant to demonstrate the government's resolve—

even if, for some, they only served to reflect its weakness and insecurity. Other measures, like a police raid on the main opposition paper and the clubbing of Muslims outside a mosque (for refusing to pay police bribes) were described by the government as "mistakes." Young people yearning for an open debate on national issues no longer watched the television news, knowing that it would start with 15 minutes of propaganda praising the ruling party. With the witch hunt for associates of the former prime minister Alassane Ouattara almost complete, the state moved to unseat civil servants who were sympathetic to the opposition or refused to contribute money to the ruling party. Increasingly, exclusion took on a regional as well as an ideological tinge. Northerners, who were mainly Muslim, were out of favor and their lives, not just their careers, were increasingly at risk.

Southerners with the "wrong" views were also in danger. Martial Ahipeaud, a former head of the National Students' Union, considered a "firebrand" because his oratory could bring a crowd of 3,000 to its feet, had been imprisoned in 1992 for running an illegal organization. Now, the Minister of Security called him to his office and warned him that he would be jailed again if he did not temper his criticism of the government. Ahipeaud and I had become friends, and shortly afterward he invited me to his wedding. This puzzled me, as brushing shoulders publicly with the World Bank representative was not likely to endear him to his fellow militants. But it became plain that I had been invited so as to prevent a police raid. The next week, he slipped out of the country and began a six-year exile in the United Kingdom. To discredit him, government gossips put out the story that he had been "bought off" by people in power. (In fact, I had quietly paid for his airfare and tuition fees in the UK, where he began a doctorate in history.) He would return briefly after the 1999 coup, but for the time being he was one of many talents the new government had purged from national life.

Instead of a government of national unity, the country had to suffer through a government of national division. During the next year, the new president (who, formally speaking, was completing his predecessor's five-year term) did everything he could to exclude Alassane Ouattara from the upcoming elections in October 1995. Ouattara's father had been born in Burkina Faso, which at the time was part of a much larger colonial entity, French West Africa. Ouattara himself was born in the Ivory Coast, but had dual citizenship. He had studied in the United States and worked at the International Monetary Fund in Washington, DC, as a Burkina national; but when Houphouët named him governor of the West African Central Bank, a position reserved for nationals of the Ivory Coast, Ouattara was issued an Ivorian passport. No one had questioned his citizenship when he served as prime minister and, quite frequently, as acting president from 1991 to 1993.

Using a buzz-saw instead of a knife, Bédié altered the electoral code in three ways, each sufficient to knock his rival out of the ring. All candidates for political office would have to have both parents born in the country. They could never have held a foreign passport. And they needed to have lived in the country continuously for the previous ten years. When it was learned that 20 sitting members of parliament, most of them from the ruling party, would also be disqualified under the new rules, they were promptly changed to apply only to presidential elections.

In mid-1994, Ouattara established his own party and won a number of seats in the new parliament, mainly from the north. But, because the new electoral code excluded him from the contest, the only serious challenger to Bédié in the 1995 elections was the socialist candidate, Laurent Gbagbo, whose support was confined mainly to the west and Abidjan. As a result, Houphouët's "dauphin" won easily. Yet, the new president was so greedy and egotistical that, before long, tongues started wagging within his own party. Referring to corruption, some murmured, "Houphouët had a large appetite, but at least he let some crumbs fall off the table." Although times were hard for most people, Bédié also sponsored lavish construction projects in his home village, which people began calling "the new Yamoussoukro."

Resentment had reached such a pitch that even democrats cheered when General Gueï overthrew the government on Christmas Eve, 1999. Friends of the country hoped this would be a positive event for Africa, but that optimism soon foundered. The next elections were scheduled for October 2000 and within weeks, despite his reassuring words, the new president was taking positions similar to those of his predecessor. On the all-important issue of

who would be allowed to run for president, Gueï remained am-
biguous, but he ultimately sided with those wanting to exclude
"foreigners" from the political process.

Ouattara was shut out as a candidate for the second time in
five years, and the former ruling party's candidate was also disqualified (on the grounds that he had been charged with corruption).
This left two horses in the race—the neophyte general and the
great survivor of the 1990s, Laurent Gbagbo, head of the supposedly progressive Ivorian Popular Front. As a democrat, Gbagbo
could have been expected to oppose the rigging of the rules, but he
knew that his chances of winning a proper race were limited. So
he made a pact with the devil instead, leaving the field conve-
niently narrowed by the restrictions. On Election Day, when early
returns showed that Gbagbo was winning his gamble, the general
ordered the counting of the vote to be interrupted, and all hell
broke loose. For six days, Gbagbo's supporters filled the streets of
Abidjan. Troops tried to control the situation, but Gueï was not
prepared for a bloodbath, so he retreated to the countryside with a
few hundred soldiers. Laurent Gbagbo became the country's fourth
president.

Although Gbagbo's supporters were ecstatic and many people
were brought into the government who had been excluded from
the political process all their lives, his government now opened
another ugly chapter in the country's history. Once an interna-
tionalist, the new president pushed the idea of "Ivoirité" to new
extremes. The former student union leader, Martial Ahipeaud, returned from London to run for Parliament. Soon after, he told me
how shocking he found the tone of the campaign. "How can a
party of the Left be anti-immigrant?" he asked dejectedly. Instead
of aligning himself with Gbagbo, he stayed close to Gueï, hoping,
like many, that he would turn out to be enlightened. During the
melee of the election count, friendly soldiers took Ahipeaud to the
airport for his own "protection," and he was forced into exile
again.

The country went steadily downhill after that. Despite efforts
to achieve "national reconciliation" with his rivals (Bédié, Ouattara, and Gueï), Gbagbo presided over a harshly repressive
regime. Mysterious murders and mass graves became an almost
normal part of life. There were recurrent army mutinies, and on

September 19, 2002, an attempted coup d'état against the government degenerated into civil war. Gueï, supposedly the instigator of the coup, was dragged from his home and killed in the street with nine members of his family. The northern half of the country essentially seceded, as the retreating rebels set up strongholds in the cities of Bouake and Korhogo. Later, another set of rebels took over western parts of the country.

Negotiations between the factions took place under various auspices, including, rather obscenely, the doyen of African tyrants, General Eyadéma of Togo. The French sent a peacekeeping force, essentially to keep the rebels from sweeping into Abidjan and taking power. But Gbagbo and his supporters were hardly grateful. Anti-French rhetoric and demonstrations prevailed, along with harassment of life-long French residents. In late 2003, the rebels agreed to enter a coalition government, but the chances of success were doomed from the start. One of the conditions set by the rebel leaders was that each of their ministers should be accompanied to Abidjan by 35 bodyguards. They soon threw up their hands at the lack of real cooperation and left the government to return to their northern strongholds. The UN and human rights groups denounced the government's "death squads," but Gbagbo and his people ignored the international outcry. On March 25, 2004, 120 people were killed in an anti-government demonstration in Abidjan. When the UN Security Council condemned the violence, thugs loyal to the government—high on drugs and spouting "gangsta-rap"—demonstrated against the UN.

What general conclusions can be drawn from this sorry tale? Certainly, one is tempted to think that the country was better off under a benevolent dictator (Houphouët-Boigny) than under his supposedly elected successors. In fact, the suppression of political debate through the first 30 years of the country's history built up the passions and jealousies that erupted with such ugliness at the end of the century. The self-absorption and self-enrichment of political leaders also set a pattern for others to follow. Even a man like Ouattara, already rich through marriage, felt that history had tipped him to be president, ignoring the fact that his own playing of the regional card after Houphouët's death had ruined his reputation as a detached technocrat devoted to his country's well-being. Others (like Gbagbo) who had been excluded from power were prepared to accept a rigged electoral code to squeeze their way into high office. In just ten years, four stubborn people—three politicians and a general—had brought a once-proud country to its knees. Some, like Ouattara and Gbagbo, had shown real promise, but both had been blinded by power and put expediency ahead of principle. They knew that a closed and corrupt political system was unlikely to give them a second or third chance.

The absence of checks and balances, including a free press and an independent judiciary, had allowed personal ambitions to weaken the foundations of the nation, rather than serve as rushing water at a mill of national debate and growth. By late 2004, like a microcosm of Africa, Abidjan had become a backwater. Even worse, following a flare-up in fighting in November 2004, Ivorians for the first time sought safety across the border in Liberia—once a synonym for bloodshed and chaos.

CHAPTER 7

DISCORD IN CENTRAL AFRICA

For different reasons, Tanzania and the Ivory Coast deserved the international attention they attracted, even if they also came to illustrate Africa's major problems. Other countries were less famous but also suffered the effects of dictatorship, petty squabbling, and a mammoth indifference to economics.

In 2000–2002, I worked closely with the Central African Economic and Monetary Community. Despite its title, it represented a feeble effort to weave together six very different nations united only in mutual detestation. The largest, Cameroon, was not on speaking terms with the richest, Gabon. Chad found Cameroon domineering, and the Central African Republic distrusted Chad. The Republic of the Congo (the large Congo's small neighbor) was riven with political discord and harbored people who were trying to overthrow the government of the Central African Republic. And Equatorial Guinea, the only Spanish-speaking country in Africa, had been spurned by the international community for its barbarous human rights record. After discovering massive oil reserves off its coast, it no longer needed its neighbors. The best-known book about the country was *Tropical Gangsters*.

It is difficult to say which of the six countries had the saddest history. Cameroon once showed considerable promise. It had one of the best school systems in Africa, a bicultural French–English tradition that strengthened its relationships with the outside

world, and an array of natural resources any other developing
country would have envied. Cameroon and its neighbor, Gabon,
accounted for half of Africa's forestry exports. But politics and ethnic divisions rotted the apple. Cameroonians are a talented, gre-
garious, and eloquent people. They have probably exported more
communications professionals (writers, broadcasters, advertising
and marketing experts) than any other African country. But their
own president, Paul Biya, did not communicate with them. Next
to Kim Jong-il of North Korea, he was arguably the most reclusive
head of state on earth. Traumatized by an attempted assassination
in 1982, he saw almost no one. Instead, he was transported by military helicopter from his mountain fortress in the capital to his
home village. He occasionally granted audiences to international
business people, but preferred to see them individually, rather than
in groups. Worse than that, he twisted the political system to his
purposes, stole the 1992 elections, was re-elected easily in 1997
when the opposition boycotted the sham elections, and won again
in 2004. Moreover, while the French reduced their presidential
terms from seven to five years, he did the opposite and increased
his own.

Cameroonians vented their disgust and impatience with Biya
through vitriolic humor: stand-up comics told stories they would
have been reluctant to put into print. And the press was so outspo-
ken that its own stridency protected it from credibility and hence
censorship. Taxi drivers spat out their denunciations of the situation with such force, you would think their throats were in a vise.
And, in a sense, they were. What irked Cameroonians most was
the world's indifference to the sham democracy they lived in. Foreign leaders were still on good terms with their president. In January 2002, France repaired roads in the capital so that Yaounde
could host the France–Africa Summit Meeting without too many
bumpy limousine rides. In March 2003, President Bush appealed
for Biya's vote—along with that of two other tyrants in Guinea
and Angola—for a crucial UN Security Council vote on the Iraq
war. Under pressure from international citizen groups like the
Christian Jubilee 2000 Campaign, Cameroon was given debt relief
of more than $100 million a year in October 2000. Yet, 15 months
later, not a cent had been added to social and economic services
for the poor. Also in 2000, the World Bank prepared a major

HIV/AIDS program for the country in just four months, but the government spent nine months completing the formalities to use the assistance. The state school system and basic health services were in tatters. Fortunately, 40 percent of Cameroon's schools and clinics were run by private, mainly religious, charities that still offered reliable services.

Not everyone regarded the role of the churches as positive. In April 2002, I met with 700 Catholic, Protestant, and Muslim leaders to discuss how they could work with international organizations and their own government to serve the poor. You could feel the pent-up interest in the room. Never before had these men and women been given the chance to know, let alone question, their government's health and education policies. The delegates were also keen to criticize the international institutions for not drawing on their expertise earlier. However, the government representatives were much less interested. Everyone but the Minister of Health left after the opening ceremony, and even he slipped away before lunch. "I don't know what this will accomplish," he told me as I escorted him to his car. "These are the very people responsible for this country's poverty in the first place, by conditioning everyone to think that Heaven—or the government—will look after them." Not usually at a loss for words, I was too aghast to react.

Among the general public, it was hard to determine whether shame or anger had the upper hand. When Cameroon was judged the most corrupt country on earth by the international watchdog agency Transparency International in 2000, many people found the assessment amusing or accidental. Some questioned the methodology used. But when Cameroon led the league again the next year, more people took notice, including the decision-making elite. Suddenly, they spotted a direct connection between foreign investor opinion and their own prospects for continued prosperity.

If there was mutual contempt between Cameroon's president and his people, it was hardly surprising that Paul Biya was also disliked by his neighbors. His fiercest critic was Omar Bongo, the president of Gabon. To begin with, there was some traditional African rivalry between the two men, based on relative seniority. Although Bongo was several years younger than Biya, he felt that Biya should show him more respect as he had been in office longer.

Bongo had taken power in 1967, 15 years before Biya, and was attracted to grand schemes and influencing events across Central Africa.

Gabon had once been an important oil exporter, but its reserves were running out. Besides, apart from Bongo's personal fortune (which was said to exceed a billion dollars), the country's wealth was only skin deep. Outside the country's ports, where oil, logs, and manganese were loaded on foreign vessels, there was little economic and social development. Elephants grazed within a few miles of the capital, Libreville. Gabon's distribution of income was the third worst on earth, after Brazil and South Africa. Yet, Gabon managed to pile up a debt so large that the country sought to be included in the general debt relief program for poor countries in 2000. Even Gabon's old friends at the French ministries of finance and foreign affairs scoffed at the idea, knowing that Bongo had enough money in his own bank accounts to reduce his nation's obligations by a substantial amount.

Gabon's problems did not prevent Bongo from stirring up trouble. With barely a million people to Cameroon's 15 million, and a tenth of the total output of the sub-region, Gabon wanted to host a new regional stock exchange. When the World Bank suggested that Cameroon was a more logical location, Bongo invited four fellow presidents to Libreville to sign a resolution choosing it as the site of the regional institution. Cameroon's President Biya was not even invited. When his prime minister showed up, he was also excluded from the final meeting. So much for regional cooperation. Cameroon has since opened its own exchange.

Gabon also had its differences with the Central African Republic. The country enjoyed brief infamy in the late 1970s when its megalomaniac president Jean Bedel Bokassa declared himself emperor and was enthroned with great pomp in 1977. The French government footed a large part of the bill, including a scepter and crown fashioned by a famous Paris jeweler. (Bokassa supplied the diamonds, but France paid for the magnificent settings). Two years later, embarrassed by his erratic behavior, including reports that he had used his scepter to bludgeon young student demonstrators to death and served their flesh to visiting dignitaries, the French sent paratroopers to overthrow him. When Bokassa flew to France to take refuge in his chateau south of Paris, he was kept waiting in his plane for three days at Evreux airport while the government decided what to do. Despite being a French citizen and war veteran, he was refused entry and began a political exile in the Ivory Coast.

By the year 2000, not much had changed. Many people insisted that the situation was actually worse and they wished Bokassa, now dead, were still in power. "At least he maintained some order," they groaned. The current president, Ange-Marie Patassé, had been Bokassa's prime minister and had been elected head of state a few years before, mainly by his own ethnic group. But the capital city, Bangui, was not in his pocket. Strikes and army mutinies had severely weakened his capacity to govern. "You insisted that we become a democracy, and see where it has got us," locals protested to foreign visitors. During an attempted coup in June 2001, led by a former president now living in the Republic of Congo, Patassé lay on his stomach for four hours, with his family beside him, as rebels raked his house with automatic fire. He was rescued by Libyan troops and rebel soldiers from across the river in the Democratic Republic of the Congo, who were eager to overthrow their own government. It was one set of rebels fighting another. After the shooting stopped, these supposed defenders of the government piled furniture they had looted from homes and offices onto boats, and returned across the river to their own country. A former army chief of staff, operating out of another neighboring state, Chad, finally ended Patassé's rule in March 2003.

Patassé had fewer delusions of grandeur than his famous predecessor, but he still had an appetite for personal enrichment. During one visit, I suggested he give up his latest venture, the distribution of oil products in the country. The conversation took place at one of his country homes, an hour's drive outside the capital. The first part of the meeting took place in a conference room, in front of his newly appointed economic team. Patassé talked for almost an hour and a half, denouncing French and World Bank advice over the years and the "unfair" treatment of his country. At the other end of the table, I saw the new Minister of Finance and his colleagues staring into space, or with their hands folded over their heads, suggesting they had heard it all before. Raising his voice and wagging his finger at me, Patassé said that he would not stand for "neo-colonialism" and "savage privatizations." Then he looked severely at his colleagues and said: "You see, if I can talk this way to the World Bank, you can imagine how I will behave if you ever let me down."

Later, in a small room just down the hall, with no one else present, Patassé was all sweetness and charm.

"Mr. President," I began, "some things are considered normal here which others would regard as strange." He smiled as I continued. "Now, what are the chances of your giving up your oil business and awarding it to someone else through competitive bidding?"

"We've already tried that," he protested, "and no one else came forward."

"That hardly surprises me," I answered. "I doubt that I would compete with you if I were a businessman here. I'm talking about inviting bids without your taking part."

"Impossible," he continued. "Someone had to do this. Otherwise, we'd be at the mercy of the multinational companies."

I changed tack: "Well, in that case, would you consider putting your profits into a fund for charitable purposes?"

He looked at me for a few seconds, with a faint smirk, to make certain I was serious. "Do you really expect me to lose money in the service of my country?"

One of those present at the meeting that day was the new prime minister, Martin Ziguélé. President Patassé had appointed him on April 1, but as he had lived abroad and was unknown outside a small circle, the local papers thought the announcement was an April Fools' joke. In fact, Ziguélé was a very serious man, 44 years old, part of a new generation who saw possibilities rather than just a cursed future for his country. But he needed time to change the environment around him.

On our way back to the capital, Ziguélé defended his president. "Please ignore half of what he just told you. Most of it was for show. He knows we need help and must make concessions to outside views. He just doesn't understand why you have seized on this particular issue."

I repeated a point made earlier in the visit. "There may be no law in this country against politicians doing business while in office, but it is certainly contrary to evolving international norms."

Ziguélé persevered: "Other African leaders, including President Biya in Cameroon, have personal businesses and no one complains about it. The president of Togo owns half the gas stations in his country. The difference is that he acquired them fifteen years ago and everyone's forgotten about it."

"Those presidents are not asking the World Bank to invest in their businesses," I replied, rather feebly.

The prime minister would be in office for less than two years, swept away by the same coup that overthrew Patassé. He escaped with his life, but his house was ransacked and he had to start life over as a political refugee in France. In April 2005, he ran second in his country's presidential elections. He had no illusions that the contest would be clean, but he faced a barrage of dirty tricks that surprised even him. He is now back in Paris looking after his family rather than his country.

On another visit, apparently wanting to show how popular he was, President Patassé took me on a tour of the capital. From behind the closed windows of his SUV, he waved at people along the way. Some recognized him and waved back; just as many turned down their thumbs. At an AIDS clinic, where a small crowd had gathered, his guards had to shove people aside with their rifles to clear a path for him. All he really demonstrated that day was his tenuous grasp on both reality and power.

In November 2001, President Bongo of Gabon spoke dismissively of his fellow head of state, not even referring to him as "President" anymore: "I asked Patassé recently why there have been so many mutinies and coups against him since he came to power. 'Because I'm so popular,' he told me, 'and my enemies are jealous of that.'"

"Can you believe it?" Bongo asked with deep disdain.

That disdain is contagious. In a region where there are few legitimate presidents, why should one head of state cooperate deeply with another? Would the Central African economic community work better if the member governments were more trusted by their own citizens? Undoubtedly. To begin with, one state would take greater notice of another government's positions if they were grounded in some public support or debate. But there are other factors that need to be overcome. One of them is petty competition among enlarged egos. Like corruption, this kind of rivalry exists elsewhere on earth but seems disproportionate in Africa, given the small sizes of many of the states involved.

During almost 20 years in power, Paul Biya of Cameroon had not set foot in Chad. He did so for the first time in October 2000 for the start of construction of the Chad–Cameroon oil pipeline. It had taken a $3.5 billion investment and considerable pressure from Chad's president, Idriss Deby, to convince Biya to leave his mountain fortress in Yaounde. Even then, Biya kept his fellow head of state guessing until the very last moment, holding off until Biya's security advisers, pilot, weather forecasters, and even astrologers had assured him that the conditions were propitious.

At about the same time, Gabon's President Bongo was furious that three international organizations (including the World Bank and International Monetary Fund) had each appointed nationals of a single African country, Burkina Faso, as their representatives. Indifferent to the international training and experience of the individuals involved, Bongo regarded the small Saharan country as too poor and primitive to offer advice to his more "sophisticated" economy. When one of the organizations offered to appoint a Cameroonian instead, Bongo was not amused.

Such pettiness among immediate neighbors explains why much larger schemes of regional cooperation in Africa have floundered. Allowed by their own citizens – and by the international community – to feather their own nests, most African leaders have focused on expanding their control over resources and events close to home rather than taking risks to enlarge the possibilities of progress for their people.

PART III

FACING THE FACTS

CHAPTER 8

DEFYING ECONOMICS

One of my favorite memories of Abidjan is of a woman near my office who sold fried bananas to passers-by all week, even on Sundays. She stayed there 12 hours, making a profit of perhaps $2 a day, and never took a holiday. One afternoon, I spotted her in a thunderstorm, undeterred, keeping her fire lit and stirring the bananas in her pan, sheltered only by a large sheet of plywood that she balanced on her head while the rain ran off it in all directions. She seemed the very image of Africa, persistent and good-natured in the face of difficulty.

The people who governed her were less resourceful. If African politics have been divisive and repressive, economic policy has followed close behind; but most economies have been "managed" by inertia or pure neglect. How could Africa lose half its markets, or $70 billion a year (in 1990 dollars), without noticing it? And why are most Africans and international observers still unaware that these cumulative losses are the greatest setback of the last 30 years?

One reason is pure ignorance. Even when they were aware of the economic forces at work, most African governments never shared the basic facts with their citizens. Another factor was the cushion of international aid. Why worry about the $700 per family per year that Africa had lost through poor policies? Never mind that this was more than twice the average household income in the rural areas. Instead, governments preferred to pressure aid donors to increase the "pittance" of $40 per person that Africa was receiving. A third cause was the already familiar one of political correctness. Foreign donors were not prepared to tell African governments that two and two made four.

In November 2000, Africa's trade ministers met for the first time in history to discuss whether they wanted a new round of international trade negotiations. It was a clear sign that the continent's governments had been living in another world. Incapable of understanding the crucial link between trade and development, indifferent to Africa's place in the global economy, and strangling their business sectors rather than promoting them, governments had been content to let others worry about international trade policy. The vice president of Gabon, the host country for the meeting, told delegates not to worry about facing anti-globalization demonstrators, as they were a long way from Seattle and Geneva, where there had been riots in the previous year.

In the end, no demonstrators were needed to subvert the meeting. For three days, the delegations argued among themselves as Mike Moore, the director general of the World Trade Organization and former prime minister of New Zealand, gazed like a leashed bulldog at a cat gamboling before it. The meeting ended before the ministers could agree on a position. A communiqué duly appeared the next day, expressing faint interest in better trade rules, but *not* calling for a new round of formal negotiations. Moore disguised his dismay at this lack of collective action: "This meeting has been everything I expected and much more. It has been a meeting run by Africans for Africans. It is an historic first. It has enlivened the debate on trade issues for Africa."[1] Nearly three years later, in September 2003, when international trade talks collapsed in Cancun, Mexico, African delegations were largely responsible. And they were the only ones who cheered.

Some critics of globalization suggest that Africa has suffered more than others from international trade rules that are biased against poor countries. Unfortunately, this is not the case. If so, the solution to the continent's problems would be relatively simple. Lifting all remaining foreign trade barriers would provide a dynamic boost to Africa's fortunes, while more complicated cultural, institutional, and, yes, structural adjustments could be introduced more gradually.

In fact, Africa has not been a victim of globalization. With only a few exceptions, it has refused to concern itself with foreign markets. This may reassure those who believe that trade is undesirable, but also confirms that most of Africa's handicaps are inbred. The continent has both wittingly and unwittingly walled itself off from the rest of the world, with the result that its economy is now rather small—barely the size of Argentina's. Excluding South Africa, the continent produces only as much as Belgium. Africa's gross domestic product is $400 billion per year, and drops to less than $200 billion if we exclude South Africa and Nigeria.[2] By 2000, the typical African economy had an income no larger than the suburb of a major American city, like Bethesda, Maryland, outside Washington, DC ($2 billion). The World Bank's headquarters uses more electricity to light its offices than is consumed in the whole of Chad, a country twice the size of France.

Africa's economy is small for two reasons. First, governments have hobbled and even persecuted small farmers, and second, they have been only slightly more encouraging to private investors. Most foreign earnings come from oil, minerals, forest products, and tropical commodities, such as coffee, cocoa, cotton, palm oil, and rubber, which were first introduced in colonial times. Only four countries (South Africa, Zimbabwe, Mauritius, and Ghana) have significant manufacturing sectors, and only one (Mauritius) has been a steady exporter of textiles and, recently, electronic goods; as a result, excluding South Africa, only a tenth of black Africa's exports are manufactured ($6 billion). Tourism is small and shallow—few people return to the continent for a second or third visit—and the list of most popular destinations (Kenya, Tanzania, Botswana, Senegal) has remained the same for 40 years. Except in Zambia and Zaire, where the state drove oncemighty copper operations back into the ground, Africa's extractive industries have survived (even in war zones like Angola) because most were run by multinational corporations. But Africa's main industry, agriculture, has been dragged down by mismanagement of every kind.

Following Independence, agriculture was considered an archaic way of earning a living, an inheritance of colonialism, rather than a real expression of Africa's wealth. Unimpressed by the important role farming still plays in the economies of rich countries like Australia, Canada, Denmark, and New Zealand, African planners were keen to move on to the "next stages" of economic development, namely manufacturing and services. Governments could defy economics, but eventually it was like ignoring gravity. By 1990, indifference to agriculture had cut Africa's already small share of world trade in half. Black Africa now accounts for barely 1.5 percent of international trade.

In addition to losing customers, Africa was bypassed by private investments—the most effective means of creating industries and reaching new markets. In the 1980s alone, total foreign investment in the world increased four times faster than world output and three times faster than world trade. Much of that foreign investment went to China and India, other Asian countries, Latin America, and even, despite its problems, Eastern and Central Europe. Very little went to Africa. Investors were deterred by high exchange rates, which made it cheaper to import some goods than produce them locally, as well as by dizzying taxes, outlandish regulations, administrative inertia, the legal system, the labor code (which complicated the hiring of temporary or seasonal workers), monopolies, corruption, and fraud.

To be sure, there were variations among Africa's economies. Countries near the coast, with abundant rain, forests, and short distances to market, felt little pressure to make economic decisions. The desert countries, like those in the Sahel region (Mali, Chad, Mauritania, Niger), had to be more resourceful, unable to leave things to chance. This showed in official behavior. Meetings started briskly in Mali and Chad. There were few pictures on the walls. Coffee or soft drinks were rarely offered to visitors. People wanted to get down to business. On the coast, all was formality and hot air—in the metaphorical sense. Hospitality was impeccable and air freshener was piped into the waiting rooms outside ministers' offices. But the results were usually the same. Investors and aid officials were generally seen as bearing gifts, rather than new ideas, useful challenges, and market expertise. The pickings may have been smaller in the desert, but among government officials there were as many flies as along the coast.

The first investors to be cautious were Africans themselves. Like anyone else, they used simple litmus tests: What did nationals of a country do with their savings? Did they splurge on fancy cars, invest at home, or stash money away in Switzerland or France? If laws were well-drafted, how were they applied and were the courts reliable, efficient, and honest? Did police and customs officers conduct themselves properly, or did they ask for bribes? If governments gave their word, what was it worth?

Investors found that, while some other developing countries were trying to become lean and nimble, like Greco-Roman athletes, African economies were becoming bloated, like Sumo wrestlers, confined to competing in a limited space according to strict rules. Countries like Tanzania hampered business and agriculture from the start, sometimes for an apparently good cause—such as moving farmers away from their original land into new villages where they could be reached by government services. This was not disruptive for annual crops, if new land was provided; but it led to the decline of tree crops, like cashew nuts, which took years to grow and needed upkeep. Other countries, like the Ivory Coast, started on a strong note—encouraging exports and building modern infrastructure—only to become flabby and listless by the time disaster struck.

Disaster came in the early 1980s, in the form of a sharp drop in prices for tropical commodities, and the use of substitutes in industrial countries (such as synthetic for natural rubber and plastic for sisal twine). The obvious solution in Africa was to cut costs or develop new industries. But the continent was already tuning out of the international economy.

It took the 14 countries of the French African franc zone seven years (from 1987 to 1994) to accept international advice and devalue their currency. During that time, the high exchange rate made electricity so expensive that it was cheaper to send local wood to Italy to dry. Training an engineer at home cost twice as much as it did at Harvard. Industrial labor costs were double those in Morocco or Malaysia. And the West African rice industry simply disappeared, since it was cheaper to import rice from Thailand and the United States.

Even after the devaluation, there were home-bred obstacles to overcome. Shipping services in the Ivory Coast cost more than twice what they did in other developing countries, absorbing up to ten cents on the dollar. The basic reason was that, by law, 40 percent of the country's commerce was to be carried on nationally owned ships. But local lines did not have enough vessels—not even a single refrigerator ship—to carry the Ivory Coast's exports to market. So local shippers sub-contracted that tonnage to a French company that already dominated the rest of the traffic.

Costs were inflated further by a series of offices in the port of Abidjan that allocated tonnage among competing shippers to ensure a "fair" distribution of the work. This involved delays, paperwork, and bribes, all of which added to costs. Another purpose of these offices was to "protect" the national shipping industries of neighboring countries like Burkina Faso and Mali, which had no ships and—more absurdly—no coastline or ports.

Once a supplier of 90 percent of the European market for bananas and pineapples, the Ivory Coast lost ground steadily to Costa Rica and other producers. In a desperate effort to recover those markets, the country's fruit producers asked to charter their own ships and even compensate the national company for lost income; but the prime minister's office turned them down.

Fruit exporters also had to buy cardboard boxes from a single local producer (a French firm). Choosing their own ships and packaging would have allowed them to gain new customers and increase production. They pointed this out to the government at the time: "For bananas alone, without investing any more money, we could produce 200,000 tons in 1993 and 250,000 tons in 1994. On the face of it, these figures are worth more than the granting of a structural adjustment loan and would create thousands of jobs for young farmers."

Small farmers also suffered. Cocoa and coffee producers had to buy jute bags from a local factory that imported the raw material from Bangladesh. Fifty miles away in Ghana, farmers could buy jute bags made in Asia. The difference in costs robbed Ivorian farmers of $15 million a year, supporting perhaps 400 manufacturing jobs in Abidjan but at the same time taxing 450,000 rural families. Machetes, too, had to be bought from a single firm.

Another obstacle to economic growth was the government's stance toward small business—the so-called informal sector. Most rural people who moved to town had to create jobs for themselves. Some imported cheap clothing, repaired cars on the side of the road, or like the woman described at the beginning of this chapter, sold food in the streets. Jobs like hers supported whole families and offered workers things they could not afford in official markets. But these small businesses were fiercely opposed by government and large enterprises as tax evaders, smugglers, and "unfair" competitors.

As these policies took their inevitable toll, government revenues began to drop, state budgets became strained, and people in high places began looking for scapegoats rather than adjust. Africa's friends tried to staunch the bleeding but received no thanks. The World Bank and IMF's "structural adjustment" programs were intended to alter the sources of growth and promote agriculture and rural development as launching-pads for more diverse activity. They knew that good policy could turn things around relatively quickly.

Take the example of Nigeria. Preoccupied with its oil wealth, the country neglected agriculture during the 1970s. As a result, by 1980 Nigeria was importing $2.5 billion in food a year. Starting in 1986, the situation was transformed through better prices for farmers and heavy investments in rural infrastructure and agricultural support services. People began returning to the rural areas, and even educated Nigerians suddenly became interested in agriculture as a career. Within five years, food imports had dropped to $400 million per year, a sixth of what they had been in 1980. Cotton, cocoa, rubber, palm oil and peanut production also increased, and textile mills that had previously imported fiber were now using local cotton. Much of this success was the result of introducing more competition into transport and processing, thus giving farmers a greater share of the final price. Political will eventually flagged, as dealers, processors, truckers, and other intermediaries regained the ear of decision-makers, or paid them off. By the late 1990s, Nigeria was again in trouble, importing food and raw materials that it could produce itself.

Instead of tackling the root problem of inefficiency and monopoly, African governments began quarrelling with international institutions about how to divide the shrinking spoils of past prosperity. They also threw dust in the eyes of their own citizens to suggest that foreigners were making them do things that went against the grain. There were many intelligent and honest policy-makers who knew what was happening and accepted that town dwellers would have to make some sacrifices to allow incomes to rise in the rural areas. But they seldom got the upper hand. Entrenched interests usually triumphed. Foreign donors poured money into government budgets to allow African decision-makers some breathing space—including the time for better policies to take effect—but government spending still needed to be trimmed. The major controversy was how to do this without harming the poor.

In fact, very few programs were helping the poor. Ninety percent of the typical national budget went for government salaries, leaving only ten percent for everything else (vehicles, gasoline, electricity, schoolbooks, medicines, bandages, and the like). Many subsidies were wasteful rather than helpful. In Tanzania, for example, free fertilizer was squandered on whitewashing rural homes, or was left outside to deteriorate in the rain. In other countries, it was used excessively, with detrimental effects upon soils and water sources. Subsidized food did not go to the poor; instead, it was hijacked by soldiers and civil servants with connections in high places. Price controls in the towns robbed farmers of a fair price for their produce. Targeted subsidies used elsewhere, such as free textbooks for school girls in Bangladesh, could not be tried in Africa because of low political commitment and stealing.

In the early years of structural adjustment, health and education services took the brunt of government cuts because they were a large part of the budget and no one insisted they be protected. Later, the World Bank and other donors pronounced a mea culpa and added another condition to their lending: that basic health and education services should be cushioned from budget cuts. Yet not all education and health spending was important for reducing poverty.

In the late 1980s, the Ivory Coast was devoting half its national budget to education and health, more than any other country on earth. But 60 percent of women were still illiterate; only 12 percent of girls were enrolled in secondary schools; and barely one in two infants was vaccinated against common illnesses. There were other problems. Primary school enrolments were falling, clinics had no bandages, and schools had no chalk. A key reason was that national spending was slanted toward universities and hospitals that served the better off.

In 1991, the government agreed with the World Bank to shift a small amount of spending (only four percent over four years) toward basic services, which were important for the rural areas and the poor. Inevitably, the program was controversial among the relatively rich. University admissions and scholarships were frozen at their existing level. Salaries of new teachers were realigned with those for the general civil service. (Previously—and rather admirably—they had been 50 percent higher.) There were positive reforms as well. Textbook prices were reduced and cheap generic drugs were to replace brand-name products.

Two years later, however, very little had changed. Basic services were still short of funds. Administrative costs and hospitals still swallowed up more than half the health budget. And there were delays in introducing generic drugs in private pharmacies. The government had been given $150 million in budget support but had not built or repaired a single classroom. Obviously, policymakers did not believe as strongly as outsiders that national priorities had to be adjusted. They wanted to fill a hole in the budget rather than reduce the travel time to the nearest clinic.

Such behavior reflected Africa's larger problem. There was just not enough money in international aid budgets to stem the economic losses that Africa was facing. Any recovery had to be based on better management and clear priorities. The West would provide additional assistance for a while, but only as long as it could be confident that it was bridging temporary gaps rather than pouring money down dark holes. No one was explaining to Africans why some of these remedies were necessary.

Even apparently harsh measures, like the introduction of small fees at clinics, had a rationale. Research showed that poor people were prepared to pay up to ten percent of the cost of basic services, if those services were actually provided and the local community kept control of the money raised. People recognized that "free" services were not worth very much if clinics had neither doctors nor medicines. Yet many Africans (and sympathizers elsewhere) complained that Western donors were forcing governments to gouge poor people.

Certainly, everyone made mistakes. Aid officials, like African governments, sometimes lost sight of the broader objective of reforms. One evening in the Ivory Coast, a Ministry of Education official, who was also the wife of the secretary general of the ruling party, approached me at a diplomatic reception to request a favor. "What's the problem?" I asked. "One of the conditions of your last education loan," she said, "was that we should charge parents an $8 registration fee for each child in school. Very few parents are paying, and we think it unreasonable to insist."

I was surprised to hear this, as it made neither economic nor social sense to raise the price of schooling. So I reassured her: "I'll suggest to my colleagues we drop the condition, because if I were the father of six children and had already paid for their school books and uniforms and knew that students from rich families were attending university entirely at public expense, even while repeating grades three or four years in a row, and that real estate taxes had never been collected here in the wealthiest neighborhood of the country in 30 years of independence, I certainly wouldn't pay those registration fees either!"

Her eyes popped a little, as if she had heard more than she wanted, and the next time we met, at another reception, she merely shook hands and moved off to another part of the room. She knew as well as anyone else that there were issues of social justice, not just efficiency, at the heart of economic reform.

In trying to correct Africa's problems, no one was satisfied or vindicated. Donors saw themselves offering a safety net to someone in free fall; Africans thought they were being hounded all the way to the ground. Hoping to stabilize the situation, aid agencies sometimes felt they were pouring concrete into quicksand. Meanwhile, Africans believed they were undergoing painful procedures without anesthetics and being asked to stop wriggling and whining on the operating table. It was a colossal misunderstanding.

In talks to young people at the time, I compared a country to an individual. If his income dropped suddenly, I pointed out, he would have to adjust his standard of living. If he ran a handicrafts shop and his customers stopped coming, he needed to respond constructively. If the shop was on the third floor and customers didn't like climbing the steep and slippery stairs, he should move it to the ground floor. If the display room was gloomy and hard to reach, the owner would have to brighten up the place and put up notices to direct visitors. If the staff greeted customers coldly, he would have to teach them good manners and remind them that no one was obliged to enter the shop. And if the bookkeeper was putting money into his own pockets, the shop owner had to fire him. Even then, the owner could not expect customers to start streaming back. In the meantime, they would have found other stores.

Sadly, no country in Africa—even the most reform-minded—has cleaned shop like those in Asia or Latin America. While I was talking to young people in the early 1990s, the Coca Cola Company tried to move its West African headquarters to Abidjan but it was refused permission to install its own satellite communications facilities. A French non-profit organization helping small enterprises had to shut down its operations because the central bank had no appropriate regulations to govern them, and refused to develop any. And a Canadian team prospecting for nickel in the northwest waited through six weeks of an eight-week drilling season for its equipment to clear the port. The team had also been pestered at police roadblocks for "tips" all the way from Abidjan.

"Africa hands" know how to play the game, but few of them have the fresh ideas, technologies, and approaches that are needed to transform an economy. New investors, including Africans, do not want to be subjected to initiation rites. They want to understand the rules quickly and see them respected by everyone.

Africa needs to shock the world by its determination to do better. Instead, it has shocked the world in other ways, and little has changed. Many countries are growing again, but barely enough to keep pace with population increases. Only two countries, Ghana and Uganda, have clawed their way back to the level of real income they had in 1970. Forty percent of Africa's private savings are held abroad because people do not trust their own governments and banks to treat them fairly. And the climate for private investment remains bleak. In Angola in 2003, it took 146 days and $5500—eight times the country's average annual income—just to meet government requirements to set up a business.[3]

There are certainly some bright spots. In countries which have managed themselves well (South Africa, of course, but also Ghana, Uganda, Botswana, and Mauritius), investment opportunities can be lucrative. In 2003, the Ghana Stock Exchange was the fastest-growing exchange in the world. But, in most parts of the continent, high returns still reflect high risk. South Africa's experienced and energetic business people are among those who have run into mud walls in other parts of the continent. "Even Africa is not equipped to do business with Africa," one of them has admitted dispiritedly.[4]

CHAPTER 9

THE TROUBLE WITH FOREIGN AID

Dictatorship and a defiance of economics have set Africa apart, but the consequences were obscured by decades of Western generosity. Other countries in the world, including the Arab sheikdoms of the Persian Gulf, could survive such tendencies because of their oil wealth, but only a few African states were lucky enough to do the same. All of them squandered that wealth. In the late 1970s, Nigeria was so flush with oil money that a tenth of the world's champagne was reportedly consumed in the capital, Lagos—some of it merely for bathing. Most African countries did not have such good fortune, but the world's response to their needs was sometimes odd.

I first heard of the Mufindi project in December 1976 in the lobby of Dar es Salaam's Kilimanjaro hotel. I had just arrived in Tanzania to work at the Canadian embassy and was being evicted from my room, as my reservation had run out and the hotel was fully booked. Or so I was told. At the reception desk, I noticed a familiar figure at the other end of the counter, just off the plane from Washington with his shirt hanging out of his jeans. It was Jim Adams, the World Bank's loan officer for Tanzania. "Hello, Jim," I said rather cheerfully. When I asked what he was up to, he said he was checking in. "They're full," I replied. "I know," he continued, "but the manager's a friend of mine, and he's just kicked someone out for me." I kept my composure and asked the purpose of his visit. From his back pocket, he pulled out a hand-scribbled design of the Mufindi plant.

It was a $200 million proposal to build a pulp and paper factory near timber plantations in the southwest that had also been financed by the World Bank. The logic was appealing enough. Given Tanzania's firm commitment to universal primary education and its fast-rising population, the country would need a growing supply of textbooks. Why import the paper when it could be produced locally? But there was a yawning gap between theory and practice. The investment was so large and the technology so advanced that no one, including the Tanzanians, believed they could manage it themselves. Technical assistance was planned, but it was not included in the project budget. If it had been, the costs would have outweighed the expected benefits and the project would not have been approved by the World Bank's Board of Directors.

Even without the technical assistance and despite very generous assumptions, the project barely paid for itself. Three years later, with the factory about to open, the World Bank proposed another loan of $20 million to operate the plant. In narrow financial terms, the project now looked "economic," as the $200 million already invested were considered a thing of the past and assigned no financial value. All future benefits were weighed against the additional $20 million, rather than the total cost of the plant. The safety valve was to be the export market. If Tanzania could not absorb the full production of the plant, the surplus would be shipped to India - one of the largest markets for paper in the world. Unfortunately, India itself was already a large producer, and transport costs would make Tanzanian paper very expensive.

By then, I was the World Bank's loan officer for Tanzania in Washington, DC, and believed the project should be abandoned. My division chief thought the same, and his boss did, too. But the Bank's senior management felt the institution had gotten Tanzania into this situation and could not walk away from it. A few days before the Board discussion, I had a worried telephone call from the corporate secretary's department. It had used an outdated cover for the project documents, carrying the broad disclaimer: "The World Bank does not accept responsibility for the completeness or accuracy of this report." My colleague on the phone asked me: "Should I recall the documents and change the

cover?" "Not at all," I replied. "You could not have chosen a better project for the mix-up."

The Bank's Board approved the technical assistance but, even
with it, the project never worked. Conceived at a time when state
industries were still considered respectable, even at the World
Bank, and financed with "hard" money, that is, the Bank's own
borrowed funds, the Mufindi pulp and paper project entered the
lore of foreign aid "white elephants." With the possible exception
of iron and steel mills in Nigeria (most of which never saw the
light of day), there cannot have been worse investments in all of
Africa. And Tanzania paid the bill for this foolish experiment for
the next 20 years.

At the time, there was strong interest in cracking open the
narrow options that African countries faced. Before the phrases
had even entered the business school lexicon, aid officials were
trying to "think outside the box," use "stretch" objectives, and
launch "big ideas." Like other aid officials, I wanted Tanzania's
strategy to work. I even recommended that Canada participate in
the pulp and paper project; fortunately, in Ottawa, saner spirits
prevailed.

One would think that a paper mill would do some good—creating jobs and avoiding unnecessary imports—or that helping poor
countries would be as easy as fishing in an aquarium. In fact, helping other nations successfully can be like looking for pearls in a
murky sea.

Take an example from another continent. In the 1980s, the
World Bank spent hundreds of millions of dollars helping to improve urban slums in Indonesia. The objective? To introduce modest changes like rubbish removal, street lighting, and storm drains
that would make these poor neighborhoods safer and cleaner. The
result? Poor people were pushed out by rising rents. The reason?
Access roads intended for garbage trucks proved just large enough
for sedan cars, allowing better off people to buy the ramshackle
dwellings, improve them, and lease them to higher-income tenants. The law of unintended consequences operated superbly.

Ten years later, in the northeast corner of the Ivory Coast, the
United Nations Development Programme (UNDP) spent $900,000
over three years trying, unsuccessfully, to show farmers how to grow
onions. Just 90 miles away, in the neighboring country of Burkina

Faso, farmers were growing onions in similar agricultural conditions quite profitably—without aid.

The difficulty of providing effective aid is not a reason for not trying. The most elementary case for foreign aid is founded on familiar Judaeo-Christian values. With two billion people in the world—a third of all humanity—living on less than $2 a day, how can the affluent begrudge a portion of their wealth to help others? Can Americans or Germans or Italians truly be said to prosper until Indians and Brazilians and Nigerians are also making steady economic progress? This notion of equity also underlies familiar aspects of internal economic policy in developed countries, such as the progressive income tax, unemployment and other welfare programs, and regional development schemes.

There is an economic case for foreign aid, too, best expressed in the establishment of the World Bank in 1946. The International Bank for Reconstruction and Development, as it was then called, was set up to promote the continued expansion of world trade after World War II. Its purpose was not charity but self-interest. Rebuilding the war-battered economies of Germany and Japan and helping other much poorer countries climb the economic ladder were seen as fundamental to ensuring global prosperity. Everyone was expected to benefit from the process: Rich countries would have ready markets for what they already produced, while poor countries would supply raw materials and eventually move into light manufactures (such as shoes and textiles) as richer countries shifted into more sophisticated products (appliances, electronics, and eventually computers). The logic of enlightened self-interest also inspired so-called tied aid for capital projects such as roads and power plants, using experts, construction companies, and equipment manufacturers from the donor country. Tied aid is now out of fashion, as it is particularly wasteful and inefficient, but it dominated international assistance from the 1950s through the 1980s.

Aid can also appeal to other aspects of self-interest. Sharing may make us more secure. In the late 1970s, the hard-driving president of the World Bank, Robert McNamara, insisted that foreign aid (about $50 billion a year) was a better investment in international security than the $400 billion spent on the arms race.[1] More recently, it has been argued that poverty is the breeding ground for mass migration, disease, and terror, and that we ignore it at our peril.

Despite such reasoning, foreign aid has remained stagnant over the last 30 years and, measured by what it can buy, it has declined considerably. Only five countries (Denmark, Luxembourg, the Netherlands, Norway, and Sweden) have met the United Nations' target of providing 0.7 percent of their gross national income in aid to poor countries. The United States has never spent more than one quarter of one percent of its national income on foreign aid, and two thirds of that has been devoted to just two countries: Israel and Egypt. As other regions have become more self-reliant, about half of the world's aid has been directed to Africa. A dizzying series of international meetings and task forces, including UK Prime Minister Tony Blair's Africa Commission Report in March 2005, have called for higher spending, but these appeals have collided with mounting public skepticism about the lasting effects of aid.

Thirty years ago, it was easier to demonstrate the benefits of economic development, and—by implication—foreign aid. Between 1950 and 1975, life expectancy in poor countries rose by fifteen years—from 35 to 50. Adult literacy increased from 30 percent to more than 50 percent in some countries. Access to health services, schools and clean water also improved.[2]But debt crises in Latin America and poor policies in Africa made the 1980s a "lost decade" for progress in the world, and in Africa the 1990s were also lost. By the end of the century, the most populous countries on earth, China and India, were charging ahead on the strength of domestic demand, strong exports, private investment, and normal borrowing rather than foreign aid. The extent of the transformation is difficult to encapsulate, but one eloquent measure was the rapid growth of China's foreign reserves. In the mid-1990s, stewards of the world's aid budgets were wondering how they could continue to justify providing grants to an economy holding over $45 billion in its central bank. By mid-2005, China's foreign reserves had reached $700 billion.

Elsewhere in East Asia, smaller countries had demonstrated the power of good economic policies, solid public finances, low inflation, and clear investment rules. In 1960, South Korea was as poor as Ghana; 30 years later, it was rich enough to offer aid to Africa. Hong Kong, Malaysia, Singapore, Taiwan, Thailand, and, more gradually, Indonesia joined the group of "newly industrializing" countries. By the 1980s, it was trade, not aid, that was causing these economies to bloom. While its foreign aid budget was small, the United States was running some of the largest trade deficits in its history and importing 40 percent of what East Asia produced. Imports of cheap electronic goods, clothing, and other light manufactures kept inflation low in the United States and improved the general standard of living, while creating hundreds of thousands of jobs overseas. East Asian economies, in turn, became avid markets for high-value US and European exports, such as capital equipment, computer software, luxury goods, and entertainment services. By 2004, 40 percent of US exports were going to Asia. This was how the international distribution of labor and capital was expected to function at the time the World Bank and International Monetary Fund were created.

By the end of the twentieth century, the World Bank and the European Union were the two largest sources of foreign aid. The Bank had also become the main conduit of global knowledge on how to promote economic growth and reduce poverty. At international aid meetings, including those for individual countries, the Bank and the rest of the international aid community—consisting of 40–50,000 officials in 20 rich countries and the UN system— distilled the lessons of trial and error, introduced and resisted fashions in development lending and tried, usually unsuccessfully, to harmonize their approaches.

Aid agencies tried everything. They went from supporting state-owned industries in the 1960s and 1970s to promoting private investment in the 1980s and 1990s; from offering lines of credit to specific sectors such as agriculture, industry, and housing to supporting national financial systems and leaving detailed lending decisions to local professionals; from bankrolling complicated rural development projects in particular locations to financing broad national services to achieve similar purposes indirectly. For a time, in the interests of speed, governments exempted major investment projects from local taxes, regulation, and decision-making; afterward, these exemptions were judged unwise, as they landed governments with infrastructure they did not understand or could not maintain. Donors set up special units to run projects, poaching talent away from other ventures; later, Africa's friends recognized they were weakening governments by creating islands of well-paid specialists in seas of mediocrity.

There was nothing capricious about these changes of approach. They were a genuine response to lessons learned in thousands of development projects around the world and reflected the limits rich countries themselves were encountering in using government as an engine of economic activity. Aid planners drew on experience in Latin America and Asia, where agricultural research, road construction, and cheap energy (such as hydroelectricity) were seen as the main building blocks of economic growth and, eventually, of a more even distribution of wealth. In the 1960s and 1970s, aid was offered mainly through individual projects, such as supporting family planning programs or building technical training schools. This ensured that aid resources were used not only productively but also clearly, and that donor parliaments, auditors, and taxpayers could understand how public money was being invested.

By the late 1970s, the most generous aid donors—the Netherlands, Sweden, and Denmark—were arguing for broader ("program") assistance to governments that had kept their promises. Those donors did not abandon individual projects, which were benchmarks for broader programs and kept aid specialists in touch with realities on the ground. But the overall trend was toward loosening the strings on aid and trusting the young institutions of developing countries to use it properly. Some countries would struggle under the burden of this trust, but—it was argued elegantly—this was the process of development.

Even before these experiments were tried, skeptics had argued that they would fail. Conservatives suggested that countries needed to find their own ways to prosperity and that outside help would distort priorities, discourage domestic savings, and create dependencies. In 1981, the economist P. T. Bauer summarized the case against aid in three powerful sentences: "The argument that aid is indispensable for development runs into an inescapable dilemma. If the conditions for development other than capital are present, the capital required will either be generated locally or be available commercially from abroad to governments or to businesses. If the required conditions are not present, then aid will be ineffective and wasted."[3] Liberal and socialist critics saw aid as a form of "imperialism," or as "an attempt to preserve the capitalist system in the Third World;"[4] instead, they preferred to see wealth redistributed in the world without strings and conditions.

For 40 years, aid agencies struggled hard to prove both sets of critics wrong. They argued that outside assistance was essential, despite its drawbacks. Some aspects of social progress, such as rural roads, primary schools, vaccination programs, family planning services, sanitation and clean water, would never attract private investment. Good policies deserved tangible support, not just a pat on the back. Project quality could be promoted through monitoring and evaluation, including impact studies. Lessons learned would be applied through follow-up efforts. As for the charge of "imperialism," aid agencies argued that it would be unconscionable to hand out public money without trying to channel it to the intended target. Technological advances, such as high-yielding crop varieties in South Asia in the 1960s, gave heart to aid practitioners. But by the end of the twentieth century, the "Green Revolution" that had transformed the food supply situation in India had yet to occur in Africa, for all the billions in aid money that had been spent there.

Increasingly, influencing the national policy of a developing nation was judged to be more important than providing it with projects and technology. Sector-wide programs, in which donors financed portions of the entire national budgets for agriculture, education, or health in exchange for specified reforms, became the preferred means of promoting development. An example of this sector-wide approach is the Ivory Coast education and health program that I described in Chapter 8. The number of countries that could be trusted to respect their agreements was very small, and this "carrot and stick" approach contradicted the findings of years of research on the effectiveness of aid.

In fact, experience showed that aid works best where governments are already on the right track, establishing priorities, implementing policies, and developing key institutions for their own reasons rather than trying to impress people in foreign capitals. In Africa, few countries have been so clear-sighted and plucky. The few that made serious efforts to reform themselves were those that had hit rock bottom and acted out of pure shame or desperation.

By 1981, Ghana, the first African country to achieve independence in 1957, was in such sorry straits that foreign businessmen would pack essential items like toilet paper before traveling there. When Ghanaians began doing the same before returning home from overseas trips, they realized that they had had enough. A new coup brought to power a determined soldier named Jerry Rawlings, who stayed in office for 19 years. From the early 1980s on, Ghana adopted more credible economic policies and began reversing the decline which it and the rest of Africa were suffering. Soon, the country became the poster child of Africa's future, backing common sense for its own sake rather than cowering in submission to international pressures. Rawlings even demonstrated that he was serious about fighting corruption by having members of his own family executed for dishonesty.

By 1986, after 15 years of dictatorship and disorder, Uganda, too, had had enough. The new president, Yoweri Museveni, cleaned house from top to bottom and ushered in a period of steady reform and economic growth. By the end of the century, Uganda had become the first African country to wrestle its way back to the per capita income it enjoyed in 1970. Upset by the deaths of many military comrades, Museveni was the first African head of state to become personally involved in fighting HIV/AIDS. As a result, by the year 2000, Uganda was also the first country to have reduced infection levels in some districts.

Other determined countries, such as Ethiopia and Eritrea, went from winning fierce wars of national freedom to introducing major social reforms. Again, they did this for their own purposes. The Ethiopian leader, Meles Zenawi, believed that apart from the security of the food supply, inflation was the principal enemy of small farmers. He also said he found it easier to ask his people to cross the metaphorical minefields of economic reform than to have his troops cross real ones a few years before. Eritrea, the country next door, swept away the cobwebs of government regulation so decisively that it shone briefly like a comet in the sky of African policy. Without foreign consultants and expensive studies, it not only reduced the size of its civil service but also improved salaries and working conditions for those who stayed in government. The reforms paid for themselves. Eritrea slashed the staff at the agency that issued business licenses from 250 to 35 and reduced waiting times from six months to 24 hours. Measures like these would transform the rest of Africa, if only they could spread. Unfortunately, soon after making these leaps, Ethiopia and Eritrea were locked in a new war with each other and their defense budgets soared accordingly. Both leaders are resented by large numbers of their citizens, who regard them as victorious soldiers rather than representative politicians. Many Ethiopians also saw Meles as advancing the interests of his own ethnic group, the Tigrayans, rather than those of all Ethiopians.

Do these relatively successful cases suggest that the road to reform must pass through national humiliation or war? Perhaps not. But they certainly illustrate that self-propelled change works best and that the West must alter current approaches to aid.

On Easter Sunday, 2001, I was driving deep into the forest of the Central African Republic with three Africans from other countries who worked there. As they discussed the local situation in the car, I could barely believe my ears. One asked: "Isn't it time this country was placed under a UN mandate?" The others agreed. This was not a cynical outburst, but a sober assessment of the problem. Their suggestion was a reference to the international arrangements set up after World War I to govern Germany's former colonies. At the time, the UK was asked to administer Tanganyika and German Cameroon; Belgium was given control over what is now Rwanda and Burundi; and South Africa governed South West Africa (now Namibia). Africans have always been Africa's harshest critics, but disgust with its institutions had now grown so deep that these sophisticated, independent voices were prepared to contemplate re-colonization as a solution.

Ten days later, on the 27th floor of an office building in New York, the UN Secretary General's Special Representative for the Central African Republic made a similar suggestion. A strikingly intelligent and idealistic man (and now the president of Mali), he asked: "Why should one help a country that does not seem willing to help itself?" His answer was that the international community should still try to help, for the sake of the people of the country and the stability of the sub-region. But, since a full-blown UN mandate was politically out of the question, he suggested that the World Bank and the IMF put advisers in the president's and prime minister's offices. I pointed out politely that such a solution had been tried—and had failed—in many other countries.[5]

Both of these anecdotes point to a yearning among Africans for continued help and guidance from the international community. Ensuring that new aid money really helps Africa may indeed resemble colonialism—not one in which foreign powers extract what they can from tropical forests and soils, but one in which still-generous nations do what is right for Africans and the world.

Foreign aid in Africa must be changed for a number of reasons. The first is that, as a whole, it has not worked. The one clear success has been the fight against river blindness in West Africa, which took 25 years and a concerted partnership between donor governments and international pharmaceutical companies (sustained by an active international secretariat) to overcome the parasite that was ruining the sight of millions of Africans, as well as the region's agriculture. Other ventures have been judged controversial rather than promising. The Chad - Cameroon Oil Pipeline, which was nearly blocked by international environmental and human rights groups, will transform the economy of Chad if the revenues are managed properly. Cultural exchange programs, particularly study trips to the United States for thousands of African intellectuals and professionals, and small grant programs supporting democracy and human rights have had a very positive impact in expanding the horizons and boosting the hopes of African reformers. But in areas meant to tackle poverty directly—clinics, schools, literacy programs, clean water supply, and sanitation—the foreign aid record in Africa has been deeply disappointing. Successes have been small, ephemeral, or too expensive to reproduce on a larger scale.

Few aid initiatives are really local and well thought out, and money rarely reaches its intended target. Even Uganda, one of the few African countries with a functioning government, found in 1998 that less than 30 percent of the funds dedicated to primary education was actually reaching the schools. Not all of the missing money was stolen or wasted; some if it was re-appropriated to other priorities by middle-level officials. Another complicating factor is the basic clash of values between Africans and Westerners (see Chapter 11). African leaders are now willing to talk about "poverty" and will even wrinkle their brows about "governance," but they prefer to have these discussions with foreign visitors rather than their own countrymen. In some countries, poverty studies have been suppressed to prevent leaks of embarrassing information. In the meantime, aid agencies keep churning out projects, some African officials try to cooperate, others try to derive personal advantage, and the African public keeps staring in disbelief at the ineffectiveness of the whole process.

Although they put on a brave face, aid practitioners have actually admitted defeat. In the 1990s, the World Bank's African department refused to cite economic growth figures for Africa as a whole because a weighted average would reflect the poor performance of the largest countries (Nigeria, Congo, Sudan, Ethiopia, and even South Africa). Instead, trying to be encouraging, the Bank referred to developments in a "typical" economy and said that Africa was "on the move." A veteran observer of Africa called this convenient use of statistics and misleading language Africa's "Potemkin deception," referring to Prince Grigori Potemkin's creation of mock villages in the Crimea to persuade Catherine the Great that her empire was thriving.[6]

Some of the best economists in the world worked hard on Africa's problems, to little avail. In 2000, the World Bank published its third major study in 20 years on the continent's economic prospects ("Can Africa Claim the 21st Century?"). Its prescriptions were essentially the same as those of 1989—and 1981.

One of those prescriptions was more "capacity-building," a persistent theme of aid planners. Since 1980, about four billion dollars a year have been spent on training, technical assistance, and assorted institutional studies. In the meantime, Africa's latent capacity has barely budged—remaining just below the surface, waiting for real opportunities to assert itself, or seeping away to other countries.

Since 2000, a frequent theme of international meetings has been how to measure the impact of aid more effectively, a disguised complaint that current yardsticks are not giving the right results. This is like hoping that a better thermometer will halt global warming. In one of the latest developments, some donors—including the World Bank—have tried to turn themselves into charitable organizations. Effectively bypassing African governments, they seek to put resources directly into the hands of beneficiaries through "community-driven" programs and to use non-governmental actors to administer them. But there are obvious limits to how far governments will allow aid organizations to run circles around them.

The ultimate indictment of foreign aid is that few Africans themselves believe in it. Shortly after I arrived in Abidjan to head the World Bank's regional office for Western Africa, a leading businessman—tough, American-trained, and plain-spoken—nearly knocked me out of my seat when I visited him with some rather sharp words: "What do you know about our government that we don't? I hope you don't believe in all these musical chairs they call 'democracy' around here. Why are you lending them any money? I certainly wouldn't." That challenge rang in my ears during the next three years in the country—and still does.

The question came in a different form in 2002 in the Central African Republic, where I met with business leaders, trade unionists, high school students, and human rights activists (who arrived late because they had taken separate taxis to confuse people who were following them). When the students heard how important education was to foreign donors, they asked if the World Bank could take over the running of the country's schools. I pointed out how impractical that would be—even as it reminded me of the two desperate school children from Guinea I described at the start of this book, who had died to draw Europe's attention to the same problem. "Then, why don't you give money directly to people rather than governments?" they persisted. I explained that even if that were physically possible, the World Bank's annual aid to Africa would meet the direct needs of the very poor for only ten days. Instead, governments and donors needed to invest in policies, projects, programs, and public debates that would help the poor improve their own lives. The students did not understand this. The way they saw it, their needs were immediate and their own government was certainly not listening to them.

If aid is largely ineffective, it is also demeaning. Unlike Shakespeare's mercy, which "blesseth him that gives and him that takes," foreign aid disfigures and corrupts at either end. Aid officials grow accustomed to flying business class and holding seminars on poverty in luxury hotels; at the same time, they complain about government extravagance. Facing a wide variety of conditions and regulations, they lose a sense of proportion. In 2002, a World Bank official came across Chadians attending a three-day training course in Niger who had stayed in the country for a whole week. Incensed at their apparent dishonesty, she berated them publicly; in fact, there was only one flight a week back to Chad. Several of the travelers had exhausted their daily allowances and were sleeping on the floor of the airport.

Equally demeaning in Africa is the lopsided "dialogue" between donors and governments about economic and social policy. Many local officials lack the training and political wiggle room to argue an issue. Knowing this, some aid staff are tactful, while others get right to the point. But the outcome is the same: Africans need the money more than donors need to persuade them; as a result, a full consensus is rarely reached. Elsewhere in the world, aid agencies have it less easy, as countries can draw on other sources of money and advice, including private investors, commercial banks, and international consulting firms. For the most part, Indonesian and Brazilian policy-makers make their own decisions—and mistakes. In contrast, policy errors in Africa have a disputed parentage.

In trying to please aid officials, African countries feel debased, like circus dogs forced to perform tricks. Governments try to defend their actions, but the public only sees the hoops they are jumping through. In March 2000, I showed a group of African church leaders a British television documentary about the World Bank's work in Uganda, hoping to reassure them about efforts to curb defense spending there. The message was lost on them. Instead of being relieved, the Ugandans in the audience complained about the harsh way in which Bank staff had spoken to their president in the film. In my view, the Bank had been polite to a fault.

For a long time, aid critics complained that policy reforms and projects were imposed on countries and that governments, like ventriloquists' dummies, said only what the donors wanted to hear. Aid professionals retorted that there was more to the process than met the eye and that some solutions were dictated more by circumstance than by foreigners. Both sides now occupy common ground, stressing the importance of increasing country "ownership" and "partnership." Yet, few African governments are more in control of anything now than they were in 1960.

This lack of control can have bizarre consequences. At a meeting of African heads of state in January 1998, two of the most intelligent among them described how it felt to be at the mercy of aid officials. President Chissano of Mozambique had asked the World Bank to finance a bridge across the Zambezi River, which divides his country in two. Transport experts prepared a traffic survey and concluded that too few cars used the road on either side to justify such an investment. "Of course, there were no cars," spluttered the President. "We have few of them to begin with, as we're poor, and without a bridge they are not likely to go in the direction of the river!" President Museveni of Uganda offered his own anecdote: "A few years ago, World Bank experts decided that telecommunications was a higher priority for us than roads. So we ended up with very nice telephone booths in remote villages where people could call their cousins in the capital to say, 'Well, it's good talking to you, but I can't come visit as the road's washed out . . .'"

If aid is both ineffective and demeaning, large amounts of it are also simply wasted. Even aid agencies have acknowledged repeatedly that there is greater pressure to commit money grandly than to spend it wisely. Of course, there are limits to what foreigners can control without taking the place of governments; supervision procedures are costly; and even apparently sophisticated accounting procedures can be mere fig leaves in an administrative jungle. Without trust and a common purpose, much aid is bound to go astray.

This record has not daunted Western donors. Aid officials are generally sympathetic, spirited, and imaginative people. It is part of their job to do the impossible. If programs stall, senior managers in donor agencies think there is something wrong with the country director rather than the country. Donors believe they are being tough with governments, but really they are constantly letting them off the hook. A recent novel by an experienced observer of Africa has parodied this self-delusion vividly. Here is his description of government and donor officials meeting behind closed doors to hammer out a public statement:

"The men in the room—there was not a single woman—knew each other well, and for the most part respected each other. Yet each joke came with a barb, and there was a story behind each witticism or verbal sally. For the insiders of the aid business, every line of the communiqué that would emerge from the talks, drafted paragraph by paragraph, was a battleground. To the uninformed eye the official statement would emerge as a bland resume of discussions; but to anyone with an insight into 'donorspeak' the result spoke volumes."[7]

According to the story, complimenting a government on its "efforts" to stabilize the economy meant "it should have tried harder." References to "initial" or "recent" successes had to be taken with a grain of salt: "Two more weasel words, used very cleverly. 'Initial' shows that the donors doubt that what has been started will be continued. And 'recent' is the way donors show their frustration that it has taken the government . . . so long to getting round to putting promises into practice."[8]

Even firm-minded people can be trapped into being too considerate or understanding. Once committed to a difficult country, aid managers tend to look for the silver lining. In 2002, the World Bank learned that Chad's Ministry of Health had used debt relief money to buy overpriced hospital equipment from a single firm, without competition. The Minister of Finance reacted promptly, canceling the contract, calling for proper bids, and eventually having the Minister of Health fired. Unimpressed, the IMF insisted that all other recent contracts be audited. I argued that the Minister of Finance had shown he was serious and should be given some leeway in rooting out other abuses. In the end, the IMF got its way. I had wanted to give the Chadians the benefit of the doubt (after all, it was Chadian health officials who had blown the whistle), but I now recognize that most Western taxpayers would agree with the IMF's approach.

Aid agencies have tried to avoid waste and inefficiency by being more focused and selective. But it is difficult to draw a line between what is important and almost important, between the root causes and the exacerbating factors of poverty. As a result, aid programs have been stretched across too many countries and activities, watering weeds as well as flowers, giving false hope to some and inadequate support to others.

Sometimes, however, fresh eyes and a can-do attitude can overcome complexity. In May 2002, the US Treasury Secretary Paul O'Neill toured four African countries with the Irish rock star Bono, who wanted to show him how difficult the development challenge was on the continent. The international press described them as an "odd couple." Bono, a tireless campaigner for international debt relief, seemed at ease with crowds, looking cool behind his dark glasses. O'Neill, a former chairman of two major corporations, was dressed for a board meeting, hesitant even to don traditional chief's clothing in one village, perhaps fearing he would look ridiculous the next morning on the front page of the *New York Times*. But, on the first day of the tour, he reacted with boyish wonder to the discovery in Ghana that only half the population had access to clean water. Here was something that could be fixed with a relatively small amount of money. As he pointed out, "Without good water, people get sick, crops don't grow . . . you can't get started *developing* anything."[9]

Eventually, Bono began to lose patience with the secretary's single-mindedness. By the time they were in Uganda, O'Neill was telling the country's president that his entire population could be given clean water for a cost of $25 million. The president's advisers showed him a consultant's study that put the bill at closer to $2 billion. "President Museveni," O'Neill said, shaking his head, "this is recommending you build a water system like in Detroit or Cleveland. You won't need that for a hundred years. You just need to drop wells, and mostly maintain them. Your people can handle the rest. We can do this quickly, maybe a year or two."[10] Like Bono, many aid officials found O'Neill's conclusions simplistic. But he had a point. Parts of the development puzzle are more important and tractable than others; solving them requires clear purpose rather than a great deal of money.

Indeed, throughout the world, it is uncompromising governments that have made good use of aid. Yet, in Africa, aid officials have been prone to muddling through and political correctness. The best example is population policy, which was prominently discussed in the 1970s and 1980s but disappeared from polite conversation during the 1990s. Africa has the youngest and most sexually active population on earth. In many countries, one in two Africans is younger than 15, compared with one in eight in Canada and the United States.[11] Thirty-four of the 40 most prolific countries on earth are African. Yet aid officials stopped quoting these numbers when Africans resisted, complaining they were already poor enough without losing their offspring ("our only wealth"). African women have been open to practicing birth control, but their governments and husbands have failed them. Public services have been slow to provide condoms and counseling services, while fathers insist on having larger families—or at least more sons.

The number of African countries where population policy has been effective remains woefully small. As part of the World Bank's first structural adjustment program in 1980, the president of Kenya agreed to head a National Council on Family Planning. That high political commitment allowed Kenya to become one of the few countries in Africa to reduce its population growth significantly by the end of the century. However, that reduction hardly represents a trend.

At the family level, the costs of having too many children are plain enough: Many are malnourished and denied the opportunity to grow in intelligence and strength. At the national level, population growth has eroded the fragile health and education facilities that existed in the early years of independence. Hundreds of thousands of primary school children sit in classes of 150–200, and enrollment and literacy rates are dropping. The population issue is delicate, but the consequences of ignoring it are severe.

A good friend of Africa prophesied, 40 years ago, that: "If Africa rejects colonialism, birth control and the big push needed to develop fast, it has only one way out: to send away all the doctors, and re-establish a high mortality rate."[12] This was long before the spread of HIV/AIDS, which could have been slowed if more women had been in control of their reproductive lives and more Africans had been familiar with the use of condoms.

Political correctness is hard to resist, especially thousands of miles from the hardship that it covers up. Most Africans are prepared to hear the truth. In fact, they are so accustomed to doublespeak and gobbledygook—when their rulers design to give them even that—that they are relieved to hear another point of view. Unfortunately, one of Africa's greatest handicaps is the lack of involvement and understanding of Africans themselves. It is true that few developing countries outside Latin America and India are guided by public opinion. But democracy is spreading elsewhere and in Africa it is barely inching forward. Repressive governments and uneducated populations are keeping the continent mired in tradition rather than open to dynamic forces.

Shortly after joining the World Bank, Jim Wolfensohn visited a water and sanitation project in a squatter settlement just outside the Brazilian city of São Paolo. While the deputy governor of the region showed him around, a large group of women followed at a short distance, joyfully waving papers in front of them. "Do you know why they are so happy?" the Brazilian asked. "Because they no longer have to drag buckets of water up these steep hills on their shoulders?" surmised Wolfensohn. "That's true," the deputy governor replied, "but that's not why they're showing you those papers." "Is it because they are proud to have contributed to the costs of the project?" "Yes," the host said, "that's also true. But they are waving their first bills for water service. It is the first time they see their names and addresses on an official document and feel *included* in government programs they had only heard about on the radio."[13] That sense of connection with national policy and programs is still largely absent in the African public.

Aid officials have tried to force that connection by establishing their own "contact groups"—consisting of journalists, business people, trade unionists, environmentalists, human rights activists, and other community leaders—to offer unvarnished advice to donor agencies. But they are no substitute for an informed free press, a strong parliamentary opposition, and governments that can speak for all shades of public opinion. Donor advisory groups grow stale and lose their independence, with members sometimes curbing their tongues because they value the opportunity—and financial perks—of continuing to be heard. To meet their own agencies' requirements for consultation, donors hold large "public workshops" that are often prepared hurriedly and are not particularly incisive. Participants rarely know the issues to be discussed ahead of time and seldom feel afterward that they have been heard.

Unlike photographs, economies cannot be developed in a dark room. Although there is no inherent connection between democracy and economic growth, there is certainly an intimate link between open political systems and equal access to economic opportunities and public services. Some countries, like South Korea and Taiwan, have postponed political pluralism until their economies were strong—China withstands it still—but even they promoted basic health and education as an integral part of encouraging economic growth. In Africa, most economies did not grow at all during the 1980s, struggled in the 1990s, and even now are expanding well below their potential. For these countries, there is no alternative to insisting on honest elections, strong parliaments, and an energetic free press as a means of promoting economic reform and an equitable sharing of the benefits of growth.

For a long time, development agencies avoided issues of democracy and human rights. Finally, beginning in the late 1980s and in Africa, where the situation was worst, aid officials became publicly concerned about "governance." This delicate phrase avoided the central issue. Using such jargon allowed Western governments to comment on internal matters such as government accountability and information, decentralization of authority, judicial systems, civil service reform, military expenditures, corruption, and relations with nongovernmental organizations. But the watered-down discourses did little to enforce the rule of law and a culture of openness and equality among citizens. In some cases, they made things worse. By training judges and clerks, computerizing records, and consolidating laws and regulations, governance projects created an illusion of modernization.

In the last five years, official statements from world bodies have grown tougher. For example, in March 2002, the UN International Conference on Financing for Development in Monterrey, Mexico came close to linking aid levels to explicit political reforms. Yet little has changed in practice. The European Union has cut off aid to small countries like Togo that were no longer even trying to appear democratic, and to larger countries like the Ivory Coast and Zimbabwe that have been on the verge of civil war. The Europeans have also sent election observers to many countries.

But most tyrants in Africa continue to enjoy a holiday. Under "smart" sanctions aimed at senior officials, Zimbabwe's Robert Mugabe has been barred from visiting Europe and the United States. But even he has been able to attend UN meetings in Geneva and was welcomed to a gathering of African presidents in Paris by President Chirac in 2003. As long as governments get away with tyranny, foreign aid will be a palliative rather than part of the cure for poverty.

The drawbacks of government-to-government aid are now obvious, but private individuals and charities continue to make an important contribution to the development of Africa. People-to-people contacts convey values and set an encouraging example surpassing the immediate effect of small projects. Private aid is not always more efficient than public assistance, but its motives are clear and it is delivered with pluck and determination.

For example, in early 1993, I visited some Italian Catholic nuns 30 miles northeast of Abidjan (the same sisters who were robbed by the dishonest hospital accountant). Several months before, they had told me they wanted to construct an AIDS clinic and nutrition center next door. I had promised to help revise their proposal for submission to local embassies and charitable organizations, but I had been too busy to follow through. After lunch, the Mother Superior said she wanted to show me something. A few hundred yards behind the house, the large AIDS clinic was now almost complete. "How did you finance it?" I asked admiringly. "Half the money came from the French International School in Abidjan, and the other half," she said with a grin, "was scrounged from our relatives in Italy." They weren't prepared to wait for anyone, including me.

Of course, private individuals have faced their own frustrations and "white elephants." A Scottish missionary in Nyasaland (now Malawi) complained in the 1920s: "Sometimes we have encouraged the people to erect a brick building. These require much stimulus, many visits, constant superintendence during their erection. But not long after all the labor has been rewarded by a magnificent structure in bricks and clay, the villagers have followed their ancient practice, and shifted their huts to a new site, and lo! the palace of bricks stands alone in the bush with no people to warm it, and no congregation to give it life. Then the European says that never again will he spend so much tireless energy in works for so temporary a purpose."[14]

The missionary got over his disappointment, as have many volunteers since. In early 2004, my brother, a surgeon, worked in Kenya for a week at a rural hospital. There, he was reunited with an old friend. My brother told me his story: "After graduating from university with a degree in forestry, Bob Swann moved here in the early 1980s with his wife and three-month-old son. He is not your typical pious, well-intentioned but impractical missionary. He has a lot of hands-on practical skills that he put to use in the Somali

Muslim world of eastern Kenya." Over the next 12 years, Swann built homes, schools and medical clinics, installed water pumps, and started tomato, banana and mango farms with members of the local communities. For a couple of years, he and his family lived willingly in the Somali slum of Eastleigh in Nairobi, which my brother described as "a congested filthy mess."

In the early 1990s, when the war in Somalia intensified, Swann was sent to the border region to help set up refugee camps. His wife Anne, a nutritionist, had the task of feeding over 16,000 children a day. Swann was fluent in Swahili and Somali, and had survived malaria, amebic dysentery, and scorpion stings; but after working 20 hours a day for months on end, he contracted both typhus and typhoid fever, which forced them to return to Canada. They settled in Toronto where they lived and worked with the growing Somali community, which is now 130,000 strong in Canada.

Swann's efforts did not end there. In 2000, a church in downtown Vancouver hired him. He started a shelter program for the street people. Every Tuesday evening, 150 people lined up outside for a free hot meal and 30–40 of them spent the night in the warm church gymnasium. As my brother reported, "He knows the names of the squeegee boys and beggars on the street and treats them like human beings. He befriends the friendless, loves the unloved and even the unlovable, and draws on a deep and unshakeable faith in serving others."

There are few people like Bob Swann in official aid agencies except in humanitarian organizations like the UN emergency relief agencies and volunteer groups like Doctors Without Borders. Aid staff are quiet heroes at best, somewhat like police officers and fire fighters in business suits, trying to make a small difference in the face of daunting odds.

However, there are exceptions. Hans Binswanger spent much of his career working on Latin America and joined the World Bank's African staff in the early 1990s as director for agriculture and rural development. In just ten years, he left a major mark, inspiring a five-fold expansion of the Bank's work on HIV/AIDS and promoting "community-driven development" programs, which are meant to turn traditional aid processes on their head. He is also HIV-positive and talked openly about the disease, galvanizing villages and volunteer groups across Africa into replacing fear with practical prevention. Another giant is Peter Eigen, who left the World Bank in the early 1990s after heading the Bank's regional office in Nairobi to found Transparency International, the watchdog agency that is now the pace-setter in international efforts to expose and control corruption.

In the shadow of such impressive contributions, most aid officials accept the limits of the possible and assume that real development progress will be gradual. Or they adopt an historical perspective, like the writer James Morris who visited Ethiopia in 1963 and came away with the following reflection. "It took some nine centuries of consistent national development for the British to reach the moment of their mechanical revolution," he wrote, "and even before their emergence as a people they had benefited from a foreign tutelage so advanced that to this day few States in Africa can compare with Roman Britain for order, inventiveness and logical government."[15] Fortunately for Africa, there has been a constant rotation of aid staff. Fresh troops are regularly deployed to the front line, sobered but not paralyzed by what the "old hands" have told them. Yet the room for optimism and imagination has almost run its course.

CHAPTER 10

THE CHAD-CAMEROON OIL PIPELINE

What direction should foreign aid to Africa now take? One of the few options left is to be more demanding, even intrusive, with governments, and to impose more, rather than fewer, conditions. This idea runs counter to modern instincts and the wishes of African officials, but it is certainly consistent with past experience and mounting concern among economists, human rights activists, and environmentalists about the current way of doing things. An alternative would be to drop the whole idea of foreign aid, but that would be like giving up the search for a cure to cancer.

In 2000, a highly controversial project, the Chad–Cameroon Oil Pipeline tested a more assertive approach to planning major infrastructure projects in Africa. The story of the project shows the real difficulties of promoting development on the continent, suggests a way of managing other aid projects in the future, and illustrates the odd turns international debates can take in promoting the interests of poor countries.

Chad sits at the very heart of Africa. More than twice the size of France, with only 200 miles of paved roads and few natural resources other than sand, it is one of the poorest countries on earth. In the dry season, mothers in southern Chad become so desperate that they raid termite mounds for larvae to feed to their children. Yet, since 1970, major oil reserves in the region sat undeveloped because of a withering civil war, a brutal dictatorship that no investor could trust, and world oil prices not quite high enough to justify transporting the oil almost 700 miles through Cameroon to the Atlantic Coast.

Finally, in the mid-1990s, the United States' largest corporation, Exxon-Mobil, and the world's most important aid agency, the World Bank, joined forces to resolve the problem. Along the way, they faced fierce opposition from a constellation of nongovernmental organizations that demonstrated both the strength of international public opinion and the strange tactics some can use in fighting a "good" cause.

It is hardly surprising that the Chad–Cameroon Pipeline attracted controversy. To begin with, the cast of characters was simply combustible. Exxon had been responsible for the environmental disaster at Valdez Bay in Alaska in 1989. Shell, a partner in the project, had caused major environmental and social damage in Nigeria's Ogoniland region, and bloodied its hands in trying to suppress local opposition to its activities there. And Elf, the formerly state-owned French oil company, had supported heavy-handed regimes in West and Central Africa for decades, sometimes at its own initiative, at other times on the instructions of the French government. As the project was being prepared, an array of prominent French businessmen associated with Elf were being tried for corruption in France. One of the alleged African beneficiaries of Elf's largesse, the unscrupulous and irrepressible president of Gabon, Omar Bongo, was also suing the French government for defamation. For most good-hearted people, this line-up was already discouraging enough. The fact that the World Bank, which was having trouble defending its own environmental record, and Chad, an authoritarian state with a history of human rights violations, were also involved made the entire enterprise an obvious, almost ideal, target of criticism. For four years, I was on the front lines of the controversy, first as the World Bank's spokesman for Africa and then as its Country Director for Central Africa.

Ironically, the World Bank would not normally have become involved in such a project. Its sole interest was in ensuring that the lessons of past oil investments in Africa would be reflected in the design of the project, that it would meet the highest international standards of environmental and social protection, and that the oil revenues would be used for the good of the people of Chad rather than wasted on "prestige" projects or siphoned off to foreign bank accounts. At a total cost of $3.5 billion, the project was to be the largest private investment in Africa in a decade. That investment would add 50 percent to Chad's annual government revenues.

Conscious of possible criticism from public interest groups, the media, and its own shareholders, Exxon-Mobil was keen to have an international "seal of approval" for the project. Getting it right was important not just for Chad. In a sense, it was also vital for all of Africa.

Critics were less certain of the project's importance. They felt that no project design, however promising on paper, could work in a country with a violent political history and little respect for the opinions and welfare of its citizens. They were also doubtful that there were useful lessons to be applied from elsewhere. Except in developed countries like the UK and Norway and a handful of developing ones, namely Botswana and Indonesia, natural resource booms had led to waste and disruption rather than social progress. In a sense, the critics were right. What had to be avoided in such circumstances was clearer than what should be done instead. New solutions, rather than established ones, would need to be tried. Furthermore, no one could guarantee that the government in Chad would live up to its obligations. And once the pipeline was built, outsiders would not be able to shut it down.

Despite these problems, there were encouraging signs, which the World Bank felt were more than just straws in the wind. Chad had held its first multi-party elections in 1996. International observers thought that the President Idriss Deby's majority had been exaggerated, but no one doubted that he had won most of the votes. Since then, the government had respected its economic reform agreements with the Bank and the IMF—not an easy task for a small, impoverished country. It had privatized or shut down 45 of the country's 50 public enterprises. It was now devoting 70 percent of its spending to basic services like education and health, which were key to improving the lot of the poor. And, despite a lingering secessionist movement in the north of the country, it had cut the size of the national army in half.

This was a respectable track record, but it was only four years long. Critics were less trusting, and felt the government should face re-election before the pipeline project went ahead, hoping that a government more to their liking would manage the project instead.

But the Bank was eager to proceed, as time was not on the project's side. Political improvements in Nigeria and new offshore discoveries in the Gulf of Guinea threatened to make the Chad deposits less profitable. The mediocre quality of the oil, the extra costs to refine it, the distance to market, and the international controversy itself could make the project so marginal as to kill it altogether before the next elections were held. There would also be a human cost to any postponement. Sixty thousand children died of malnutrition in Chad every year. Putting off the project two years, on top of the two years needed to build the pipeline, meant that almost a quarter of a million young Chadians would die before the government could receive additional revenues. Of course, there was no certainty that any of these children could be saved. Not just more public money, but also better policies and stronger institutions would be necessary to improve basic services and economic opportunities. But there were more than theoretical reasons for proceeding promptly with the investment.

Several dark clouds hovered over the project. The first was esoteric and highly political, but allowing it to prevail would almost certainly have proven fatal to the enterprise. The two countries involved in the project, Chad and Cameroon, were highly indebted and had no international credit rating, so the Bank intended to use funds from its soft loan facility for the poorest countries on earth. But major contributors to that facility, like Germany and the United States, let it be known that they would oppose the use of such funds–which were normally devoted to schools, clinics, child nutrition, and other "direct" poverty projects—for a large private-sector energy project. This view was economic nonsense. The purpose of soft loans was to support a country's progress without adding unduly to its debt burden. The nature of a project was less important than whether it would contribute directly to a country's economic and social development.

No one could doubt that the pipeline project, if properly managed, could transform the Chadian economy from one entirely dependent on fickle weather conditions and international aid to one with a chance of charting its own future. Other oil deposits in the country were being explored, which could add to the revenues flowing into the national development budget. The Bank's small share of project costs (five percent) could prove to be the most important single contribution it had made to Chad's development.

But economics are often less powerful than politics and personal vanity. In November 1997, the terms of the Bank's funding were quickly resolved. During a visit to Stuttgart, the German government informed the publicity-conscious World Bank president, Jim Wolfensohn, that unless he wanted to throw away the popularity he had won in Western capitals during his first two years in office, he should drop the idea of using soft loans for the project. Even then, the Germans would not commit themselves to supporting the project. In fact, when a new World Bank publication boasted of special measures to protect the pipeline construction workers against HIV/AIDS, the Germans objected strongly to the assumption that the project would go ahead. On his return to Washington, Wolfensohn ordered his financial staff to lend "hard" money to the two uncreditworthy countries.

Other doubts about the project were more familiar. Given the petroleum industry's environmental record and the Bank's own checkered history in that department, how could the international community be satisfied that there would not be oil leaks from the pipeline, that opposition groups would not blow it up, or that fragile ecosystems and indigenous peoples along the route would be respected?

Exxon had prepared a thorough environmental assessment, and defenders of the project made much of the fact that it took up 19 volumes. But its size was less important than its contents. The assessment acknowledged that the project presented a series of major challenges. But all of them were manageable. It was not like building a power dam in an earthquake zone. The pipeline was to be buried and would follow mainly existing roads and railway lines. Not a single house was to be destroyed along the way. Only about five square miles of forest were to be disturbed. To compensate for this, two new national parks, covering 2,000 square miles, were to be established in Cameroon. Farmers, too, would be compensated for the temporary loss of their land during construction. And it would be Exxon, not the governments, which would implement the environmental plan under local and international supervision. For all their limitations, the oil companies were more competent, accessible, and responsive to international public opinion than the two governments involved.

World Bank staff examined the draft assessment and identified 66 "issues" or "clarifications" that needed to be discussed. The debate lasted for 18 months, during which time neither the Bank nor Exxon-Mobil was certain of the outcome. The Bank's environmental staff and, even more so, those in the Bank's private sector arm who also wanted to finance the project, at times doubted the seriousness of the oil companies, wondering whether they simply wanted the Bank's "rubber stamp." For their part, Exxon managers thought that Bank staff were "picky," shifting the goal posts as time went on, and asking for more and more changes to the pipeline route, each of which would add to the cost.

In late 1998, the Bank's vice president for Africa put his foot down. Yes, he admitted, there had been some escalation of the Bank's requirements over the previous year, as international best practices and the Bank's own safeguard standards had evolved, but there was no question of taking any shortcuts in protecting the natural and human environments of the two countries. "We want a pipeline," he said, "which would be built in New Jersey, not just one which is suitable for Africa."

Thereafter, the logjam was broken. The pipeline route was changed in forty locations and improvements were made in the way local people would be consulted and compensated. In May 1999, Wolfensohn met with major environmental protection groups. He said that he sympathized with their concerns, but informed them that he was now inclined to support the project. The same day, he shook hands with Chad's President Idriss Deby and said they had a deal. But the roller coaster ride had only begun.

Another key issue, human rights, remained unresolved. How could the Bank favor expanding the budget of a country that had emerged from a 40-year civil war and still treated opposition groups roughly? In his meeting with the nongovernmental organizations, Wolfensohn said he, too, was worried about human rights in Chad and more generally across Africa. But how could outside agencies stop short of helping countries that seemed on the right track in developing democratic institutions and proper legal systems? If Chad began to brutalize its people again, or refused to investigate and punish human rights violations, then of course the Bank and other donors would not be able to support the oil pipeline or anything else. This was more than Wolfensohn could say in public, as the Bank is formally prevented from imposing political conditions on its lending. But his private views checked that line of criticism for a while.

The remaining problem with the project was the most serious and complex. How could anyone guarantee that the oil revenues would be used for national development? In December 1998, at the urging of the World Bank, Chad's National Assembly passed a law allocating ten percent of the revenue to a Future Generations Fund to be managed offshore, five percent to the producing region, and 80 percent of the rest to agriculture, education, health, and infrastructure projects. To ensure openness in the use of the funds, Exxon was to deposit the government's share of revenues in an overseas account. A "watchdog" committee, consisting of Chadian public officials, parliamentarians, religious bodies, human rights groups, and other nongovernmental organizations, would vet the government's spending plans, authorize the release of the oil revenues to the national budget, and track the actual use of the funds. The Bank would undertake annual studies to suggest more efficient ways of funding the priority sectors. There would be annual published audits of the oil accounts. The Bank would supervise the project frequently and intensively. Furthermore, it would fund three companion projects to strengthen the Ministries of Finance and Environment in the two countries. And an International Advisory Group, consisting of highly reputable people from Senegal, Canada, the United States, and the Netherlands, would visit Chad two or three times a year for the first ten years, to make certain that the letter, not just the spirit, of the project agreements was being respected. Their reports were to be published on the Internet within minutes of being submitted to the World Bank's management and board.

These arrangements were so elaborate and unusual that many people began talking of them as a possible model for managing aid in other areas. Some skeptics were won over. The Scandinavian on the Bank's Board, a doubter until then, quoted a Chadian adage of the desert: "This is as good as it gets before the rain comes." Others felt that the Bank had gone overboard in its efforts to be rigorous. A Latin American on the Board cautioned against thinking of this a precedent. "Few countries," he warned, "will be as poor or as patient as Chad."

In the meantime, international environmental groups were having a field day. Led by the Environmental Defense Fund, the Center for International Environmental Law, and the Bank Information Center—all based in Washington DC, a worldwide campaign had been whipped up against the project. Some international groups with limited exposure to the Bank's work or dated information on the project had genuine concerns that needed to be addressed. But the Washington, DC, groups, who should have known better, simply twisted the facts. They blithely suggested that Bank staff were promoting the project to advance their own careers—an almost comical distortion of the long hours and pointed questions the same staff were facing within their own organization. Just days after making such remarks, the Environmental Defense Fund requested a briefing from those staff members. The Fund got a thorough one, with a smile.

Early in the controversy, a list of the Bank's concerns about Exxon's draft environmental study was leaked, suggesting that the institution's own experts were being overruled. In fact, that list was a simple reflection of the lively professional debate underway within the institution. In September 1999, during the annual meetings of the Bank and IMF, the Bank organized an unprecedented public briefing on how the project was evolving. Instead of participating in the session, the Environmental Defense Fund stationed someone outside the room to hand out a press release denouncing the Bank's "public relations exercise." Two weeks later, they wrote to the World Bank president to complain that they had not been invited to the meeting.

Critics blew minor issues out of proportion. A typical concern was how much farmers should be paid for fruit trees cut down along the pipeline route. The idea of compensating them at all was rather original, as most of them were subsistence farmers and consumed the fruit themselves. A scale of prices was devised, based on the type and age of the tree and the time required to replace it. The winner of the sweepstakes in Chad was a full-grown mango tree, worth $1,500, or five times the annual income of most rural families. Jealous farmers in Cameroon wondered what was so special about Chadian mangoes. Yet, citizen groups in Chad and Washington, DC, argued that such compensation was not enough. I asked Exxon staff how many mango trees would be cut down during construction. The answer was between one and seven.

Another cause célèbre was the way villagers had been asked their views. Early in the consultation period, Exxon employees visited settlements along the pipeline route, accompanied by soldiers or armed security personnel. Critics argued that the presence of the guards had prevented the Chadians from expressing their views freely. At the time, remnants of a secessionist army were still operating in the area. A kinder reading of events was that Exxon staff, mostly security-conscious Americans who were new to Africa, were risking life and limb to find out what farmers and their families thought. Aid officials knew, too, that in Chad, as elsewhere in Africa, people found a way of expressing themselves subtly and sometimes quite bluntly, even in the presence of government officials or the army. Once security improved in southern Chad and the complaints of Washington-based groups became deafening, Exxon dropped the armed guards.

Such antics were bad enough. But, in the summer of 1999, another organization, the California-based Rainforest Action Group, embarrassed even the Washington, DC, environmental bodies. Some of its efforts were ingenious and even amusing. They dressed someone up as a gorilla, supposedly endangered by the project, to hand out leaflets in front of the World Bank. Despite intensified security, they smuggled a large helium balloon into the Bank's headquarters that they released into the enclosed central atrium of the building. It floated upward beyond the reach of security personnel, where it remained suspended for several days, spelling out a protest message to the Bank's senior decision-makers on the 12th and 13th floors.

In other ways, they went too far. They bought full-page ads in the West Coast edition of the *New York Times* while the Bank's president was visiting Stanford University, depicting him as wanted for "murder and corruption" in connection with the "African" pipeline project. Similar posters were pasted on trees and street corners at Jackson Hole, Wyoming, where Wolfensohn was spending his summer holidays. And a zealous Rainforest Action staffer, who had asked questions about the project at Stanford and walked out as they were being answered, delivered a series of protest letters to Wolfensohn's home in Washington, DC.

This over-exuberance backfired. Once an unqualified supporter of nongovernmental organizations of every kind, Wolfensohn began drawing distinctions between "good" and "bad" NGOs. The critics of the project tried to arouse a sense of drama, portraying themselves as David fighting several Goliaths. Behind the scenes, the real drama was the struggle within the Bank between those who were applying all their professional skill and scruples to keep Chad's hopes alive, and those who preferred to walk away from a high-risk project.

Meanwhile, a change of tack by the project's opponents revealed just how much progress had been made in improving the design. Environmental groups were now focusing on human rights issues and the political risks, tacitly accepting that most of their technical concerns had now been met. Only one environmental issue was outstanding: how detailed the oil spill protection plan should be two years before it was needed. By November 1999, the Bank was ready to submit the project to its board.

Then the bottom fell out from under the project. For reasons that were never disclosed, Exxon's two partners, Shell and Elf, suddenly pulled out. An angry crowd in Chad's capital attacked the French embassy and began to burn Elf's service stations in the city. Trying to quell the riot, the army shot four demonstrators. But Exxon stuck to its plans and tried to identify new partners. In April 2000, the Malaysian national oil company, Petronas, and the US company Chevron signed up to the project, and the Bank geared up to make its case again to its board and—through the media—to the world.

The Bank had been through many controversies before. In 1983, as the Bank's loan officer for Indonesia, I had negotiated the last "transmigration" project, part of a national effort to move poor farmers from Java to less populated parts of the country. Critics argued that poor people were just being moved around rather than given new lives, that the new soils allocated to the migrants were less stable and productive than the ones left behind, and that in opening up new lands the government was causing irreparable damage to virgin forests and wildlife. Like the Chad–Cameroon project, there was a basic misunderstanding at the heart of the controversy. All the project would finance was site selection studies applying stringent environmental standards. Four-fifths of the studies eventually recommended against new settlements and the government ended up abandoning the whole program. That summer, however, while the project was still being considered, 400 people—many of them Australians—wrote protest letters to the Bank. I answered each of them personally. It was a busy summer.

That was before fax machines and e-mail became weapons of mass instruction. The Chad–Cameroon Pipeline controversy was much larger. In the last year of the debate, the Bank received more than 50,000 letters opposing the project. Sixteen thousand came from a single organization, Working Assets, a public-spirited telephone company in California that devotes part of its earnings to good causes and urges its subscribers each month to join specific protest movements. In October 1999, it denounced the "provision of low-interest loans to wealthy oil companies to decimate the tropical forests of Central Africa." As the World Bank spokesman for Africa, I sent every one of these protesters a detailed letter explaining the efforts being taken to protect people and nature along the pipeline route. Some wrote back to say how much they appreciated the response.

Notwithstanding all of these efforts, the battle was far from won. Despite the good technical work of Bank and Exxon specialists, and the Bank's openness about the risks and proposed solutions, the fate of the project hung by a thread. US organizations such as the Environmental Defense Fund were still determined to stop the project, as if it were a litmus test of their strength as a public interest group or a trophy for display in their entrance hall for future donors. Public relations staff close to the Bank's president were also concerned that persevering with the project would affect the institution's "brand image." This was a remarkable line of reasoning. Most Bank staff were proud to work for an institution that supported difficult but worthwhile causes, while most outside critics thought the Bank's reputation was already beyond repair.

Two special factors saved the project. A personal chemistry had developed between the World Bank President Jim Wolfensohn and Exxon-Mobil's Chief Executive Officer Lee Raymond. Wolfensohn was convinced that Raymond was firmly committed to doing the project properly and acting similarly in other international ventures. The Bank had been pressing international companies to become better "corporate citizens," so Wolfensohn could not easily drop the project if someone he trusted was doing all he could to heed the Bank's advice.

The other saving factor was an even larger controversy. The Bank was preparing a project in Western China that was similar to the Indonesian transmigration program of the 1980s. It included putting poor Chinese farmers on new land. The problem was that the areas to be occupied were part of what was, until the European sixteenth century, the Tibetan Empire—a fact of which the Bank was unaware. While these lands were outside the borders of modern Tibet, which had been occupied by the Chinese in 1950, they were in an area where the current head of Tibetan Buddhism, the Dalai Lama, had been born. These discomforting circumstances came to the attention of the Free Tibet movement during the final months of work on the Chad–Cameroon project, and the activists pounced. They turned a well-intentioned agricultural development project into Bank collusion in China's illegal occupation of Tibetan land and its efforts to suppress Tibetan culture and religion. The fax machines of the Bank's Board members were so overloaded with overnight protest messages that they jammed each morning and could not be used for hours.

The stakes were raised to the equivalent of nuclear war. US government officials reportedly warned Wolfensohn that if he went ahead with the Chinese project they would not support him for a second term as Bank president. In the opposite corner, China—which was the Bank's largest borrower and was infuriated by this intrusion into its "internal" affairs—warned Wolfensohn that they would withdraw from the Bank if he did not present the project to his board. Chinese ambassadors around the world were instructed to inform their capitals, especially in Western Europe, that a vote against the project would be interpreted as an unfriendly act and be taken into account in awarding future commercial contracts. To signal its displeasure with the US action, China even held up a key vote in the UN Security Council on the situation in Kosovo for three days. The project passed, but the controversial component was dropped and the Chinese financed it themselves.

A little country like Chad had no such leverage in the international community. But a certain war weariness had set in, especially when the pipeline's critics saw that the Bank was prepared to go ahead, despite the row over the Western China project. The pipeline did not exactly slip by in the shadow of the larger controversy. There was suspense about the final result until the very end. But, in the homestretch, there was more concern with fine-tuning the design than overcoming any important hurdles. The storm had broken, and there was a sudden stillness in which reasoned arguments rather than sensationalist claims could again be considered.

In the meantime, the US Treasury was having trouble coordinating views in Washington. The State Department and the Commerce Department supported the project, but the Bank's natural allies, the US Agency for International Development and the Environmental Protection Agency, were opposing the project for political, not technical, reasons: They simply refused to believe the government of Chad. Larry Summers, the US Treasury secretary, called Wolfensohn to ask for a postponement of the Board meeting. This made the Chadians—and Exxon-Mobil—nervous again. To allay their fears, Wolfensohn decided to spread the discussion over two meetings rather than postponing the first one.

Media interest remained intense. A former French prime minister, Michel Rocard, published an article in the Paris daily *Le Monde,* supporting the Pipeline. The day before the first Board meeting, an editorial in *The Washington Post* also endorsed the project. It was entitled "Undoing Oil's Curse." I fielded questions for seven and a half hours from the French- and English-language services of Radio France Internationale, the BBC (also in English and French), National Public Radio ("Marketplace" and "Morning Edition"), Voice of America, and other media. Even the Australian Broadcasting Service called; until then, they had shown no interest in the subject.

The vote on June 6, 2000 (D-Day) seemed almost an anti-climax. The project was approved all but unanimously. No one opposed it, and only Italy abstained, for reasons that had nothing to do with the environment, human rights, or the use of the oil money. The Italians were concerned about the inflationary effects of all that sudden revenue.

One reason for the consensus was that the international debate had shed a bright light on every nook and cranny of the massive project. There were no surprises around the corner. And the Bank had made its case successfully. On NPR, I summed up the merits of the project in a single sentence: "No one can guarantee that a hundred percent of the oil revenues will be used responsibly, but one thing is certain: if the oil fields are not developed, not a single penny of that money will go to reducing poverty."

Following the vote, the Chadian government did two things that raised confidence further. They expanded the number of non-governmental members on the oil revenues oversight committee, without increasing the total size of the committee. And the president of Chad announced that they would manage other project earnings—including a $25 million "bonus" that they were to receive from the project sponsors at the signing of the final agreements—the same way as the eventual oil revenues.

That was in mid-June. By August 2000, rumors were already beginning to spread that the government was using the signing bonus secretly. I was now the Bank's Country Director for Chad, Cameroon, and three other Central African countries. I told my staff to be patient. Chad had been under an international spotlight for four years, and the government was entitled to some breathing room. If they were using the bonus, it was a problem of their own creation, and one which they would need to solve for themselves. After all, those funds were not covered by our agreements, and the Chadian president was entitled to change his mind. But I knew that if the rumors proved true, they would blow a massive hole into the hard-won consensus on the project.

By September, the speculation was unquenchable. So, in my first meeting with Chad's president that month, I asked him about it. He didn't miss a beat. Yes, he said, they had used $15 million of the bonus to fund food imports, repair flood damage in the capital, supply fuel oil to the nation's key power plant, and—this was the clincher—to purchase arms and military equipment. These were urgent needs, he argued, and he could not wait for the oil revenues oversight committee to be set up. But he seemed to have no idea of the firestorm his actions would cause; it was this innocence—or cynicism—that worried me most. I advised him to get ahead of the critics by informing Parliament of his actions and freezing the remainder of the bonus. I also told him that he should put it in the hands of the Ministry of Finance (the first money had been spent outside the normal budget process), and issue a full public statement summarizing the reasons for the spending.

Even if he did this, I told him, the damage to Chad's credibility would be hard to repair. While the bonus money was not covered by any legal agreement, the Bank would probably need to postpone Chad's access to debt relief for six months until the government was able to demonstrate that they were back on the right track. The international community had recently approved a major program of debt reduction for poor countries, which required governments to put every penny of the new money into programs aimed at the poor. If Chad had used supplementary funds from the private sector secretly and haphazardly, how could it be trusted to manage debt relief responsibly?

Neither the Christian lobby group Jubilee 2000, which wanted to cancel as much debt as possible before the end of the Biblically symbolic millennium year, nor the Bank and IMF, which were keen to comply, could help Chad. As a result of its misstep, the country had to wait until May 2001 for debt relief. This was ironic in many ways. Before the fiasco over the bonus, Chad had done more to improve its policies in a few years than other candidate nations had done in a decade. And some of the countries that beat it past the post, such as its neighbor Cameroon, had done much less to strengthen basic services for the poor.

Throughout this period, the president of Chad showed no signs that he understood the bargain he had made with the rest of the world. The same week I talked to him about the bonus, he summoned me to his office for a lecture. Since our first meeting, he had received a copy of a letter I had written to the Minister of Planning challenging the award of a mobile telephone license without competition to an Egyptian company close to the president. I suggested he cancel the license and invite international bids, for the benefit of the country and his own sake, as many would think he had profited from the deal.

The minister had told me earlier that he regretted my sending the letter. "You didn't need to put this into writing. You know that we have an oral culture in Africa." I wanted to say that I preferred a moral culture, but I bit my tongue. The president was even more livid. For two hours, in his opulent palace, he defended himself against suspicions of corruption. When he denounced donor overreactions to "rumors," I pointed out that the one about the bonus had come true. I urged him to be more open with his own people, if he wished to head off suspicions and unpleasant letters in the future.

But openness was not in his nature. Three months later, there had still been no parliamentary briefing or public statement on the use of the bonus. Behind the scenes, the government had frozen the remainder of the money and taken steps to set up the oversight committee. But the Chadian people and the press were still in the dark.

So, in December 2000, when a French reporter asked me whether Chad had used some oil money for military purposes, I had little choice but to tell him the whole story. I explained the extenuating circumstances, but did not defend the government's actions. The next week, I did the same with *The Washington Post*, which almost retracted its original endorsement of the project. Most observers were pleased that the Bank had taken strong action, but they wondered what would happen when the "real" money began to flow. Although I was unpopular in Chad for a while, the episode proved salutary. Chad now knew that the world, not just the World Bank, would be following their every move. And there was little doubt that the Bank meant business.

More disappointments lay ahead. After the first round of presidential elections in May 2001, just days after Chad's debt relief had been approved, the president locked up the six opposition candidates twice in the same week, once only briefly and then for a couple of days. International pressure, including a call from Wolfensohn, forced a change of mind, but only after one of the candidates had been physically beaten. In addition, a demonstration of women in the main street of the capital was broken up violently. But the president won the second round of elections.

The pipeline was opened in October 2003 and remains controversial. Some local citizen groups have dismissed the elaborate pipeline agreements as "papier mâché" and complained that oil revenues have not yet had a significant effect on poverty. In July

2005, the World Bank said it was "very concerned" by the delayed delivery of services to the poor and by the opaque procedures still being used in awarding some government contracts.[1] And, in September 2005, Amnesty International issued a rather theoretical report speculating that the human rights of Chadians were now in the hands of unelected multinational corporations rather than the government.[2]

The story will not end there. Until Chad's political culture is more open and safe, question marks will remain about the future use of the oil. In the meantime, the sometimes topsy-turvy partnership between oil companies and an international development institution has proved fruitful. Not only has it offered pointers to making future development projects more promising, but it has also created real possibilities of progress for one of the poorest countries on earth.

CHAPTER 11

A CLASH OF VALUES

Unfortunately, international good will and imaginative arrangements like the Chad–Cameroon pipeline will not help Africa, as long as Westerners and African governments disagree on what is important. This clash of values takes many forms.

In November 1992, I spent four days in the Tai National Park in the western Ivory Coast, near the borders of Liberia and Guinea. The first day, we sweated heavily as we hiked up an airless track under the low canopy of the primeval forest. Suddenly, one of the group, a World Bank vice president, who was also a passionate birdwatcher, stumbled in front of us. As we helped him up, we saw he had landed on both his hands just inches above a bamboo stake pointed straight at his heart. The bamboo had been slashed with a machete by those clearing the way ahead of us. The skin on his chest was broken, but only superficially, so no harm was done. But I could not understand why our visitor had dropped like a stone. That evening, I found out. As we stretched out on a large tarpaulin after dinner, he removed three mammoth bird encyclopedias from his knapsack to identify species we had encountered during the day. I wished international conservation groups could see this senior World Bank official curled up like a boy under a Christmas tree, lost in an adventure story, in the flickering light of the hurricane lamps.

Tai is one of the few remaining clusters of forest in Central and Western Africa dating back 50,000 years. The rest of Africa's forests were wiped out by a major drought 8,000 years ago and grew back later. So the area is rich in botanical and zoological life, including red colobus monkeys, leopards, chimpanzees, and pygmy hippopotamuses. The young park director accompanied us, along with four armed guards on the look-out for dangerous poachers, not animals. We enjoyed being in one of the few parts of the country where loggers and farmers had been kept at bay. The whole of the time, we were conscious that it was the rough terrain and absence of good roads—not government policy or local good will—which were keeping this area intact.

If there was any doubt about this, as we left the park, we were reminded of just how difficult it is to promote conservation, even among the people responsible for it. On arriving in the area the previous Thursday, we had learned that forest guards had confiscated 25 gray parrots from poachers. We asked to see them and discovered the magnificent birds crowded together, nearly suffocated, in a long covered wicker basket. The park director instructed the guards to release the birds that day. When we came out of the forest three days later, I asked my driver (who had stayed behind) what had happened, and he said with bright innocence: "Oh, they have been kind enough to give me two to take back to my children in Abidjan." I kept quiet, knowing we would accomplish nothing if we gave the birds back to the guards. So the World Bank team released the two birds the next morning at a monkey research station 20 miles to the north. I didn't know what happened to the other 23, but the park director reacted grimly to the news and was clearly going to lower the boom after we left.

Sometimes, earnest Western-run conservation schemes can turn into simple protection rackets. In February 2001, I "adopted" two giant sea turtles on the Cameroon coast for $15 each. A Dutch-supported biodiversity project had persuaded local fishermen to hand over turtles caught in their nets, for a fee that was intended to compensate the fishermen for lost income and dissuade them from selling the turtles in the market. Restaurants in town were urged not to buy the turtles for meat, and hotel owners encouraged their guests to sponsor the creatures as part of their visit to the region. Tourists received "certificates of adoption" as sou-

venirs and were given a chance to see their turtles tagged and returned to the water. If they strayed again into the fishermen's nets,
they were to be put back into the sea. But it was all too easy to see
that this conservation formula was illusory. Fishermen could always tear off the tags and sell the luckless turtles in the market. In
fact, as I turned away from "my" turtles flapping with plodding ea-
gerness to freedom, I spotted two fishermen at a distance turning
their small boat sharply and moving steadily toward the creatures.

If parrots and turtles can illustrate opposing Western and
African values, the indifference of governments to broader issues
of poverty and democracy is even more graphic. In fact, poverty
in Africa is more of a Western issue than an African one. Most
African governments consider poverty to be as natural as the
wind or the rain, rather than something they can do anything
about. In the Ivory Coast, in the early 1990s, the Minister of Finance dozed with his head in his arms as his officials negotiated a
national policy statement with World Bank and IMF staff. He
stirred when he heard the word "poverty" mentioned. "Do we really need to use that word? Our people are not really poor." Told
that 60 percent of his fellow citizens were now below the poverty
line, he relented–and went back to sleep. Six years later, he left in
such a hurry during a military coup that American dollars littered
his bedroom floor, hours after he had emptied his safe and stuffed
his bags.

The same week the minister dozed, a senior Chinese official
visited the country. Later, he told me: "You know, people think my
country is authoritarian, but if we had ministers sporting French-
made suits and gold watches, and squalid slums right up against
garish mansions, we would have another revolution in 24 hours."

Despite mounting poverty, African politicians have regularly
increased their salaries—often discreetly, but sometimes brazenly,
too. In June 1993, the Ivory Coast's National Assembly doubled
the salaries of its members without a public announcement or debate. The pay increase and even the secrecy might have been
overlooked at other times. But civil service salaries had not been
adjusted for 12 years; people had rioted when the government
tried to reduce salaries by ten percent; and farmers' incomes had
been cut in half as a result of low world prices for cocoa and coffee. Were the parliamentarians embarrassed when word got out?

Not at all. Even the ten opposition members, who were heavily outnumbered in a chamber of 175 seats, defended the pay increase serenely.

Asked for an explanation, the opposition leader said he stood for better working conditions for everyone. So why should he pass them up for himself? He added that no great leader, religious or political, had ever led his people out of their misery by being miserable himself. "Neither Moses, nor Christ, nor Mohammed was poor. Nor were Marx, Engels, Lenin, De Gaulle, Mitterrand or George Washington." He was a history professor, but I wondered how recently he had consulted his sources. His defiance was reminiscent of the civil rights leader Ralph Abernathy's reported remark during the 1969 Poor People's Campaign in Washington, DC, when asked why he was staying in a hotel while his followers were in drenched tents on the National Mall: "My job is to dream dreams, and you don't dream dreams in the mud."[1] Then and now, Africans could not be consoled with zany historical parallels.

No matter what the state of their countries' economies, African ministers almost always travel first class. In the late 1970s, as a young diplomat visiting Somalia, I remember walking with my ambassador from the economy cabin to the forward section of the plane, as the local officials were waiting for us at the bottom of the first class stairway. That was where dignitaries were supposed to descend. Twenty-five years later, tight budgets have yet to affect ministerial travel. Such perquisites are considered part of public life. Even the nongovernmental organizations sitting on the Chad oil watchdog committee insisted on travelling first class and receiving diplomatic passports. The government refused their request; but its own ministers continued to travel in comfort.

Major African institutions can also stare absurdity in the face without blinking. In January 1994, the West African franc zone devalued its currency by 50 percent, meaning that the price of every imported article doubled automatically. But not everything was imported, and most employers decided against adjusting salaries until actual inflation was known, so as not to fan the flames of price increases. This included outside agencies like the World Bank, which had pressed hard for the devaluation and did not want to make matters worse for the economies of the zone. Its "little brother," the African Development Bank in Abidjan, felt no such sense of social responsibility. It doubled staff salaries immediately, leading to grotesque scenes of secretaries shopping along Abidjan's main streets, their purses bulging with banknotes.

Even senior African officials in international institutions at times let down their guard. I traveled once to Chad with one of the two Africans on the World Bank's Board of Directors. In a meeting with nongovernmental organizations on the controversial oil pipeline project, my senior colleague adopted a near-threatening tone. "Don't press your case too hard," he told them, "or you may simply scare away the investors." While there was a kernel of truth to this, he could have found a more considerate way of saying it, and at the same time encouraged a public debate. On the way back to Washington, we stopped in the Ivory Coast, where the president was trying to disqualify his leading opponent from running in the upcoming elections. As we left the airplane, my colleague said: "I don't know why he doesn't behave like all other African heads of state: Rig the elections, say 'sorry,' and then carry on as before." There were no signs of a "new Africa" that day.

Six years before, the same president expressed similar sentiments to me. He had invited me for a farewell lunch at the end of my three-year posting in Abidjan. Toward the end of the lunch, he asked for some parting advice. I suggested he set up an independent commission to organize the next elections. "Do you have such a thing where you're from, and does it work?" he asked me sharply. "Yes," I replied, "and it works very well." "Well, what's good enough for Haiti, Burkina Faso and Burundi is good enough for me." (He could not have chosen three more dubious models for crafting his country's electoral code.) Then I suggested he expand his interest in family planning into heading the national effort to combat HIV/AIDS. "I'll think about it," he said serenely. By the time the new century dawned, he had done almost nothing about it, and his country's infection rate was out of control.

In a sense, he was only reflecting public indifference. A year before, I had attended a three-day meeting on HIV/AIDS at the national parliament, along with 1,500 other people, all of them supposedly interested in combating the disease. One of the first speakers, a woman doctor, reported on a recent survey at the university that suggested that 30 percent of students still did not use contraceptives. This seemed surprisingly low to me, and probably untrue; but, of course, the doctor's concern was that the level was still too high. She added that some students had as many as 14 different sex partners per month. I gulped. But the crowd of researchers, health workers, and public officials erupted in a wave of laughter at the antics of these young people. Humor is one of Africa's greatest resources. But, that day, the ripples of enjoyment in the audience seemed to say that the coin had yet to drop.

On another occasion, I talked to 600 business students in the French cultural center. At the end of a long presentation, I appealed to their sense of public awareness and service: "Too many women are illiterate in this country. They are pregnant too often and too many of them contract AIDS. You can do something about this." Even before I had finished the sentence, there was a hubbub in the hall, signaling embarrassment that I had raised these "sensitive" subjects. Even the cabinet minister sitting next to me leaned over and groaned, "Oh, why did you have to bring *that* up?" But I stared the audience down, and continued: "If nothing is done about this, it will be a catastrophe for the whole society." Inwardly, of course, I was sad that young educated people, in a position to set an example, should be so uneasy talking about these issues even among themselves.

In other respects, too, senior government officials live such detached lives that even basic gestures to the business community, let alone the poor, can seem superfluous to them. In 2002, I toured a community road project in a poor district of Gabon's capital, Libreville, with the Minister of Planning. It was his first visit to the neighborhood. Even more surprisingly, later that day he set foot in the country's main port for the first time. He had been planning minister for 14 years, and prime minister before that, but had never found time to explore one of the basic arteries of the economy. Even then, it was almost by accident. The only reason he had left his office that day was that I was accompanied by the second most important official at the World Bank.

The higher African officials go in the hierarchy, the greater their sense of entitlement. I have been in very poor villages that offered goats, poultry, or rice to us as a mark of their hospitality. Not wanting to offend our hosts, we would invent an elegant excuse for not accepting the gifts (our vehicles were too small, for instance) or ask if we could donate them in turn to a local women's group. But, half the time, the local officials, who earned six or seven times what the villagers did, would mutter under their breath: "If you can't accept their hospitality, we'll be happy to do so instead." Sometimes, they would even nab the goats and put them in their cars before we had a chance to object.

The distance between government officials and their subjects was made plain during a trip I took to the central Ivory Coast in September 1993. Earlier that year, I had been asked by a young friend whether I had ever been to a village in the interior. I said, "Of course, to quite a few." He persisted: "But have you ever spent the night there?" When I shook my head, he said "Well, that doesn't count," and he invited me to a tree-planting event in his home village the following month. I accepted immediately.

Shortly afterward, my young friend invited me to lunch at his sister's home in the capital. Neither she nor a second brother believed that the World Bank representative was prepared to spend a weekend without running water or electricity. Two days later, I had a third visit—this time from their eldest brother, upset that the "young people" had invited a "personality" to the village without consulting him. A retired civil servant, he tried to convince me to stay at a nearby hotel and commute to the village each morning.

I explained that I had camped in the bush and doubted his village would be less comfortable than that. But my prospective hosts were facing problems of protocol. The district governor was reluctant to let me spend two days in his area without accompanying me. I asked my visitor to tell the district governor politely that I would stop by to say hello, but that he should not feel obliged to leave his wife and family for the weekend on my behalf.

A few days later, we stopped off to greet the governor, who also tried to persuade me to stay at a hotel rather than carry on "deep into the country"—just 15 miles away. He said that he would come for a couple of hours the next day to make certain that the villagers were looking after me properly.

He needn't have worried. When we arrived after dark, my driver was asked to keep our headlights lit, while young girls brought flowers, older women swayed their hips in celebration, and a large crowd applauded. Behind the house where I was to spend the night, several groups of dancers showed off their skills and one of the village elders started to greet me on six-foot drums. One of his welcomes, translated for my benefit, went as follows: "A World Bank representative is like the pangolin [a cross between an ant-eater and armadillo] which spends most of its life in dark holes in the forest floor. When the pangolin emerges from its hole, everyone gathers around to admire it." This was a polite way of saying: "Where have you been all this time?"

The next day, I helped plant trees around the village and was made an honorary chief. Then, under a roof of palm leaves, I gave a talk to several hundred people about protecting the local environment and creating economic opportunities for young people. The talk lasted three hours, as my remarks (in French) were translated successively into the local language and then again into a regional one for the benefit of the immigrant population of the village.

During the ensuing debate, I shocked my host's eldest brother, who I now learned was the senior representative of the ruling party. Someone asked why their village of 3,000 people still had no clinic after years of asking for one. I said that every village of their size had the right to at least *one* dispensary, but that the World Bank was as helpless as the villagers in ensuring this would happen. I explained that we had provided $50 million to the government's health and education budgets to improve basic services in the rural areas, but very little progress had been made. Our only recourse was to hold back the remaining $100 million. The current Minister of Health, I said, was certainly a serious man, but somewhere between him and this village—and hundreds of others as well—the wrong choices were being made. As my words were translated, I heard a collective gasp in the audience. These figures were immense, compared with the $400-$500 they earned each year. But just as unbelievable was the extent of the waste, disorganization, inertia, and dishonesty I had revealed to them.

The party official protested that it was unfair to ask such questions as I was not in a position to make any decisions. The village needed to be patient. Eventually, it would be included in the government's plans. I countered that I would be glad to speak for the village back in Abidjan, as we needed to cite concrete examples in general policy discussions in the capital. Later, I learned that my persistence had given people hope that solutions were possible. But the party official remained incensed that I had shared these facts. I had come out of my "hole," but he did not want the villagers to come out of theirs.

Five years later, American journalists in Uganda commented on a new World Bank training program that required managers to spend a week in a village somewhere in the world becoming familiar with the day-to-day facts of poverty. "I wish," said one of the correspondents, "that more government officials spent time in villages, too."

Officials in many countries do spend time in villages, but the surroundings are almost too familiar to them. Where visitors see misery, they see the slow march of progress. Or they shower their families and home villages, if they can, with "favors" like roads and clinics that other parts of the country must do without. African leaders water their roots, but their sensitivity, imagination, and ambition do not stray very far from home.

Fortunately, some of Africa's positive values thrive despite adversity and poor leadership. As I prepared to leave the Ivory Coast in late 1994, I was struck by the image of university students walking slowly between streetlights in our neighborhood, with books in their hands memorizing their lessons for upcoming examinations. Why were they studying outside? Because the families they lived with, their parents or guardians, could not afford to keep the lights switched on long enough for late-night studies. I had seen this many times before but the scene now seemed more poignant—and hopeful. Here was determination, not privation, and the resilience that Africans needed in fighting for political freedom and economic opportunity.

The warmth and generosity of Africans were also on display. I invited four hundred people to a farewell reception, but not everyone could come. The last day I was at the office, the phone rang:

"It's Simon here . . ."

"Oh, hello, Mr. Birba. How are you?" [He was a successful restaurant and hotel owner in the Western region whose spirit I had admired during a visit six months before. He was also illiterate.]

"What a memory you have, Mr. Calderisi! I'm calling because I have just this minute received the invitation to your cocktail, and I want you to know how touched I am. If I had known in time, I would have walked all the way to Abidjan, if necessary, to attend it. I'm just a little mosquito and you wanted me among your guests!"

"Mr. Birba, you're not a 'mosquito'," I insisted. "You're accomplishing great things."

A major newspaper printed a farewell article about me, saying that I had been a "great friend" of Ivorian society, that I had opened the Bank office to people from all walks of life, and that I had never "kept my tongue in my pocket." (That is a compliment in French West Africa.)[2]

The same week, my secretary told me that "some villagers" were waiting downstairs to see me. It was a delegation from nine villages I had visited a couple of times that year. They were carrying a typewritten "resolution," with four pages of signatures attached, expressing their appreciation for my help and using the local names that had been given to me and my partner during our stay. The resolution raised me to the rank of honorable member of their cooperative ("because we have nothing else to offer you"), prayed that the Almighty would give "Gode" (Jean Daniel) and "Bobo" (me) prosperity and a long life, and ended: "May the new earth that receives you be like honey."

PART IV

FACING THE FUTURE

CHAPTER 12

TEN WAYS OF CHANGING AFRICA

Given all the obstacles to mutual understanding, economic progress, and effective aid, how should Westerners and Africans react to the 40 years of disappointment they have suffered since Independence in the 1960s?

The rest of the world can now do very little for Africa, except support those already fighting for better government and a decent life there. Maintaining the status quo may well ease the West's sense of historical and racial guilt, and slow down migration to a degree. But there should be no illusion that current policies will make a lasting difference to the daily lives of most Africans. In 2025, Western consciences will still be itching and there will still be floods of immigrants moving north, because Africa's underlying problems will not have been solved. The following suggestions are meant to change that.

Few of these recommendations are original, but some highlight issues that have been treated as marginal until now; others take current trends in international affairs to a more logical, starker conclusion; still others challenge conventional prescriptions, like the need for more aid. Some are radical and may appear unreasonable. Undoubtedly, they will violate tradition and political correctness; but the time for half-measures is past.

Africans need the clear support of their friends abroad. If Western governments are reluctant to alter their ways, citizen groups can take up the cause and press for such improvements. Some of these initiatives will be disruptive in the short term, but will help the continent more than billions of dollars of foreign aid have done in the past.

1. INTRODUCE MECHANISMS FOR TRACING AND RECOVERING PUBLIC FUNDS

The world's greatest gift to Africa's democrats would be to stop the amassing of illegal fortunes by its politicians and senior officials in foreign banks. Serious controls in this area would have to resemble current global efforts to undermine terrorist financing networks. The laborious process of tracking down the assets of military strongmen like Mobutu of Zaire has only served to hearten other high-level thieves across the continent. In October 2003, the Nigerian authorities were forced to sue the British government in the civil courts to secure assistance in recovering up to $5 billion thought to have been stolen by the country's late dictator, General Abacha. More than three years earlier (June 2000), the Nigerians had asked the British government for bank statements and other evidence to trace funds laundered through UK banks; they received nothing. Even the Swiss, renowned for their secretiveness, had been more cooperative. To Africans, who for years have been told to fight corruption, such inertia seems hypocritical. Closing safe havens for illicit money would be a major building block of political reform in Africa.

2. REQUIRE ALL HEADS OF STATE, MINISTERS, AND SENIOR OFFICIALS TO OPEN THEIR BANK ACCOUNTS TO PUBLIC SCRUTINY

Openness about personal finances would build confidence within the African public and identify those with something to hide. Would this mean prying into the private affairs of thousands of African officials? Yes. But the tracking system does not need to be very sophisticated. In a continent as poor as Africa, there should not be many legitimate millionaires in government—not yet, in any case. As African corruption is the worst in the world, officials should long ago have lost the right to have unexamined bank accounts. If countries refuse to accept such constraints, they should not be asking for aid. Regardless of the positions taken by outsiders, Africans themselves should press for such a reform.

3. CUT DIRECT AID TO INDIVIDUAL COUNTRIES IN HALF

Contrary to conventional recommendations, direct foreign aid to most African countries should be reduced, not increased. Out of necessity, leaner budgets would be better managed. There would be greater competition for resources among nations and more time to select, prepare, and supervise projects in the few countries that met stringent criteria.

Some of the savings from direct country aid could be channeled to more general purposes such as the establishment of regional universities, multi-country infrastructure projects, agricultural research, and cross-border HIV/AIDS initiatives. Such efforts would benefit several countries at a time or, for that matter, the entire continent.

Abundant aid offers false hope, dampens the initiative to develop the continent's own resources, including its people, and calms Western consciences while dulling them to the even greater horrors that lie ahead. Bad policy and the continued departure of trained personnel will exacerbate the spread of disease, famine, unemployment, and desperation. Only political change can offer hope of a turnaround on those fronts.

4. FOCUS DIRECT AID ON FOUR TO FIVE COUNTRIES THAT ARE SERIOUS ABOUT REDUCING POVERTY

Serious countries should be taken out of the "intensive care" unit. They no longer need the close monitoring they have received until now; instead, they should be given more generous and flexible support. Unfortunately, there are only five of them: Uganda, Ghana, Mozambique, Tanzania, and perhaps Mali. The number could grow as political systems throughout the continent are opened up, corrupt leaders are replaced, and the benefits of self-directed development become clear. In contrast, governments that are indifferent to poverty, cannot guarantee basic education for their citizens, or offer only lip service to fighting HIV/AIDS, should not be helped at all. Governments that lie in between these two extremes should still receive aid, but with strict conditions until their own sense of determination impresses the rest of the world.

The international community should give the five serious countries the equivalent of blank checks. They have earned that latitude. If they meet certain desired objectives, the assistance can be repeated in two or three years' time. If they do not, they will need to fall back into the pack and have international bodies look over their shoulders again.

The international community should stop providing *any* form of budget aid, except to those five countries, and then on such a massive scale as to allow them to reap permanent benefits from their policies and programs. If they prove unable to use it all in the short term, the rest of the money could be put into an endowment fund that would be drawn down over time. Some countries would "graduate" from the group once they no longer needed aid; but the group would remain small and the criteria for entering the group would be exceptionally tough. All new aid should be in the form of grants.

5. REQUIRE ALL COUNTRIES TO HOLD INTERNATIONALLY-SUPERVISED ELECTIONS

It is time for aid to become more openly political. All African countries receiving assistance should now be expected to meet minimum standards of open political debate and fair elections. The merits of this suggestion will be obvious to Western readers, but it will nettle African leaders who have insisted on their own pace and style of political progress. They have reason to resist. In a true contest of talent, knowledge, and values, most of them would be booted out of office

International supervision of elections would need to be highly organized and well-staffed, and would have to begin months rather than days before elections took place. Among other things, election supervisors would have to give close attention to the preparation of voter registration lists and ensure that the opposition had access to state-owned media.

Political, economic, and social reforms should be promoted in parallel. For a long time, American insistence on democracy as a central feature of development was regarded in Europe as simplistic and fundamentalist. Skeptics pointed to autocratic countries such as Korea, Taiwan, China, and Indonesia that had achieved major economic and social progress before introducing political reforms. For a time, there was also a reasonable hope that African countries could be coaxed into changing their ways. Instead, like people on their deathbeds, most African leaders are still in denial or in a mood to bargain. They still want to be "rewarded" for doing the right thing, rather than doing it for its own sake.

Over the years, donor agencies have learned the importance of public participation and open debate in everything they do. Yet they have been bound by old-fashioned rules to talk about "governance" rather than government and to avoid direct links between politics and economics. Even Jim Wolfensohn, the imaginative and tireless president of the World Bank, was unable to drag human rights to the center of the development debate, as he did with corruption and debt relief.

Western reluctance to interfere in the political process was based on sound principles. Like individuals, countries were considered to have a right to privacy, unless they invaded their neighbors or committed acts of genocide. It was understood that one was not to do in Chad what was unacceptable in China. But Africa has suffered terribly as a result of such restraint, and Africans themselves have long been impatient with foreigners who reinforced dictatorships by their "neutrality."

Now it can be argued that African governments *are* committing acts so reprehensible that past courtesies should be abandoned. Referring to the 30 million African children who have died of preventable diseases in the last ten years, the former Africa editor of the *Financial Times*, Michael Holman, has said: "It is true that they are not victims of genocide. But they are victims, nonetheless, of neglect on a genocidal scale."[1] Holman believes the "stench of hypocrisy" marks Western governments that have not honored their solemn promises of greater aid to the continent. But, in my view, Africa needs a shake-up before those promises can be kept, and the old "hands-off" rules should be set aside for at least the next 20 years.

Aid should be denied to all governments which refuse to hold internationally supervised elections, suppress minority views, or tamper with a free press. Such a change of policy might cause some governments to fall, and jolt others into realizing that they can no longer count on Western guilt to bail them out of their difficulties. The international community has been moving toward more in-trusive rules and cross-country comparisons on "governance." These need to be toughened further —and enforced. If this results in lower aid than planned, so be it. Africa needs new leaders, ideas, approaches, and technologies much more than it needs money. Smaller aid budgets will nurture real political—not just economic—development.

Some Westerners still think that Africa is not "ripe" for democracy. They should consider the long lines of people in elec-tion after election, waiting in the searing sun for hours to cast their votes. In Ethiopia, in May 2005, the voter turnout was 85 percent; unfortunately, the election results were not announced until September 2005 and in November 2005, 33 people died, protesting alleged irregularities in the vote. Africans are prepared to make their choice. They just need to be offered one.

6. PROMOTE OTHER ASPECTS OF DEMOCRACY, INCLUDING A FREE PRESS AND AN INDEPENDENT JUDICIARY

Proper elections are not enough. Laws that protect heads of state from insult are an insult to Africans. They reinforce a leader's tra-ditional right to swagger and stamp out independent views and dissent. Thin-skinned Africans should stay out of politics.

Similarly, governments that put even one journalist in prison for expressing personal views should face the court of international public opinion within 24 hours. Where governments persist in such tyranny, aid projects and even commercial transactions carry-ing some official Western stamp should be interrupted within 48 hours. Should those pressures fail, international corporations deal-ing with such governments should be forced to account to their shareholders or consumers. Also, governments refusing to hold independent inquiries into the death or disappearance of journalists should be placed in quarantine. It is strong, concrete responses like these that have lagged behind verbal Western appeals for better government, and left most Africans wondering how much foreign governments really care about their freedom.

Granted, such measures would be harsh. It is difficult to interrupt construction of a power dam without raising costs or creating engineering risks. But few actions are more damaging to a nation's health—and emblematic of a government's values—than the rough treatment of journalists. Better to raise the cost of major projects than devalue the importance of an independent voice in public policy.

Another initiative the international community should undertake is increased support for credible pressure groups in Africa. This support is vital for the emergence of a more open society. Cultural exchange programs, such as those of the United States Information Agency, which have hosted thousands of African intellectuals and professionals on study tours of the United States and Europe, have had a profound effect. Small grants to support democracy and human rights groups are also valuable. Novel approaches, such as subsidizing the cost of newsprint for small publishers, should also be tried.

7. SUPERVISE THE RUNNING OF AFRICA'S SCHOOLS AND HIV/AIDS PROGRAMS

Every aid official knows enough about the links between schooling and the health and prosperity of entire societies to make primary schooling an absolute priority. How feasible would this be across 48 very different countries? As feasible as any other major project where firm purpose and massive resources are applied—such as the overthrow of the Taliban in Afghanistan in 2001.

What would this mean? Most officials currently involved in administration and teaching would stay in place, but they would be supervised by international personnel—100–150 per country—to prevent the siphoning off of funds and abuses at the local school level. These supervisors do not all need to be Westerners. Many expatriate Africans would undoubtedly be willing to return home for extended contracts on attractive salaries, in order to be part of such a noble enterprise.

The goal of such a system would be to keep everyone of school age enrolled and improve the quality of teaching and learning. Support measures would include eliminating all school fees, subsidizing textbooks and uniforms, and compensating poor families for the loss of their children's labor; upgrading the quality of teachers and raising their salaries; building safer and cleaner schools; and making curricula more suitable to local cultures. Little new research would be needed. Current knowledge just needs to be put into action. The resources already being approved by national parliaments must be made to reach the schools.

In 20 years, it might be possible to restore full control to Ministries of Education, but in the interim an entire generation—the first since the 1970s—would be given a fair chance to make it on its own. If there is success at the primary level, a similar formula could be applied to secondary, vocational, and university education.

The fight against HIV/AIDS is also too important to leave to the whims of African governments. The scale of organization needed to provide information to vulnerable groups, and the logistical network required for storing and distributing pharmaceutical products, is without precedent for most countries. Reductions in the price of HIV/AIDS drugs have created opportunities yet to be exploited in Africa, partly for practical reasons, but also because of inadequate political commitment. Countries that have put themselves on a war footing, for flimsier reasons, in the past need to be accompanied by the international community on this new battleground rather than left to react as local resources, fatalism, and prejudice allow.

8. ESTABLISH CITIZEN REVIEW GROUPS TO OVERSEE GOVERNMENT POLICY AND AID AGREEMENTS

Donor efforts to consult public opinion in African countries are admirable; however, they are also makeshift, superficial, and unrepresentative. African countries should see the value of establishing independent sounding boards that would offer the public—and even parliamentarians—a detached view on national issues. Such citizen groups could review proposed government agreements with outside interests, including Western donors and private investors, and offer their support, or a rationale for backing out of such arrangements.

Many African countries have economic councils stuffed with "eminent personalities," that is, friends of current and former regimes. As a result, these councils are usually an uncritical elite, sitting on their privileges rather than exercising any independent judgment. Even properly elected national parliaments can have odd priorities. Soon after taking office, Nigeria's Senate and House of Representatives voted themselves large increases in salaries and benefits and threatened to hold up passage of the national budget if their demands were not met. The government was chagrined but could do little about it.

Citizen review groups, like the oil revenues watchdog group in Chad, would be above politics, oversee government officials, and act as a filter for public initiatives. International agreements that did not pass muster with such groups would stand little chance of ratification in Parliament; if the proposals met this test, the public would be more confident that their elected representatives were acting in the national interest.

Creating such groups would not be easy. So as not to duplicate existing institutions, the members would have to be chosen on merit and seen to be independent. They would be nominated by major non-governmental bodies: religious associations, labor unions, human rights groups, women's organizations, business federations, journalist networks, environmental activists, and law societies. Not normally attracted to positions in government or politics, members should have demonstrated an interest in serving the public in other ways. To ensure their dedication and objectivity, they could serve rotating two- or three-year terms. They would have a budget for research and travel and be empowered to issue their own reports. Their audience would be the government and general public, not foreign donors.

9. PUT MORE EMPHASIS ON INFRASTRUCTURE AND REGIONAL LINKS

Aid resources not devoted to individual countries should be focused increasingly on targets of common rather than national interest, such as agricultural research, control of infectious diseases, and regional communication and transportation links.

Not enough is being done to meet the tremendous need for infrastructure–roads, ports, railways, water, power, and telecommunications facilities. Like the sinews and blood vessels of a human body, they determine the strength of the whole. When they are weak, whole economies will be stunted and poverty will remain deep and widespread. To expand markets and improve regional cooperation, the disparate parts of Africa must be bound more closely together–not just politically, economically, and culturally, but also physically.

A strong infrastructure spreads economic opportunities and social progress, permits a more even sharing of the fruits of development, and may also reduce the potential for discord. It draws together people and talent, knowledge and experience. Better roads can bring clinics or schools closer to the people who need them. Even small village bridges can make an enormous difference to people living at the margins of society.

Most of these projects will be small, and much of the financing will be domestic or private. But when such projects are large, Africa's friends must help design them in a way that protects the environment and local communities, while offering the possibility of breakthroughs to a better life.

10. MERGE THE WORLD BANK, IMF
AND UNITED NATIONS DEVELOPMENT PROGRAMME

This suggestion is more radical than it seems. The three institutions at the center of international development policy have guarded their different raisons d'être jealously. Yet their rivalry and conflicting objectives have led to confusion in the advice they give to Africa. They have ignited unnecessary arguments, sometimes put ideology ahead of the facts, wavered between clear prescriptions and polite ones, and dispersed resources over a wide field.

These three organizations are as compatible as oil and water. The Bank prides itself on investing in the long-term health of economies. The IMF's approach is more short-term, orthodox, and rigid. If international coffee prices go up, the Bank will want small farmers to get a larger share of the revenues; the IMF is likely to want governments to use them to reduce the public deficit or debt. The United Nations Development Programme (UNDP) does not take positions on such delicate matters. It focuses on supporting institutional or "capacity-building" initiatives that appear sound, but are often tame and at the margin of a country's problems (such as decentralization studies). It has very little money and more diplomats than technical specialists. To make matters worse, the World Bank and IMF are constantly quarrelling, despite negotiating a series of "coordination agreements" over the last 20 years. Both look down on the UNDP as amateur and lightweight. UNDP staff, in turn, loathe the two Washington institutions as deeply unrepresentative instruments of the wealthy countries, filled with elite analysts removed from personal contact with the poor.

All three agencies serve the broad goals of the United Nations in their individual ways. It would be more efficient and clear to consolidate their efforts, but the merger would be complicated. The IMF is responsible for monitoring economic developments not just in Africa but in all countries, including rich ones. The Bank is proud of its ability to raise funds in the international capital markets; its board is dominated by Western countries rather than subjected to the one country–one vote formula that sometimes paralyzes the UN General Assembly. And the UNDP is glad to reflect the views of all nations and be seen as everyone's friend.

A merger of the institutions would combine the strengths of all three. At least initially, Africa would be only a part of the new body's overall mission; however, all developing countries would benefit from its more coherent services. As other developing nations became self-reliant, Africa would move to the center of the new UN institution's agenda. Combining the three institutions would also free up thousands of their staff. Instead of being administrators and researchers, they could become school inspectors and election observers.

Any one of these proposals would contribute to changing the human environment of Africa. Taken together, they would provide a major boost to democracy and encourage activists across the continent to deepen their efforts and join hands across national boundaries to change the face of political discourse. Such reforms would create a real chance for young people unable to get a proper education, and also offer hope to those infected with HIV/AIDS.

The suggestion that overall aid levels should be reduced may seem mean-spirited. What is $25 billion a year for Africa (with its 600 million people) compared with the $200 billion spent in 2003 and 2004 on the war in Iraq (an oil producer, with only 25 million people)? What about the $350 billion that the European Union devotes to protecting its farmers?

The costs of the Iraq war certainly dwarf the amounts of assistance that Africa receives. But that does not justify wasting aid money. European agricultural subsidies actually achieve their objective: young farmers are staying on the land and rural landscapes are being preserved. That is not true for Africa. Aid budgets are shrinking because they have been ineffective, and the challenge is to manage those diminishing amounts more productively.

Under these proposals, some of the money denied to individual countries would go to general programs that would benefit them indirectly. If countries were prepared to hold internationally supervised elections or allow outside supervision of primary education and HIV/AIDS programs, they could receive aid for those purposes. If, on top of that, they attracted global attention by their own actions and a change of priorities (such as an interest in first-rate schools rather than first-class tickets), they could begin receiving substantial assistance for other purposes. In those circumstances, there might even be a case for pushing aid volumes back to historical levels. But that would require real change and hard evidence that governments were behaving differently.

Foreign aid, one might counter, is already dwindling. So why accelerate the process? Because aid is slowing the process of political change in Africa. For a long time, direct involvement in a large number of countries was considered necessary so as to have some influence, however refracted and obscured, on national policymaking. In the soft jargon of aid professionals, it was important to have "a place at the table." In most countries, we should now just walk away from it.

In doing so, we would respect Julius Nyerere's lucid thinking of a generation ago: "If our effort slackens, [donors] will—and they should—lose interest in cooperating with us for our benefit. And, in any case, we have no right to rely upon these countries. We can accept their willingness to help us become self-reliant; we must not think of them as sources of charity which excuse us from work and sacrifice. . . . There is a time for planting and a time for harvesting. I am afraid for us it is still a time for planting."[2]

How much influence would outsiders then have on Africa's development? Ostensibly less than before, but perhaps more in practice as the aid would be finite and Western words more believable. If support were centered on the serious countries, little leverage would be needed. The "game" would have changed. There would be no tug-of-war: Everyone would be pulling in the same direction. And if other countries needed an incentive, other than intelligent policies for their own sake, they would have the example of the serious countries benefiting steadily from self-propelled reforms.

What is so special about the five exceptions, Uganda, Tanzania, Mozambique, Ghana, and Mali? Most of these countries suffered prolonged political turmoil but emerged serious about the future; Tanzania is the only one whose government was never overthrown. Ghana, Africa's first independent nation, has shown steady purpose and real economic and social success since 1981. In a sure sign of change and confidence, Ghanaians are returning home and investing their savings there. That is also happening in Uganda, where even the Asian community, which was expelled by Idi Amin in 1971, has begun to rebuild itself. Mozambique has gone from being a backwater of Marxism to a beacon of common sense; while it is still very poor, it has reduced poverty from 70 percent to 56 percent of the population in six years. Corruption is still widespread in all five countries, but the governments are making credible efforts to combat it. These countries are not perfect— Uganda and Tanzania bought new presidential jets shortly after receiving international debt relief—but no nation in the world is beyond reproach, and they stand head and shoulders above every other country receiving aid on the continent. In short, none of them deserves to be lectured any longer.

Is it reasonable to insist on international supervision of primary school and HIV/AIDS services? Would this not be even

more humiliating than traditional aid? Perhaps. But no government that is unwillling to look after the basic needs of its citizens
should want to hold its head very high. Past aid has been generous,
but dispersed. New aid should be tough and focused. If the West is
clear about its priorities, the African public—and perhaps a growing number of African leaders—will get the point.

Could some of these recommendations apply to other parts of
the developing world, like Central Asia and the Middle East? Undoubtedly, but their wider relevance should not obscure their ur-
gency for Africa. Would it not be more logical to stop all aid to
Africa, apart from emergency relief and occasional military intervention? Definitely. But that would amount to turning one's back
on a tenth of humanity. Are the proposals realistic? Some will certainly be controversial, but not less realistic than expecting conventional solutions to work. In many cases, giving aid to Africa
has been like giving money to a drunkard down the street expecting him to spend it on food. Current approaches provide an illusion of progress while forestalling real breakthroughs.

My suggestions will do little to help Nigeria and the Sudan
(which are oil producers) or the Democratic Republic of the
Congo (formerly Zaire), which is rich not only in raw materials
but also ethnic and political rivalries. These three countries account for a third of Africa's population, and are so large that you
can walk from one coast to the other by traversing only two of
them (Sudan and the Congo).

Nigeria, like South Africa, is almost a world onto itself. Formal
democracy has been restored, but the process of creating a truly informed and open society has barely begun. It does not need aid—
in fact, until recently, good-hearted efforts to provide it have been
frustrated by bad policy and corruption. Even the World Bank,
with a strong interest in supporting the new government, has been
unable to justify serious levels of lending. Better mechanisms for
tracking graft and recovering stolen money will certainly help
Nigeria reduce the tremendous corruption that infects national
life. Debt relief may also help, but only if it is managed properly.

Sudan is governed by a reclusive Islamist regime that has per-
sistently persecuted the Christian minority in the South. During
that time, it has also become independent of world opinion
through the development of oil reserves, financed with Chinese

and Malaysian money. While Exxon-Mobil and the World Bank were making the case for the Chad–Cameroon oil project, Sudan built a similar pipeline for itself without a proper environmental assessment. Instead of consulting the local population, let alone the world, the government used helicopter gun ships to subdue recalcitrant villagers along the pipeline route. Under US pressure, linked to the war on terrorism, the government put and end to a 25-year civil war with southern rebels. But implementation of that peace settlement was slow, and new ethnic trouble erupted in the western Darfur region, where Sudan has reluctantly accepted the presence of an African Union peacekeeping force.

In the country described by some as the "backbone of Africa," more radical action is necessary to give its 50 million people some hope of a normal life. The ill-named Democratic Republic of the Congo has been a slow-motion Rwanda over the last eight years, with an estimated four million deaths from warfare and starvation. Prime Minister Blair of the United Kingdom has proposed the establishment of a European military force to intervene in such troubled situations on the continent. But peaceful countries cannot be expected regularly to insert their militaries between warring factions in Africa.

It is difficult to conceive of an effective intervention short of a UN-led multinational administration of the entire country for an extended period. Such an intervention would be resisted by the various rebel groups still hoping to win control of the national government or their own regions (through secession, if necessary). It would also face serious risks—including the specter of UN soldiers killing Congolese for the sake of other Congolese. But the advantage would be that some of the resources that the world has devoted to other trouble spots (like Iraq) could now be diverted to saving the Congolese—not through aid but through direct administration and reconstruction. Humanity calls for it, and realpolitik will also be served: it would have a salubrious effect right across the troubled heart of the continent and demonstrate the world's commitment to treating Africa as a close relative rather than distant cousin.

Such intervention may not work, in which case the Congo should be allowed to break up. It is perhaps the most unstable of all the countries created during the colonial period, certainly the one with the deepest ethnic divisions and rivalry for resources, and the one most conspicuously kept afloat by geopolitical considerations during the Cold War. If international efforts fail there again, the most humane solution may be to let nature and nationalism take their course.

CHAPTER 13

A NEW DAY

Early in the 20th century, the French Prime Minister Georges Clemenceau had a problem. A tree in the garden next door was so large that it kept his study in the shade most of the day. Even worse, the neighbor was a Catholic priest and Clemenceau was so anti-clerical that he was reluctant to ask him a favor. Taking the problem upon himself, Clemenceau's secretary suggested that the cleric trim back the tree, which he did quite graciously. The next morning, the politician walked into a suddenly bright study and asked what had happened. His secretary proposed that Clemenceau now send the priest a note of thanks. "Out of the question!" he snapped. "How could I even address it properly? He's not my 'father'!" A few days later, the secretary found a note in the out-box: "Dear Father, I take the liberty of calling you that as you have allowed me to see the light of day . . ."

Many Africans would enjoy this story, because of their sense of humor and respect for hierarchy. Few, however, would see it as a parable for their continent. Much of Africa's potential, and the causes of its current difficulties, are hidden in the shade of major misconceptions—about the slave trade, colonialism, the World Bank, and so on—which simply need to be whittled away. Individual Africans have risen to the challenges confronting them for decades, but their governments have not; even worse, most leaders have stood in the way of individual initiative and innovative solutions, fearing some loss of control. African talents—at home and abroad—need to be given a chance to prosper. They need fresh air and light.

One day in the early 1990s, I visited a number of clinics outside the capital of the Ivory Coast. Most of them were filthy, dilapidated, and bare—lacking even syringes, bandages, and medicines. The personnel were idle, listless and, for obvious reasons, demoralized. In one clinic, a mother had been torn during a difficult birth, and the midwife had been forced to mend her with electrical copper wire. By the end of the morning, I too was disheartened. But, before returning to town, I passed by another clinic where the nurse met me at the door. She was well-dressed, clean, and plainly happy to have a visitor. The place was well-equipped and in good order. She had medicines, alcohol, and bandages. Her furniture was still usable. Her notebooks for patient follow-up were impeccable. And she was in the process of replacing wooden doors and windows that had been eaten away by termites.

What made the difference? Short of alternatives and unwilling to wait for the government, the nurse had convinced the women of the village to contribute to the running of the clinic. She had no water, so she had contacted an Italian charity to repair the well. She had the conviction, energy, imagination, and charm to compensate for the lack of normal structures. Thinking that perhaps she had just arrived and that her enthusiasm was understandable, I asked how long she had been there. Eleven years, she told me. This took my breath—and my discouragement—away.

Later that year, a couple of young friends asked me to support a banana-growing project. They already had jobs in the capital–one was a schoolteacher and the other an information programmer–but they wanted to help 100 young people in their home village use land that had been given to them by their parents. They needed $2,000 to buy banana cuttings, and I gave it to them.

A few months later, I asked the schoolteacher how the project was going. "Quite well," he answered, "after a few hurdles. First, I was arrested by the district governor who was worried that we were agitating for the opposition rather than engaged in a real development activity. I was released the next day, after telling them that the World Bank representative had contributed his personal funds to the project. The government then sent the Minister of Youth and Sports to investigate. He was so impressed that he gave us a medal in front of the whole village and promised us $20,000 to expand the project."

I did not want to dampen his excitement. After all, he had gone from jailbird to decorated local hero in the space of a week! But privately I was worried that the government was doing just what it had accused the young people of doing: making political capital out of a personal initiative. I was also concerned that the banana cooperative would now have more money than it could use wisely.

Six months later, the news was even better. The cooperative had grown from 100 to 400 members. The volume and quality of production were good, thanks to technical assistance from the national agricultural advisory service. And even the marketing was proving easier than they had imagined. People were coming in trucks, by bicycle, or on foot to buy the bananas and transport them as far away as the capital.

"So the government's money came in handy," I told the schoolteacher. There was a twinkle in my friend's eye. "They never gave us a penny," he said. "After the elections, they forgot about us entirely." "Then how did you finance all of this?" I asked. "With your $2,000 and the money we raised selling banana cuttings to new members," he replied. "I'm astonished," I said. He smiled. "You shouldn't be. You always told us that money was not the major obstacle to progress in Africa."

He was forgetting that he had received the start-up capital free of charge. But he certainly demonstrated how individual initiative and determination, good organization, and improved public services (in this case, the agricultural service) could turn a small investment into major improvements for people.

In Africa, people like the nurse and schoolteacher outnumber the scoundrels a hundred to one. But, unfortunately, through military intimidation, ethnic division, and the absence of any other experience of government, the scoundrels remain in charge.

Must a suffering and smiling Africa remain part of the sad poetry of human existence? I believe not. Major openings for individual opinion and initiative, combined with solid obstacles to graft and mismanagement, will transform the outlook for individual countries. If aid levels drop, some governments will collapse under their own weight. Others will be forced to take a new measure of their countries' possibilities, draw on local resources, and follow their own path rather than rely on outside money and advice. Eventually, that path may coincide with Africa's and the world's expectations of better government.

A hard-boiled skeptic might ask: Why bother? Does Africa even have a future? It is thoroughly respectable to think the continent should be left to its own fate. The author of a recent book, called *Al Qaeda and What it Means to be Modern*, suggests a hands-off approach to international affairs: "In a world containing many regimes and several economic systems, international institutions should be charged with framing minimum terms of peaceful coexistence . . . Unless a regime was a demonstrable threat to peace, no attempt would be made to induce it to alter its form of government. Even intolerable regimes would be tolerated so long as they posed no danger to others."[1]

It would certainly be easier to forget about Africa. But the continent will not go away, and it is not just liberals or idealists who are concerned about it. Newt Gingrich, the former Republican speaker of the US House of Representatives and self-styled futurist, has talked of the "offence" to human evolution that one tenth of the world's population should be excluded from material improvement.[2] Neo-conservatives, who believe in promoting democracy and free speech in improbable places like the Middle East, may also become increasingly appalled at the lack of human progress in Africa. And, in the bewildering line-up of emerging views on such subjects, neo-conservatives may find common ground with anti-globalizers, who are suspicious of a free market in goods and services but thoroughly attached to the free flow of ideas. In the words of George Monbiot, one of the most lucid and lively critics of globalization: "These people [who do not live in representative democracies], perhaps more than anyone else on earth, need international or global assistance, both to undermine their oppressive governments and to secure the peace and material prosperity those governments tend to deny them."[3]

Africa's future is hard to predict—except to say that, if current trends continue, it will be very dark indeed. But there can be no doubt that something has to change if Africa is not to become a graveyard as well as the birthplace of the human race. Because of its late start, it may take a long time for Africa to achieve its ambitions. In a material sense, it may never "catch up" with Europe or

North America or Japan. But it should be possible for Africa to assure its peoples a real improvement in their lives and a greater harmony between their physical resources, cultural traditions, natural environments, and material expectations. When he retired, the first African American judge on the United States Supreme Court, Justice Thurgood Marshall, was asked how he wanted to be remembered. He answered, "'I would like it to be said: 'He did what he could with what he had.'" Africa should at least be given the chance to do the same.

It is difficult to be optimistic about Africa. HIV/AIDS alone is cutting deeply into the potential, resilience, and social fabric of the continent. Sometimes, a sense of the long term overwhelms even those who are immensely talented and impatient for progress. Last year, a close African friend wrote me: "I am totally convinced that, in relative time, I am at best the son, if not the grandson, of people my own age. We live in the same period of absolute time—2005—but in relative time, from the point of view of urban life, and ideas of nation, culture, and civility, the others have just arrived from the bush. There, they were alone and could afford to be uncivil—the consequences were almost negligible. In a city of three million people, it's an entirely different matter. Those who raised me had known city life for several generations. So it will be the grandchildren of my contemporaries who will have the same sense of tolerance and understanding of the relativity of cultures which I have already."

But even in a bleak landscape there are encouraging signs. Most Africans are heroes, coping with obstacles that would have flattened the spirits of others. Ingenuity triumphs daily over adversity. I once met a man who had become a millionaire by shipping West African yams wrapped in colored tissue to Washington, DC. This puzzled me, as the people who bought the yams were Central American immigrants and I assumed they preferred more familiar produce from Nicaragua or El Salvador. In fact, they had developed a taste for West African yams and this entrepreneur had discovered it.

Small countries like Lesotho, which a generation ago was literally exporting its blood and is now selling water to South Africa and textiles to the United States, have demonstrated the power of some political stability and massive private investment.

There are signs of progress within individual governments, and even degraded institutions can offer surprises. In late 2004, a judge widely regarded as captive to the ruling party acquitted the Zimbabwean opposition leader Morgan Tsvangirai of planning the assassination of President Robert Mugabe. With international support, the African Union has begun serious peacekeeping efforts in places as different as Sudan and Somalia.

Some of Africa's talents are returning home. Nigeria's finance minister (and a former World Bank official), Ngozi Okonjo-Iweala, has brought common sense to an economy that has lacked it for decades. In November 2004, she commented publicly on the *disadvantages* of the sudden rise in international oil prices, which were proving hugely beneficial for Nigeria in the short term.[4] In October 2005, using some of these windfall earnings, she negotiated the most important debt relief agreement in the country's history. Previous finance ministers would have reveled rather than worried. Individuals like her and Ghana's Kofi Annan (who was unknown outside a tight circle before becoming UN Secretary-General) are among Africa's greatest assets.

Not all politicians have been corrupt, and some have stayed home. Jean-Paul Ngoupandé, the man I quoted on slavery and colonialism in Chapter 1, led a brief government of national unity in the Central African Republic in 1996–97. Later, he escaped several assassination attempts, including once by jumping out of the back window of his house. When he visited me at the World Bank office in Bangui in 2001, he arrived in a pick-up truck guarded by three highly-armed youths. Foreign friends have often asked him why he does not drop everything and move to Europe. His answer is an earthy proverb from the African interior: "The sparrow doesn't leave its nest just because it's full of bird droppings."[5] True to form, Ngoupandé agreed to serve as Foreign Minister in his country's new government, which was elected in April 2005.

Africa has had seven Nobel Prize winners, five of them from South Africa. Their awards have been in Literature and Peace, two fields that can flourish even in poverty and war.[6] There are probably hundreds of other potential African Nobel laureates emerging in science, medicine, and economics. Many of them study or work overseas, ready to return home if conditions allow.

Often by sheer will, human determination can triumph at home. "My mother never set foot in a school," an African friend told me, "but when I was ten years old, she decided to learn to read by asking us—her children—questions. She was the pillar of support for her five sons. Two became doctors—one in the humanities and the other in medicine. Three of us became engineers."

The rest of the world can contribute to liberating Africa. But Africans must take the most important steps. First, they should stop feeling sorry for themselves and expecting others to do so as well. Sympathy for Africa, like foreign aid, is drying up. Intellectuals and politicians must stop looking for excuses for their own failures, and understand that the future lies in unleashing African talent and enterprise, regardless of its regional or ethnic origins. They must do this in such a radical way that it will attract attention at home and abroad. In order for such talent to flourish, Africans must demand much more from their governments rather than accept that they are doomed to dictatorship or mere imitations of democracy. They do not need to take up arms. Solid investigative reporting by journalists, the creation of pressure groups, appeals to international opinion, and even civil disobedience, can all play a part.

Africa's "unofficial" friends—church groups in Montana, old-age pensioners in the United Kingdom, school children in France—can also contribute by championing a free press, supporting organizations like Reporters without Borders, and putting emphasis on improving primary education and fighting HIV/AIDS. The power of international citizen opinion to sway government and corporate outcomes should not be doubted, as was shown by the near-defeat of the Chad–Cameroon Oil Pipeline. In fact, public surveillance of that project is still fundamental to whether it succeeds or fails.

Many people will say that progress in Africa will be slow and that we must accept occasional setbacks as long as the broad direction is right. Some would add, as I would have done 20 years ago, that it is better to light a candle than to curse the darkness. In my view, we now know enough to just turn on the lights.

Despite its poverty, Africa has enormous resources at its disposal to build a better future. To use just one example, with its high mountains, virgin forests, and splendid beaches, a country like Cameroon could become a major international destination for eco-tourists—if it abolished entry visas and persuaded the police to stop harassing people. Costa Rica has become popular because it is so easy to visit, despite the fact that the country once cut down all its forests and allowed them to grow back as nature reserves. There are much more fauna and flora to be seen in Cameroon.

The 40 percent of Africa's savings currently held abroad are potentially available for investment at home. And there are the thousands of talented, experienced Africans overseas who could return if the political and economic outlook brightened. Africa also continues to enjoy the good will of many governments and private charities who have been trying to reach people more directly with their money and ideas.

One thing that has yet to collapse is the African spirit. Part of this stubbornness comes from the simple human instinct for survival. Another part comes from a reluctance to face the truth. At the height of apartheid, the oppressed black majority of South Africa probably lived better lives—in material terms—than those who were nominally "free" elsewhere on the continent. Even the descendants of millions of African slaves in the Western hemisphere, though still facing discrimination and unequal opportunities in some countries, have far greater access to health, education, and jobs than the average African.

Africans now need to assert themselves. Before any country in Africa was independent, Basil Davidson wrote in his *African Awakening* (1955): "All the way up and down Africa . . . there is desire for many-sided change, for movement into the modern world, for an end to subjection and a beginning of equality."[7] Five decades later, Africa is in a state of suspended hope. Only those familiar with the human beauty, potential, and suffering of the continent will dare hope for breakthroughs in the next ten years. More than others, they know that only Africans can break the cycle of terror, poverty, and mediocrity that keeps them subdued.

NOTES

INTRODUCTION

1. Excerpts of the letter of Yaguine Koita and Fode Tourkana, dated July 29, 1999, posted on the Jubilee 2000 website (jubilee2000uk.org).
2. Jean Ziegler's best-selling 2002 book, *Les nouveaux maîtres du monde* [*The New Masters of the World*], starts with the same story, but draws conclusions very different from mine. He implies the boys died because rich countries, multinational corporations, and global financial institutions have made it difficult for developing countries to raise enough domestic resources for development.
3. Sir Thomas Browne (1605–1682) in *Religio Medici*.
4. Ryszard Kapuscinski, *The Shadow of the Sun*, introduction.
5. John Gunther, *Inside Africa*, p. xxi.
6. Map of the World (Planisphere), included in the exhibition "Caliphs and Kings: The Art and Influence of Islamic Spain" at the Arthur M. Sackler Gallery, Smithsonian Institution, Washington, DC, Summer 2004.
7. Most notably in George N. Ayittey's *Africa Betrayed*.
8. Aminata Traoré, *Lettre au Président des Français à propos de la Côte d'Ivoire et de l'Afrique en général*, p. 29.
9. See also Martin Wolf, *Why Globalization Works*; Jagdish Bhagwati, *In Defense of Globalization*.
10. Samuel Brittan, "Democracy alone is not enough," *Financial Times*, May 13, 2005.

CHAPTER 1

1. Aminata Traoré, *Lettre au Président des Français* p. 28.
2. Ibid., p. 104.
3. "Rwandan celebrity downplays role," *The Gazette*, Montreal, May 1, 2005, p. A3.
4. Paul Theroux, *Dark Star Safari*, pp. 313–314.
5. James Morris, *The Road to Huddersfield: A Journey to Five Continents*, p. 47.

6. George Monbiot, *The Age of Consent*, p. 20.
7. Catherine Caufield, *Masters of Illusion*, Chapter 12.
8. Graham Hancock, *Lords of Poverty*, Part I.
9. Susan George and Fabrizio Sabelli, *Faith and Credit*, p. 3.
10. Robert Coughlan, *Tropical Africa*, p. 85.
11. John Iliffe, *Africans: The History of a Continent*, p. 131.
12. René Dumont, *Paysans écrasés, terres massacrées*, p. 266.
13. Iliffe, p. 127.
14. Press conference of November 23, 2004.
15. Ibid.
16. Sir Donald Cameron, *My Tanganyika Service and some Nigeria*.
17. Sir Philip Mitchell, *African Afterthoughts*.
18. J. H. Oldham, *White and Black in Africa*, p. 4.
19. Dumont, *Paysans écrasés*, pp. 267–268.
20. Basil Davidson, *The African Awakening*, pp. 237–238.
21. Antoine Glaser and Stephen Smith, *L'Afrique sans Africains*, pp. 225–250.
22. Dumont, *False Start*, p. 76.
23. Ibid., p. 290.
24. Paul Johnson, *A History of the Modern World* (1983), p. 517.
25. John Reader, *Africa: A Biography of the Continent*, p. 93.
26. Ibid., p. 234.
27. J. C. Carothers, *The Mind of Man in Africa*, p. 35.
28. John Hatch, in Dumont's *False Start in Africa*, p. 295.
29. *African Regional Organizations and their Role in the Present World Context*, Closing statement of the Union of African Parliaments meeting at its 21st Conference in Niamey, Niger on 22nd and 23rd August, 1998 (www.uafparl.org).
30. *Background Paper on African Union* (October 24, 2001), prepared by Natalie Steinberg for the World Federalist Movement, p. 1 (www.wfm.org).
31. Ibid., p. 4.
32. Review of Jean-Paul Ngoupandé's *L'Afrique sans la France*, in *Le Monde*, May 17, 2002.

CHAPTER 2

1. Conversation in the US Ambassador's residence in Abidjan, Ivory Coast in September 1993.
2. *La Voie*, No. 335, October 29, 1992, p. 6.
3. *Notre Temps*, No. 172, August 18, 1994, pp. 4–5.
4. *Notre Temps*, No. 174, August 31, 1994, pp. 10–11.

CHAPTER 3

1. Henry M. Stanley, *In Darkest Africa*, p. 9.

2. Michela Wrong, *In the Footsteps of Mr. Kurtz*, p. 187
3. Omar Bongo, *Blanc comme nègre*, p. 291 (author's translation).
4. A. Conan Doyle, *The Great Boer War*, p. 22.
5. *New York Times*, February 9, 2004.
6. BBC News, January 29, 2002.
7. Quoted in John Gross, ed., *The New Oxford Book of English Prose*, p. 308.
8. Quoted in J. Mohan, "Nkrumah and Nkrumahism," *Socialist Register*, London, p. 198.
9. Gwendolyn Carter, *Independence for Africa*, p. 34.
10. Kwame Nkrumah, *Autobiography*, p. x.
11. Quoted in Ryszard Kapuscinski, *The Shadow of the Sun*, p. 103.
12. Raphael Lakpé, "Des êtres inachevés," in *La Voie*, October 25, 1993 (author's translation).
13. *The Economist*, "The World This Week," May 29, 2004.
14. African Women's Media Center inaugural conference, December, 1997.
15. Remarks made by President Nelson Mandela at the closing banquet of the South African Institute of International Affairs (SAIIA) conference on "Southern Africa into the Next Millennium," March 19, 1998, Smuts House, Johannesburg.
16. Léopold Senghor, *Ce Que Je Crois*, p. 14 (author's translation).
17. Ibid., p. 24.
18. Ibid., p. 131.
19. Ibid., p. 190.
20. Noël X. Ebony, *20 anneés de passion en 100 articles*), p. 355 (author's translation).
21. "OAU Stance on Amin 'disgrace': Nyerere," Associated Press/ Montreal *Gazette*, December 11, 1978.
22. Remarks over lunch at World Bank headquarters, Washington, DC, May 5, 1998.
23. World Bank Press Release, October 14, 1999.
24. *Financial Times*, July 1, 2004, p. 4.
25. *The Citizen* (East Africa), January 19, 2004, p. 9.
26. *The Guardian Weekly*, April 1–7, 2004, p. 3.
27. Quoted in *The Financial Times*, July 15, 2004, p. 5.
28. "Malawi president a bad choice," BBC News, May 4, 2005.
29. Anthony Sillery, *Botswana: A Short Political History*, p. 192.
30. *La Presse de Tunisie*, November 1, 2003, pp. 1 and 4 (author's translation).
31. Letter from Mr. Paul Kegne, in *BTP Afrique*, February-March 2002, p. 83 (author's translation).
32. Review of *Beyond the Miracle* (Profile Books, 2003) in *The Guardian Weekly*, November 13–19, 2003, p. 18.
33. Stephen Smith, *Nécrologie*, p. 217.

34. Transparency International Press Release: "Transparency International urges NEPAD leaders to ratify AU Anti-Corruption Convention," November 22, 2004.
35. Winston Churchill, *A History of the English-Speaking Peoples*, Volume II, Dodd, Mead & Company, New York, 1966, pp. 291–292

CHAPTER 4

1. Quoted in Ian Smith, *Bitter Harvest: The Great Betrayal*, p. 402.
2. Robert Coughlan, *Tropical Africa*, p. 17.
3. J. C. Carothers, *The Mind of Man in Africa*, p. 54.
4. Quoted in Nadine Gordimer, *Living in Hope and History*, pp. 50–51.
5. Ibid., p. 51.
6. Carothers, p. 121.
7. Talk at the World Bank, June 17, 1998.
8. Francis Parkman, *Pioneers of France in the New World*, pp. 39–40.
9. Ryszard Kapuscinski, *The Shadow of the Sun*, p. 36.
10. *Le Monde*, October 30, 2003.
11. Geoffrey Gorer, *Africa Dances*, p. 186.
12. CNN/*New Scientist*, October 2, 2003.
13. Wrong, p. 172.
14. Kapuscinski, p. 36
15. Christopher Kolade, "Corruption in Africa, in Calderisi et al., ed., *Faith in Development*, p. 80.
16. Coughlan, p. 96.
17. *International Herald Tribune*, August 9–10, 2003
18. Quoted in Basil Davidson, *The African Awakening*, p. 86.
19. Carothers, pp. 157–162.
20. Quoted in Wrong, p. 119.
21. Chinua Achebe, *The Trouble with Nigeria*, p. 33.
22. Excerpt of a speech by the President of the Club d'Hommes d'Affaires Franco-Ivoirien, "Quelle justice pour les hommes d'affaires?," Abidjan, April 8, 1993 (author's translation).
23. J. H. Plumb, *The Making of an Historian*, pp. 328–329.
24. Eric Orsenna et al., *Besoin d'Afrique*, p. 348 (author's translation).
25. Oakland Ross, "Into Africa," *Toronto Star*, May 25, 2003.
26. Editorial in *The New York Times*, December 30, 2003, entitled "Harvesting Poverty."
27. Jean Ziegler, *Les Nouveaux Maîtres du Monde*, pp. 90, 93–116, 179–202.
28. Chinua Achebe, "An Image of Africa: Racism in Conrad's *Heart of Darkness*," in *Hopes and Impediments*, pp. 1–20.
29. Talk at the World Bank, June 17, 1998.
30. Keith Richburg, *Out of Africa*, p. xviii.
31. Stephen Smith, *Négrologie: Pourquoi l'Afrique Meurt* (author's translation), p. 14.

32. Ibid., p. 23.
33. Quoted in Roy Richard Grinker, *In the Arms of Africa*, p. 77.
34. Ibid., p. 79.
35. Smith, p. 131.
36. Associated Press, September 14, 2004.
37. *New York Times*, March 1, 2004.
38. *New York Times*, June 23, 2004.
39. *Financial Times*, May 28, 2004.
40. Aryeh Neier, quoted in *The International Herald Tribune*. August 17, 2004.
41. *The Economist*, May 1, 2004, p. 8.

CHAPTER 5

1. Julius Nyerere, Ujamaa: Essays on Socialism, pp. 22–23.
2. Ibid., pp. 24–28.
3. Ibid., p. 32
4. Ibid., p. 35.
5. Ibid., pp. 30–31.
6. Ibid., p. 77.
7. Ibid., p. 67.
8. Nyerere, *The Arusha Declaration : Ten Years After*, p. 19.
9. Ibid., p. 20.
10. Ibid., p. 32.
11. Ibid., pp. 34–35.
12. Ibid., p. 35.
13. Ibid., pp. 50–51.
14. Goran Hyden, *Beyond Ujamaa in Tanzania*, p. 225.
15. *Wall Street Journal*, July 17, 1981, p. B26.
16. Bernard Joinet, *Tanzanie: Manger d'abord* (author's translation), p. 185.
17. Ibid., pp. 189–191.
18. Hyden, p. 18.

CHAPTER 6

1. Meeting at the Ivorian President's residence in Abidjan, October 31, 1992.
2. Alain Decaux, *Le tapis rouge*, pp. 238–240.

CHAPTER 8

1. World Trade Organization Press Release, November 17, 2000.
2. These are real GDP figures for 2002, using constant 1995 prices (World Bank, *African Development Indicators*, p. 15.)
3. World Bank study cited in the *Financial Times*, October 7, 2003

4. "The end of investor Afro-pessimism," *Financial Times*, May 10, 2005.

CHAPTER 9

1. Robert S. McNamara, "Development and the Arms Race," Speech at the University of Chicago, May 22, 1979.
2. World Bank, *World Development Report*, pp. 33–35.
3. P. T. Bauer, *Equality, the Third World, and Economic Delusion*, p. 100.
4. Teresa Hayter, *Aid as Imperialism*, p. 9.
5. Meeting of the "Friends of the Central African Republic," in the offices of the French Permanent Representative to the United Nations, New York, July 5, 2001.
6. Michael Holman, "Africa's Potemkin deception," *Financial Times*, January 30, 2004.
7. Michael Holman, *Last Orders at Harrods: An African Tale*, pp. 224–225.
8. Ibid., p. 226.
9. Ron Suskind, *The Price of Loyalty*, p. 245.
10. *Ibid.*, p. 254.
11. *The Economist Pocket World in Figures*, 2001.
12. René Dumont, *False Start in Africa*, p. 96.
13. "The Challenge of Inclusion," Address of James D. Wolfensohn to the Annual Meeting of the Board of Governors of the World Bank Group, Washington, DC, September 1997.
14. Donald Fraser, *African Idylls*, p. 34.
15. James Morris, *The Road to Huddersfield*, p. 107.

CHAPTER 10

1. World Bank Press Release, July 26, 2005.
2. Amnesty International, "Contracting out of Human Rights: The Chad–Cameroon pipeline project," September 7, 2005.

CHAPTER 11

1. I first heard this story in 1969 (the year after the Poor People's Campaign) from my Oxford neighbor, the British Caribbean Rhodes Scholar, Richard Jacobs.
2. "Un gendarme militant" ["A principled policeman"], *Notre Temps*, Abidjan, December 22, 1994.

CHAPTER 12

1. *Financial Times*, January 20, 2004.
2. Nyerere, *The Arusha Declaration: Ten Years After*, p. 51.

CHAPTER 13

1. John Gray, *Al Qaeda and What It Means to be Modern*, p. 114.
2. During lunch at the World Bank in June 2000.
3. George Monbiot, *The Age of Consent*, p. 79.
4. *Financial Times*, October 27, 2004.
5. Jean-Paul Ngoupandé, *L'Afrique sans la France*, p. 18 (author's translation).
6. Albert Luthuli (1960), Desmond Tutu (1984), Nelson Mandela (1993), and Wangari Maathai (2004) for Peace; Wole Soyinka (1986), Nadine Gordimer (1991), and John Coetzee (2003) for Literature
7. Basil Davidson, *African* Awakening, p. 9.

BIBLIOGRAPHY

Achebe, Chinua. *The Trouble with Nigeria.* Oxford: Heinemann, 1983.
———. *Hopes and Impediments.* New York: Doubleday (Anchor Books), 1989.
———. *Home and Exile.* New York: Random House, 2001.
Appiah, Kwame Anthony and Gates, Henry Louis, Jr. *Africana: The Encyclopedia of the African and African American Experience.* New York: Perseus Books, 1999.
Ayittey, George N. *Africa Betrayed.* New York: St. Martin's Press, 1992.
Bauer, P. T. *Equality, the Third World, and Economic Delusion.* Cambridge: Harvard University Press, 1981.
Bhagwati, Jagdish. *In Defense of Globalization.* New York: Oxford University Press, 2004.
Bongo, Omar. *Blanc comme nègre.* Paris : Grasset, 2001.
Calderisi, Robert et al., *Faith in Development.* Washington: The World Bank/Regnum Press, 2001.
Cameron, Donald. *My Tanganyika Service and Some Nigeria.* London: George Allen and Unwin, Ltd., 1939.
Carothers, John Colin. *The Mind of Man in Africa.* London: Tom Stacey, 1972.
Carter, Gwendolyn. *Independence for Africa.* London: Thames and Hudson, 1961.
Caufield, Catherine. *Masters of Illusion: The World Bank and the Poverty of Nations.* New York: Henry Holt and Company, 1996.
Chomsky, Noam. *Hegemony or Survival: America's Quest for Global Dominance.* New York: Henry Holt and Company, 2003.
Churchill, Winston. *A History of the English-Speaking Peoples,* Volume II. New York: Dodd, Mead, and Company, 1966.
Conan Doyle, Arthur. *The Great Boer War.* London: George Bell & Sons, 1901.
Coughlan, Robert. *Tropical Africa.* New York: Time/Life, 1962.
Davidson, Basil. *The African Awakening.* London: Jonathan Cape, 1955.
Decaux, Alain. *Le tapis rouge.* Paris: Perrin, 1992.
Dumont, René. *False Start in Africa.* New York and Washington, DC: Frederick A. Praeger, 1966.

———. *Paysans écrasés, terres massacrées*. Paris: Robert Laffont, 1978.

Ebony, Noël X. *20 années de passion en 100 articles*. Abidjan: Union Nationale des Journalistes de Côte d'Ivoire et Fraternité Matin, 1994.

Fraser, Donald. *African Idylls*. New York and London: Fleming H. Revell Company, 1925.

George, Susan. *Faith and Credit: The World Bank's Secular Empire*. Boulder and San Francisco: Westview Press, 1994.

Glaser, Antoine. *L'Afrique sans Africains: Le rêve blanc du continent noir.* Paris: Stock, 1994.

Gordimer, Nadine. *Living in Hope and History: Notes from Our Century*. New York: Farrar, Straus, Giroux, 1999.

Gorer, Geoffrey. *Africa Dances*. London: Penguin Books, 1945.

Gray, John. *Al Quaeda and What It Means to Be Modern*. London: Faber and Faber, 2003.

Grinker, Roy Richard. *In the Arms of Africa: The Life of Colin M. Turnbull*. New York: St. Martin's Press, 2000.

Gunther, John. *Inside Africa*. New York: Harper & Brothers, 1955.

Hancock, Graham. *Lords of Poverty: The Power, Prestige and Corruption of the International Aid Business*. New York: The Atlantic Monthly Press, 1989.

Hayter, Teresa. *Aid as Imperialism*. Harmondsworth: Penguin Books, 1971.

Holman, Michael. *Last Orders at Harrods: An African Tale*. Edinburgh: Polygon, 2005.

Hyden, Goran. *Beyond Ujamaa in Tanzania*. Berkeley and Los Angeles: University of California Press, 1980.

Iliffe, John. *Africans: The History of a Continent*. Cambridge: Cambridge University Press, 1995.

Johnson, Paul. *A History of the Modern World*. London: Wiedenfield and Nicolson, 1983.

Joinet, Bernard. *Le soleil de Dieu en Tanzanie*. Paris: Les Editions du Cerf, 1980.

———. *Tanzanie: Manger d'abord*. Paris: Editions Karthala, 1981.

Kapuscinski, Ryszard. *The Shadow of the Sun*. New York and Toronto: Alfred A. Knopf, 2001.

Mitchell, Philip. *African Afterthoughts*. London: Hutchinson and Company, 1954.

Monbiot, George. *The Age of Consent: A Manifesto for a New World Order.* London: Harper Perennial, 2003.

Morris, James. *The Road to Huddersfield: A Journey to Five Continents*. New York: Random House (Pantheon Books), 1963.

Museveni, Yoweri. *Sowing the Mustard Seed*. London: Macmillan: 1997.

Ngoupandé, Jean-Paul. *L'Afrique sans la France*. Paris: Albin Michel, 2002.

Nkrumah, Kwame. *Autobiography*. London: Thomas Nelson and Sons, 1961.

Nyerere, Julius K. *Ujamaa: Essays on Socialism*. Dar es Salaam: Oxford University Press, 1968.

———. *The Arusha Declaration: Ten Years After.* Dar es Salaam: Government Printer, 1977.

Oldham, J. H. *White and Black in Africa: A Critical Examination of the Rhodes Lectures of General Smuts.* London: Longmans, Green, and Co., 1930.

Orsenna, Eric et al. *Besoin d'Afrique.* Paris: Fayard, 1992.

Parkman, Francis .*Pioneers of France in the New World.* Boston: Little, Brown, and Company, 1925.

Reader, John. *Africa : A Biography of the Continent.* London: Hamish Hamilton, 1997.

Richburg, Keith B. *Out of America: A Black Man Confronts Africa.* New York: Harcourt, 1998.

Sallah, Tijan M. and Okonjo-Iweala, Ngozi. *Chinua Achebe: Teacher of Light.* Trenton New Jersey and Asmara, Eritrea: Africa World Press, Inc., 2003.

Senghor, Léopold Sedar. *Ce Que Je Crois.* Paris : Bernard Grasset, 1988.

Sillery, Anthony. *Botswana: A Short Political History.* London: Methuen & Co., Ltd, 1974.

Smith, Ian. *Bitter Harvest: The Great Betrayal and the Dreadful Aftermath.* Johannesburg: Jonathan Ball Publishers, 2001.

Smith, Stephen. *Négrologie: Pourquoi l'Afrique Meurt.* Paris: Calmann-Lévy, 2003.

Stanley, Henry M. *In Darkest Africa.* New York: Charles Scribner's Sons, 1891.

Stiglitz, Joseph E. *Globalization and Its Discontents.* New York: W.W. Norton & Company, 2002.

Suskind, Ron. *The Price of Loyalty: George W. Bush, the White House, and the Education of Paul O'Neill.* New York: Simon & Schuster, 2004.

Theroux, Paul. *Dark Star Safari.* Toronto: McClelland & Stewart, 2004.

Traoré, Aminata. *Lettre au Président des Français à propos de la Côte d'Ivoire et de l'Afrique en général.* Paris: Fayard, 2005.

Wolf, Martin. *Why Globalization Works.* New Haven: Yale University Press, 2004.

The World Bank. *Adjustment in Africa : Reforms, Results and the Road Ahead.* New York: Oxford University Press, 1994.

———. *Assessing Aid: What Works, What Doesn't, and Why.* New York: Oxford University Press, 1998.

———. *Aid and Reform in Africa.* Washington, DC: World Bank, 2001.

———. *Can Africa Claim the 21st Century?* Washington, DC: World Bank, 2000.

———. *World Development Report.* Washington, DC: World Bank, 1980.

Wrong, Michela. *In the Footsteps of Mr. Kurtz: Living on the Brink of Disaster in the Congo.* London: Fourth Estate, 2000.

Ziegler, Jean. *Les nouveaux maîtres du monde.* Paris: Fayard, 2002.

ABOUT THE AUTHOR

Robert Calderisi studied at the Universities of Montreal, Oxford Sussex, and London. A 1968 Rhodes Scholar, he first visited Africa in November 1975. He has had a thirty-year career in international development, principally at the World Bank, where he held several senior positions. From 1997 to 2000, he was the Bank's international spokesperson on Africa. He has lived in France, the Ivory Coast, Tanzania, the United Kingdom and the U.S. He is now a consultant and writer, splitting his time between Montreal and Paris.

INDEX

Casino Ave

mini O

Church on left

Vicwrage

by white

handings

right